Cognitive Modeling and Computational Linguistics

(CMCL 2013)

Sofia, Bulgaria
8 August 2013

ISBN: 978-1-62993-010-7

Printed from e-media with permission by:

Curran Associates, Inc.
57 Morehouse Lane
Red Hook, NY 12571

Some format issues inherent in the e-media version may also appear in this print version.

Printed by Curran Associates, Inc. (2013)

Association for Computational Linguistics
209 N. Eighth Street
Stroudsburg, Pennsylvania 18360

Phone: 1-570-476-8006
Fax: 1-570-476-0860

acl@aclweb.org

Additional copies of this publication are available from:

Curran Associates, Inc.
57 Morehouse Lane
Red Hook, NY 12571 USA
Phone: 845-758-0400
Fax: 845-758-2634
Email: curran@proceedings.com
Web: www.proceedings.com

Introduction

The papers in these precedings were presented at the Fourth Annual Workshop on Cognitive Modeling and Computational Linguistics (CMCL), held in Sofia, Bulgaria on 8 August 2013, in conjunction with the Annual Meeting of the Association for Computational Linguistics (CMCL). The CMCL workshop series provides a unique venue for work on the interdisciplinary field of computational psycholinguistics, described by ACL Lifetime Achievement Award recipient Martin Kay as "build[ing] models of language that reflect in some interesting way on the ways in which people use language". This workshop series builds on the tradition of earlier meetings, including the 1997 computational psycholinguistics meeting at the 1997 Annual Conference of the Cognitive Science Society in Berkeley, CA, and on the Incremental Parsing workshop held in 2004 at the Annual Meeting of the Association for Computational Linguistics.

We received nineteen submissions to the 2013 CMCL workshop, of which we accepted eleven for final appearance in the conference program. The overall quality of workshop submissions was extremely strong, reflecting the perennially increasing quality of work in this field. This year we also expanded the workshop by including keynote talks from two invited speakers, Dr Sharon Goldwater from the University of Edinburgh and Professor Rick Lewis from the University of Michigan, leading researchers in computational psycholinguistics. We would like to thank all submitting authors for allowing us to consider their work, the program committee for an outstanding job in reviewing and discussing submissions, and of course our invited speakers. We also gratefully acknowledge funding from the Cognitive Science Society for the Best Student Paper award, and to the Cluster of Excellence on "Multimodal Computing and Interaction" for assisting with funding of our invited speakers. Many thanks to all of you for your continued support of this workshop.

Vera Demberg and Roger Levy

Organizers:

Vera Demberg, Saarland University
Roger Levy, UC San Diego

Program Committee:

Afra Alishahi, Tilburg University
Klinton Bicknell, UC San Diego
Matthew Crocker, Saarland University
Brian Dillon, University of Massachussetts
Afsaneh Fazly, University of Toronto
Naomi Feldman, University of Maryland
Michael C. Frank, Stanford University
Stefan Frank, Radboud University Nijmegen
Sharon Goldwater, Edinburgh University
Noah Goodman, Stanford University
John T. Hale, Cornell University
T. Florian Jaeger, University of Rochester
Frank Keller, University of Edinburgh
Jeffrey Heinz, University of Delaware
Richard L. Lewis, University of Michigan
Brian Edmond Murphy, Carnegie Mellon University
Timothy John O'Donnell, Massachusetts Institute of Technology
Sebastian Padó, University of Heidelberg
Ulrike Padó, Hochschule für Technik, Stuttgart
Steven Piantadosi, University of Rochester
David Reitter, Penn State University
William Schuler, The Ohio State University
Nathaniel Smith, University of Edinburgh
Ed Stabler, UC Los Angeles
Whitney Tabor, University of Connecticut and Haskins Laboratories

Invited Speakers:

Sharon Goldwater, University of Edinburgh
Rick Lewis, University of Michigan

Table of Contents

Workshop Program

Thursday, August 8th, 2013

8:25 Opening Remarks

8:30 Invited Talk by Sharon Goldwater

Session 1: Segmentation and Phonetics

09:30 *Why is English so easy to segment?*
Abdellah Fourtassi, Benjamin Börschinger, Mark Johnson and Emmanuel Dupoux

10:00 *A model of generalization in distributional learning of phonetic categories*
Bozena Pajak, Klinton Bicknell and Roger Levy

10:30 Coffee break

Session 2: Syntax and Morphology

11:00 *Learning non-concatenative morphology*
Michelle Fullwood and Tim O'Donnell

11:30 *Statistical Representation of Grammaticality Judgements: the Limits of N-Gram Models*
Alexander Clark, Gianluca Giorgolo and Shalom Lappin

12:00 *An Analysis of Memory-based Processing Costs using Incremental Deep Syntactic Dependency Parsing*
Marten van Schijndel, Luan Nguyen and William Schuler

12:30 *Computational simulations of second language construction learning*
Yevgen Matusevych, Afra Alishahi and Ad Backus

13:00 Lunch break

Thursday, August 8th, 2013 (continued)

	Session 3: Semantics
14:00	*The semantic augmentation of a psycholinguistically-motivated syntactic formalism* Asad Sayeed and Vera Demberg
14:30	*Evaluating Neighbor Rank and Distance Measures as Predictors of Semantic Priming* Gabriella Lapesa and Stefan Evert
15:00	*Concreteness and Corpora: A Theoretical and Practical Study* Felix Hill, Douwe Kiela and Anna Korhonen
15:30	Coffee break
	Session 4: Discourse and Dialog
16:00	*On the Information Conveyed by Discourse Markers* Fatemeh Torabi Asr and Vera Demberg
16:30	*Incremental Grammar Induction from Child-Directed Dialogue Utterances* Arash Eshghi, Julian Hough and Matthew Purver
17:00	Invited Talk by Rick Lewis

Whyisenglishsoeasytosegment?

Abdellah Fourtassi[1], Benjamin Börschinger[2,3]
Mark Johnson[3] and Emmanuel Dupoux[1]

(1) Laboratoire de Sciences Cognitives et Psycholinguistique, ENS/EHESS/CNRS, Paris

(2) Department of Computing, Macquarie University

(3) Department of Computational Linguistics, Heidelberg University

{abdellah.fourtassi, emmanuel.dupoux}@gmail.com , {benjamin.borschinger, mark.johnson}@mq.edu.au

Abstract

Cross-linguistic studies on unsupervised word segmentation have consistently shown that English is easier to segment than other languages. In this paper, we propose an explanation of this finding based on the notion of segmentation ambiguity. We show that English has a very low segmentation ambiguity compared to Japanese and that this difference correlates with the segmentation performance in a unigram model. We suggest that segmentation ambiguity is linked to a trade-off between syllable structure complexity and word length distribution.

1 Introduction

During the course of language acquisition, infants must learn to segment words from continuous speech. Experimental studies show that they start doing so from around 7.5 months of age (Jusczyk and Aslin, 1995). Further studies indicate that infants are sensitive to a number of word boundary cues, like prosody (Jusczyk et al., 1999; Mattys et al., 1999), transition probabilities (Saffran et al., 1996; Pelucchi et al., 2009), phonotactics (Mattys et al., 2001), coarticulation (Johnson and Jusczyk, 2001) and combine these cues with different weights (Weiss et al., 2010).

Computational models of word segmentation have played a major role in assessing the relevance and reliability of different statistical cues present in the speech input. Some of these models focus mainly on *boundary detection*, and assess different strategies to identify them (Christiansen et al., 1998; Xanthos, 2004; Swingley, 2005; Daland and Pierrehumbert, 2011). Other models, sometimes called *lexicon-building algorithms*, learn the lexicon and the segmentation at the same time and use knowledge about the extracted lexicon to segment novel utterances. State-of-the-art lexicon-building segmentation algorithms are typically reported to yield better performance than word boundary detection algorithms (Brent, 1999; Venkataraman, 2001; Batchelder, 2002; Goldwater, 2007; Johnson, 2008b; Fleck, 2008; Blanchard et al., 2010).

As seen in Table 1, however, the performance varies considerably across languages with English winning by a high margin. This raises a generalizability issue for NLP applications, but also for the modeling of language acquisition since, obviously, it is not the case that in some languages, infants fail to acquire an adult lexicon. Are these performance differences only due to the fact that the algorithms might be optimized for English? Or do they also reflect some intrinsic linguistic differences between languages?

Lang.	F-score	Model	Reference
English	0.89	AG	Johnson (2009)
Chinese	0.77	AG	Johnson (2010)
Spanish	0.58	DP Bigram	Fleck (2008)
Arabic	0.56	WordEnds	Fleck (2008)
Sesotho	0.55	AG	Johnson (2008)
Japanese	0.55	BootLex	Batchelder (2002)
French	0.54	NGS-u	Boruta (2011)

Table 1: State-of-the-art unsupervised segmentation scores for eight languages.

The aim of the present work is to understand why English usually scores better than other languages, as far as unsupervised segmentation is concerned. As a comparison point, we chose Japanese because it is among the languages that have given the poorest word segmentation scores. In fact, Boruta et al. (2011) found an F-score around 0.41 using both Brent (1999)'s MBDP-1 and Venkataraman (2001)'s NGS-u models, and Batchelder (2002) found an F-score that goes from 0.40 to 0.55 depending on the corpus used. Japanese also differs typologically from English along several phonological dimensions such as number of syllabic types, phonotactic constraints and rhythmic structure. Although most lexicon-building segmentation algorithms do not attempt to model these dimensions, they still might be relevant to speech segmentation and help explain the performance difference.

The structure of the paper is as follows. First, we present the class of lexical-building segmentation algorithm that we use in this paper (Adaptor Grammar), and our English and Japanese corpora. We then present data replicating the basic finding that segmentation performance is better for English than for Japanese. We then explore the hypothesis that this finding is due to an intrinsic difference in segmentation ambiguity in the two languages, and suggest that the source of this difference rests in the structure of the phonological lexicon in the two languages. Finally, we use these insights to try and reduce the gap between Japanese and English segmentation through a modification of the Unigram model where multiple linguistic levels are learned jointly.

2 Computational Framework and Corpora

2.1 Adaptor Grammar

In this study, we use the Adaptor Grammar framework (Johnson et al., 2007) to test different models of word segmentation on English and Japanese Corpora. This framework makes it possible to express a class of hierarchical non-parametric Bayesian models using an extension of probabilistic context-free grammars called Adaptor Grammar (AG). It allows one to easily define models that incorporate different assumptions about linguistic structure and is therefore a useful practical tool for exploring different hypotheses about word segmentation (Johnson, 2008b; Johnson, 2008a; Johnson et al., 2010; Börschinger et al., 2012).

For mathematical details and a description of the inference procedure for AGs, we refer the reader to Johnson et al. (2007). Briefly, AG uses the non-parametric Pitman-Yor-Process (Pitman and Yor, 1997) which, as in Minimum Description lengths models, finds a compact representation of the input by re-using frequent structures (here, words).

2.2 Corpora

In the present study, we used both Child Directed Speech (CDS) and Adult Directed Speech (ADS) corpora. English CDS was derived from the Bernstein-Ratner corpus (Bernstein-Ratner, 1987), which consists in transcribed verbal interaction of parents with nine children between 1 and 2 years of age. We used the 9,790 utterances that were phonemically transcribed by Brent and Cartwright (1996). Japanese CDS consists in the first 10, 000 utterances of the Hamasaki corpus (Hamasaki, 2002). It provides a phonemic transcript of spontaneous speech to a single child collected from when the child was 2 up to when it was 3.5 years old. Both CDS corpora are available from the CHILDES database (MacWhinney, 2000).

As for English ADS, we used the first 10,000 utterances of the Buckeye Speech Corpus (Pitt et al., 2007) which consists in spontaneous conversations with 40 speakers in American English. To make it comparable to the other corpora in this paper, we only used the idealized phonemic transcription. Finally, for Japanese ADS, we used the first 10,000 utterances of a phonemic transcription of the Corpus of Spontaneous Japanese (Maekawa et al., 2000). It consists of recorded spontaneous conversations, or public speeches in different fields ranging from engineering to humanities. For each corpus, we present elementary statistics in Table 2.

3 Unsupervised segmentation with the Unigram Model

3.1 Setup

In this experiment we used the Adaptor Grammar framework to implement a Unigram model of word segmentation (Johnson et al., 2007). This model has been shown to be equivalent to the original MBDP-1 segmentation model (see Goldwater (2007)). The model is defined as:

$$Utterance \rightarrow \underline{Word}^{+}$$
$$\underline{Word} \rightarrow Phoneme^{+}$$

In the AG framework, an underlined non-terminal indicates that this non-terminal is adapted, i.e. that the AG will cache (and learn probabilities for) entire sub-trees rooted in this non-terminal. Here, <u>Word</u> is the only unit that the model effectively learns, and there are no dependencies between the words to be learned. This grammar states that an utterance must be analyzed in terms of one or more Words, where a Word is a

Corpus	Child Directed Speech		Adult Directed Speech	
	English	Japanese	English	Japanese
Tokens				
Utterances	9,790	10,000	10,000	10,000
Words	33,399	27,362	57,185	87,156
Phonemes	95,809	108,427	183,196	289,264
Types				
Words	1,321	2,389	3,708	4,206
Phonemes	50	30	44	25
Average Lengths				
Words per utterance	3.41	2.74	5.72	8.72
Phonemes per utterance	9.79	10.84	18.32	28.93
Phonemes per word	2.87	3.96	3.20	3.32

Table 2 : Characteristics of phonemically transcribed corpora

sequence of Phonemes.

We ran the model twice on each corpus for 2,000 iterations with hyper-parameter sampling and we collected samples throughout the process, following the methodology of Johnson and Goldwater (2009)[1]. For evaluation, we performed their Minimum Bayes Risk decoding using the collected samples to get a single score.

3.2 Evaluation

For the evaluation, we used the same measures as Brent (1999), Venkataraman (2001) and Goldwater (2007), namely token Precision (P), Recall (R) and F-score (F). Precision is defined as the number of correct word tokens found out of all tokens posited. Recall is the number of correct word tokens found out of all tokens in the gold standard. The F-score is defined as the harmonic mean of Precision and Recall , $F = \frac{2*P*R}{P+R}$.

We will refer to these scores as the *segmentation* scores. In addition, we define similar measures for word *boundaries* and word types in the *lexicon*.

3.3 Results and discussion

The results are shown in Table 3. As expected, the model yields substantially better scores in English than Japanese, for both CDS and ADS. In addition, we found that in both languages, ADS yields slightly worse results than CDS. This is to be expected because ADS uses between 60% and 300% longer utterances than CDS, and as a result presents the learner with a more difficult segmentation problem. Moreover, ADS includes between 70% and 280% more word types than CDS, making it a more difficult lexical learning problem. Note, however, that despite these large differences in corpus statistics, the difference in segmentation performance between ADS and CDS are small compared to the differences between Japanese and English.

An error analysis on English data shows that most errors come from the Unigram model mistaking high frequency collocations for single words (see also Goldwater (2007)). This leads to an under-segmentation of chunks like "a boy" or "is it" [2]. Yet, the model also tends to break off frequent morphological affixes, especially "-ing" and "-s" , leading to an over-segmentation of words like "talk ing" or "black s".

Similarly, Japanese data shows both over- and under-segmentation errors. However, over-segmentation is more severe than for English, as it does not only affect affixes, but surfaces as breaking apart multi-syllabic words. In addition, Japanese segmentation faces another kind of error which acts across word boundaries. For example, "ni kashite" is segmented as "nika shite" and "nurete inakatta" as "nure tei na katta". This leads to an output lexicon that, on the one hand, allows for a more compact analysis of the corpus than the true lexicon: the number of word types drops from 2,389 to 1,463 in CDS and from 4,206 to 2,372 in ADS although the average token length – and consequently, overall number of tokens – does not change as dramatically, dropping from 3.96 to

[1]We used incremental initialization

[2]For ease of presentation, we use orthography to present examples although all experiments are run on phonemic transcripts.

	Child Directed Speech						Adult Directed Speech					
	English			Japanese			English			Japanese		
	F	P	R	F	P	R	F	P	R	F	P	R
Segmentation	**0.77**	0.76	0.77	**0.55**	0.51	0.61	**0.69**	0.66	0.73	**0.50**	0.48	0.52
Boundaries	0.87	0.87	0.88	0.72	0.63	0.83	0.86	0.81	0.91	0.76	0.74	0.79
Lexicon	0.62	0.65	0.59	0.33	0.43	0.26	0.41	0.48	0.36	0.30	0.42	0.23

Table 3 : Word segmentation scores of the Unigram model

3.31 for CDS and from 3.32 to 3.12 in ADS. On the other hand, however, most of the output lexicon items are not valid Japanese words and this leads to the bad lexicon F-scores. This, in turn, leads to the bad overall segmentation performance.

In brief, we have shown that, across two different corpora, English yields consistently better segmentation results than Japanese for the Unigram model. This confirms and extends the results of Boruta et al. (2011) and Batchelder (2002). It strongly suggests that the difference is neither due to a specific choice of model nor to particularities of the corpora, but reflects a fundamental property of these two languages.

In the following section, we introduce the notion of *segmentation ambiguity*, it to English and Japanese data, and show that it correlates with segmentation performance.

4 Intrinsic Segmentation Ambiguity

Lexicon-based segmentation algorithms like MBDP-1, NGS-u and the AG Unigram model learn the lexicon and the segmentation at the same time. This makes it difficult, in case of poor performance, to see whether the problem comes from the intrinsic segmentability of the language or from the quality of the extracted lexicon. Our claim is that Japanese is intrinsically more difficult to segment than English, even when a good lexicon is already assumed. We explore this hypothesis by studying segmentation alone, assuming a perfect (Gold) lexicon.

4.1 Segmentation ambiguity

Without any information, a string of N phonemes could be segmented in 2^{N-1} ways. When a lexicon is provided, the set of possible segmentations is reduced to a smaller number. To illustrate this, suppose we have to segment the input utterance: /ay s k r iy m/ [3], and that the lexicon contains the following words : /ay/ (I), /s k r iy m/ (scream), /ay s/ (ice), /k r iy m/ (cream). Only two segmentations are possible : /ay skriym/ (I scream) and /ays kriym/ (ice cream).

We are interested in the ambiguity generated by the different possible parses that result from such a supervised segmentation. In order to quantify this idea in general, we define a *Normalized Segmentation Entropy*. To do this, we need to assign a probability to every possible segmentation. To this end, we use a unigram model where the probability of a lexical item is its normalized frequency in the corpus and the probability of a parse is the product of the probabilities of its terms. In order to obtain a measure that does not depend on the utterance length, we normalize by the number of possible boundaries in the utterance. So for an utterance of length N, the Normalized Segmentation Entropy (NSE) is computed using Shannon formula (Shannon, 1948) as follows:

$$NSE = -\sum_i P_i log_2(P_i)/(N-1)$$

where P_i is the probability of the parse i .

For CDS data we found Normalized Segmentation Entropies of 0.0021 bits for English and 0.0156 bits for Japanese. In ADS data we found similar results with 0.0032 bits for English and 0.0275 bits for Japanese. This means that Japanese needs between 7 and 8 times more bits than English to encode segmentation information. This is a very large difference, which is of the same magnitude in CDS and ADS. These differences clearly show that intrinsically, Japanese is more ambiguous than English with regards to segmentation.

One can refine this analysis by distinguishing two sources of ambiguity: ambiguity *across word boundaries*, as in "ice cream / [ay s] [k r iy m]"

[3] We use ARPABET notation to represent phonemic input.

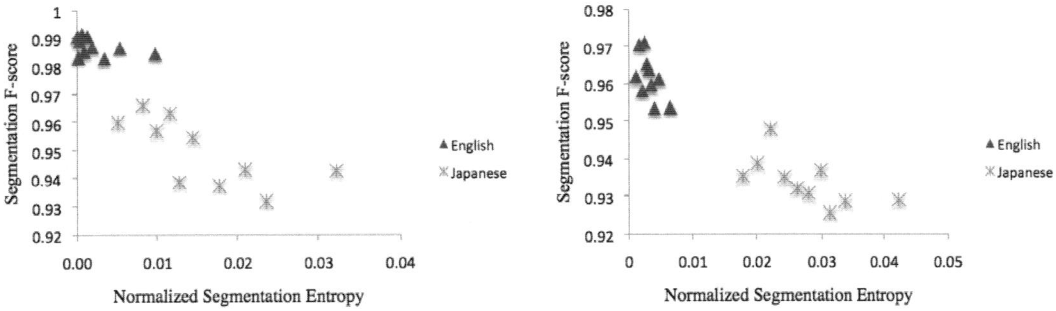

Figure 1 : Correlation between Normalized Segmentation Entropy (in bits) and the segmentation F-score for CDS (left) and ADS (Right)

vs "I scream / [ay] [s k r iy m]". And ambiguity *within the lexicon*, that occurs when a lexical item is composed of two or more sub-words (like in "Butterfly").

Since we are mainly investigating lexicon-building models, it is important to measure the ambiguity within the lexicon itself, in the ideal case where this lexicon is perfect. To this end, we computed the average number of segmentations for a lexicon item. For example, the word "butterfly" has two possible segmentations : the original word "butterfly" and a segmentation comprising the two sub-words : "butter" and "fly". For English tokens, we found an average of 1.039 in CDS and 1.057 in ADS. For Japanese tokens, we found an average of 1.811 in CDS and 1.978 in ADS. English's averages are close to 1, indicating that it doesn't exhibit lexicon ambiguity. Japanese, however, has averages close to 2 which means that lexical ambiguity is quite systematic in both CDS and ADS.

4.2 Segmentation ambiguity and supervised segmentation

The intrinsic ambiguity in Japanese only shows that a given sentence has multiple possible segmentations. What remains to be demonstrated is that these multiple segmentations result in systematic segmentation errors. To do this we propose a supervised segmentation algorithm that enumerates all possible segmentations of an utterance based on the gold lexicon, and selects the segmentation with the highest probability. In CDS data, this algorithm yields a segmentation F-score equal to 0.99 for English and 0.95 for Japanese. In ADS we find an F-score of 0.96 for English and 0.93 for Japanese. These results show that lexical information alone plus word frequency eliminates almost all segmentation errors in English, especially for CDS. As for Japanese, even if the scores remain impressively high, the lexicon alone is not sufficient to eliminate all the errors. In other words, even with a gold lexicon, English remains easier to segment than Japanese.

To quantify the link between segmentation entropy and segmentation errors, we binned the sentences of our corpus in 10 bins according to the Normalized Segmentation Entropy, and correlate this with the average segmentation F-score for each bin. As shown Figure 1, we found significant correlations: ($R = -0.86$, $p < 0.001$) for CDS and ($R = -0.93$, $p < 0.001$) for ADS, showing that segmentation ambiguity has a strong effect even on supervised segmentation scores. The correlation within language was also significant but only in the Japanese data : $R = -0.70$ for CDS and $R = -0.62$ for ADS.

Next, we explore one possible reason for this structural difference between Japanese and English, especially at the level of the lexicon.

4.3 Syllable structure and lexical composition of Japanese and English

One of the most salient differences between English and Japanese phonology concerns their syllable structure. This is illustrated in Figure 2 (above), where we plotted the frequency of the different syllabic structures of monosyllabic tokens in English and Japanese CDS. The statistics show that English has a very rich syllabic composition where a diversity of consonant clusters is allowed, whereas Japanese syllable structure is quite simple and mostly composed of the default CV type. This difference is bound to have an effect on the structure of the lexicon. Indeed, Japanese has to use

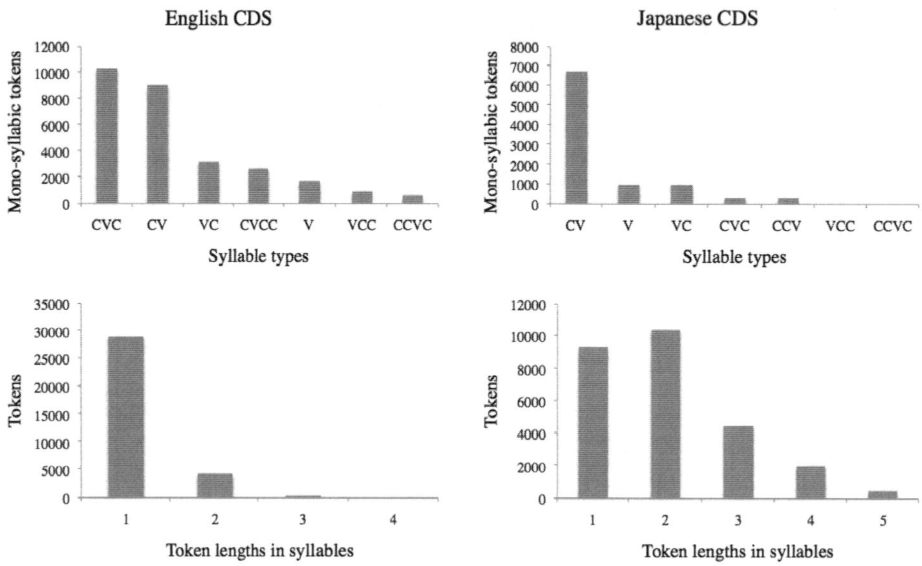

Figure 2 : Trade-off between the complexity of syllable structure (above) and the word token length in terms of syllables (below) for English and Japanese CDS.

multisyllabic words in order to achieve a large size lexicon, whereas, in principle, English could use mostly monosyllables. In Figure 2 (below) we display the distribution of word length as measured in syllables in the two languages for the CDS corpora. The English data is indeed mostly composed of mono-syllabic words whereas the Japanese one is made of words of more varied lengths. Overall, we have documented a trade-off between the diversity of syllable structure on the one hand, and the diversity of word lengths on the other (see Table 4 for a summary of this tradeoff expressed in terms of entropy).

	CDS		ADS	
	Eng.	Jap.	Eng.	Jap.
Syllable types	2.40	1.38	2.58	1.03
Token lengths	0.62	2.04	0.99	1.69

Table 4 : Entropies of syllable types and token lengths in terms of syllables (in bits)

We suggest that this trade-off is responsible for the difference in the lexicon ambiguity across the two languages. Specifically, the combination of a small number of syllable types and, as a consequence, the tendency for multi-syllabic word types in Japanese makes it likely that a long word will be composed of smaller ones. This cannot happen very often in English, since most words are monosyllabic, and words smaller than a syllable are not allowed.

5 Improving Japanese unsupervised segmentation

We showed in the previous section that ambiguity impacts segmentation even with a gold lexicon, mainly because the lexicon itself could be ambiguous. In an unsupervised segmentation setting, the problem is worse because ambiguity within and across word boundaries leads to a bad lexicon, which in turn results in more segmentation errors. In this section, we explore the possibility of mitigating some of these negative consequences.

In section 3, we saw that when the Unigram model tries to learn Japanese words, it produces an output lexicon composed of both over- and under-segmented words in addition to words that result from a segmentation across word boundaries. One way to address this is by learning multiple kinds of units jointly, rather than just words; indeed, previous work has shown that richer models with multiple levels improve segmentation for English (Johnson, 2008a; Johnson and Goldwater, 2009).

5.1 Two dependency levels

As a first step, we will allow the model to not just learn words but to also memorize sequences of words. Johnson (2008a) introduced these units as "collocations" but we choose to use the more neutral notion of *level* for reasons that become clear shortly. Concretely, the grammar is:

	CDS						ADS					
	English			Japanese			English			Japanese		
	F	P	R	F	P	R	F	P	R	F	P	R
Level 1												
Segmentation	**0.81**	0.77	0.86	0.42	0.33	0.55	**0.70**	0.63	0.78	0.42	0.35	0.50
Boundaries	0.91	0.84	0.98	0.63	0.47	0.96	0.86	0.76	0.98	0.73	0.61	0.90
Lexicon	0.64	0.79	0.54	0.18	0.55	0.10	0.36	0.56	0.26	0.15	0.68	0.08
Level 2												
Segmentation	0.33	0.45	0.26	**0.59**	0.65	0.53	0.50	0.60	0.43	**0.45**	0.54	0.38
Boundaries	0.56	0.98	0.40	0.71	0.87	0.60	0.76	0.95	0.64	0.73	0.92	0.60
Lexicon	0.36	0.25	0.59	0.47	0.44	0.49	0.46	0.38	0.56	0.43	0.37	0.50

Table 5 : Word segmentation scores of the two levels model

$$Utterance \rightarrow \underline{level2}^+$$
$$\underline{level2} \rightarrow \underline{level1}^+$$
$$\underline{level1} \rightarrow Phoneme^+$$

We run this model under the same conditions as the Unigram model but evaluate two different situations. The model has no inductive bias that would force it to equate *level1* with words, rather than *level2*. Consequently, we evaluate the segmentation that is the result of taking there to be a boundary between every *level1* constituent (Level 1 in Table 5) and between every *level2* constituent (Level 2 in Table 5). From these results , we see that English data has better scores when the lower level represents the Word unit and when the higher level captures regularities above the word. However, Japanese data is best segmented when the higher level is the Word unit and the lower level captures sub-word regularities.

Level 1 generally tends to over-segment utterances as can be seen by comparing the Boundary Recall and Precision scores (Goldwater, 2007). In fact when the Recall is much higher than the Precision, we can say that the model has a tendency to over-segment. Conversely, we see that Level 2 tends to under-segment utterances as the Boundary Precision is higher than the Recall.

Over-segmentation at Level 1 seems to benefit English since it counteracts the tendency of the Unigram model to cluster high frequency collocations. As far as segmentation is concerned, this effect seems to outweigh the negative effect of breaking words apart (especially in CDS), as English words are mostly monosyllabic.

For Japanese, under-segmentation at Level 2 seems to be slightly less harmful than over-segmentation at Level 1, as it prevents, to some extent, multi-syllabic words to be split. However, the scores are not very different from the ones we had with the Unigram model and slightly worse for the ADS. What seems to be missing is an intermediate level where over- and under-segmentation would counteract one another.

5.2 Three dependency levels

We add a third dependency level to our model as follows :

$$Utterance \rightarrow \underline{level3}^+$$
$$\underline{level3} \rightarrow \underline{level2}^+$$
$$\underline{level2} \rightarrow \underline{level1}^+$$
$$\underline{level1} \rightarrow Phoneme^+$$

As with the previous model, we test each of the three levels as the word unit, the results are shown in Table 6.

Except for English CDS, all the corpora have their best scores with this intermediate level. Level 1 tends to over-segment Japanese utterances into syllables and English utterances into morphemes. Level 3, however, tends to highly under-segment both languages. English CDS seems to be already under-segmented at Level 2, very likely caused by the large number of word collocations like "is-it" and "what-is", an observation also made by Börschinger et al. (2012) using different English CDS corpora. English ADS is quantitatively more sensitive to over-segmentation than CDS mainly because it has a richer morphological structure and relatively longer words in terms of syllables (Table 4).

	CDS						ADS					
	English			Japanese			English			Japanese		
	F	P	R	F	P	R	F	P	R	F	P	R
Level 1												
Segmentation	**0.79**	0.74	0.85	0.27	0.20	0.41	0.35	0.28	0.48	0.37	0.30	0.47
Boundaries	0.89	0.81	0.99	0.56	0.39	0.99	0.68	0.52	0.99	0.70	0.57	0.93
Lexicon	0.58	0.76	0.46	0.10	0.47	0.05	0.13	0.39	0.07	0.10	0.70	0.05
Level 2												
Segmentation	0.49	0.60	0.42	**0.70**	0.70	0.70	**0.77**	0.76	0.79	**0.60**	0.65	0.55
Boundaries	0.71	0.97	0.56	0.81	0.82	0.81	0.90	0.88	0.92	0.81	0.90	0.74
Lexicon	0.51	0.41	0.64	0.53	0.59	0.47	0.58	0.69	0.50	0.51	0.57	0.46
Level 3												
Segmentation	0.18	0.31	0.12	0.39	0.53	0.30	0.43	0.55	0.36	0.28	0.42	0.21
Boundaries	0.26	0.99	0.15	0.46	0.93	0.31	0.71	0.98	0.55	0.59	0.96	0.43
Lexicon	0.17	0.10	0.38	0.32	0.25	0.41	0.37	0.28	0.51	0.27	0.20	0.42

Table 6 : Word segmentation scores of the three levels model

6 Conclusion

In this paper we identified a property of language, *segmentation ambiguity*, which we quantified through Normalized Segmentation Entropy. We showed that this quantity predicts performance in a supervised segmentation task.

With this tool we found that English was intrinsically less ambiguous than Japanese, accounting for the systematic difference found in this paper. More generally, we suspect that Segmentation Ambiguity would, to some extent, explain much of the difference observed across languages (Table 1). Further work needs to be carried out to test the robustness of this hypothesis on a larger scale.

We showed that allowing the system to learn at multiple levels of structure generally improves performance, and compensates partially for the negative effect of segmentation ambiguity on unsupervised segmentation (where a bad lexicon amplifies the effect of segmentation ambiguity). Yet, we end up with a situation where the best level of structure may not be the same across corpora or languages, which raises the question as to how to determine which level is the correct lexical level, i.e., the level that can sustain successful grammatical and semantic learning. Further research is needed to answer this question.

Generally speaking, ambiguity is a challenge in many speech and language processing tasks: for example part-of-speech tagging and word sense disambiguation tackle lexical ambiguity, probabilistic parsing deals with syntactic ambiguity and speech act interpretation deals with pragmatic ambiguities. However, to our knowledge, ambiguity has rarely been considered as a serious problem in word segmentation tasks.

As we have shown, the lexicon-based approach does not completely solve the segmentation ambiguity problem since the lexicon itself could be more or less ambiguous depending on the language. Evidently, however, infants in all languages manage to overcome this ambiguity. It has to be the case, therefore, that they solve this problem through the use of alternative strategies, for instance by relying on sub-lexical cues (see Jarosz and Johnson (2013)) or by incorporating semantic or syntactic constraints (Johnson et al., 2010). It remains a major challenge to integrate these strategies within a common model that can learn with comparable performance across typologically distinct languages.

Acknowledgements

The research leading to these results has received funding from the European Research Council (FP/2007-2013) / ERC Grant Agreement n. ERC-2011-AdG-295810 BOOTPHON, from the Agence Nationale pour la Recherche (ANR-2010-BLAN-1901-1 BOOTLANG, ANR-11-0001-02 PSL* and ANR-10-LABX-0087) and the Fondation de France. This research was also supported under the Australian Research Council's Discovery Projects funding scheme (project numbers DP110102506 and DP110102593).

References

Eleanor Olds Batchelder. 2002. Bootstrapping the lexicon: A computational model of infant speech segmentation. *Cognition*, 83(2):167–206.

N. Bernstein-Ratner. 1987. The phonology of parent-child speech. In K. Nelson and A. van Kleeck, editors, *Children's Language*, volume 6. Erlbaum, Hillsdale, NJ.

Daniel Blanchard, Jeffrey Heinz, and Roberta Golinkoff. 2010. Modeling the contribution of phonotactic cues to the problem of word segmentation. *Journal of Child Language*, 37(3):487–511.

Benjamin Börschinger, Katherine Demuth, and Mark Johnson. 2012. Studying the effect of input size for Bayesian word segmentation on the Providence corpus. In *Proceedings of the 24th International Conference on Computational Linguistics (Coling 2012)*, pages 325–340, Mumbai, India. Coling 2012 Organizing Committee.

Luc Boruta, Sharon Peperkamp, Benoît Crabbé, and Emmanuel Dupoux. 2011. Testing the robustness of online word segmentation: Effects of linguistic diversity and phonetic variation. In *Proceedings of the 2nd Workshop on Cognitive Modeling and Computational Linguistics*, pages 1–9, Portland, Oregon, USA, June. Association for Computational Linguistics.

M. Brent and T. Cartwright. 1996. Distributional regularity and phonotactic constraints are useful for segmentation. *Cognition*, 61:93–125.

M. Brent. 1999. An efficient, probabilistically sound algorithm for segmentation and word discovery. *Machine Learning*, 34:71–105.

Morten H Christiansen, Joseph Allen, and Mark S Seidenberg. 1998. Learning to segment speech using multiple cues: A connectionist model. *Language and cognitive processes*, 13(2-3):221–268.

Robert Daland and Janet B Pierrehumbert. 2011. Learning diphone-based segmentation. *Cognitive Science*, 35(1):119–155.

Margaret M. Fleck. 2008. Lexicalized phonotactic word segmentation. In *Proceedings of ACL-08: HLT*, pages 130–138, Columbus, Ohio, June. Association for Computational Linguistics.

Sharon Goldwater. 2007. *Nonparametric Bayesian Models of Lexical Acquisition*. Ph.D. thesis, Brown University.

Naomi Hamasaki. 2002. The timing shift of two-year-olds responses to caretakers yes/no questions. In *Studies in language sciences (2)Papers from the 2nd Annual Conference of the Japanese Society for Language Sciences*, pages 193–206.

Gaja Jarosz and J Alex Johnson. 2013. The richness of distributional cues to word boundaries in speech to young children. *Language Learning and Development*, (ahead-of-print):1–36.

Mark Johnson and Katherine Demuth. 2010. Unsupervised phonemic Chinese word segmentation using Adaptor Grammars. In *Proceedings of the 23rd International Conference on Computational Linguistics (Coling 2010)*, pages 528–536, Beijing, China, August. Coling 2010 Organizing Committee.

Mark Johnson and Sharon Goldwater. 2009. Improving nonparameteric Bayesian inference: experiments on unsupervised word segmentation with adaptor grammars. In *Proceedings of Human Language Technologies: The 2009 Annual Conference of the North American Chapter of the Association for Computational Linguistics*, pages 317–325, Boulder, Colorado, June. Association for Computational Linguistics.

Elizabeth K. Johnson and Peter W. Jusczyk. 2001. Word segmentation by 8-month-olds: When speech cues count more than statistics. *Journal of Memory and Language*, 44:1–20.

Mark Johnson, Thomas Griffiths, and Sharon Goldwater. 2007. Bayesian inference for PCFGs via Markov chain Monte Carlo. In *Human Language Technologies 2007: The Conference of the North American Chapter of the Association for Computational Linguistics; Proceedings of the Main Conference*, pages 139–146, Rochester, New York. Association for Computational Linguistics.

Mark Johnson, Katherine Demuth, Michael Frank, and Bevan Jones. 2010. Synergies in learning words and their referents. In J. Lafferty, C. K. I. Williams, J. Shawe-Taylor, R.S. Zemel, and A. Culotta, editors, *Advances in Neural Information Processing Systems 23*, pages 1018–1026.

Mark Johnson. 2008a. Unsupervised word segmentation for Sesotho using Adaptor Grammars. In *Proceedings of the Tenth Meeting of ACL Special Interest Group on Computational Morphology and Phonology*, pages 20–27, Columbus, Ohio, June. Association for Computational Linguistics.

Mark Johnson. 2008b. Using Adaptor Grammars to identify synergies in the unsupervised acquisition of linguistic structure. In *Proceedings of the 46th Annual Meeting of the Association of Computational Linguistics*, pages 398–406, Columbus, Ohio. Association for Computational Linguistics.

Peter W Jusczyk and Richard N Aslin. 1995. Infants detection of the sound patterns of words in fluent speech. *Cognitive psychology*, 29(1):1–23.

Peter W. Jusczyk, E. A. Hohne, and A. Bauman. 1999. Infants' sensitivity to allophonic cues for word segmentation. *Perception and Psychophysics*, 61:1465–1476.

Brian MacWhinney. 2000. *The CHILDES Project: Tools for Analyzing Talk. Transcription, format and programs*, volume 1. Lawrence Erlbaum.

Kikuo Maekawa, Hanae Koiso, Sadaoki Furui, and Hitoshi Isahara. 2000. Spontaneous speech corpus of japanese. In *proc. LREC*, volume 2, pages 947–952.

Sven L Mattys, Peter W Jusczyk, Paul A Luce, James L Morgan, et al. 1999. Phonotactic and prosodic effects on word segmentation in infants. *Cognitive psychology*, 38(4):465–494.

Sven L Mattys, Peter W Jusczyk, et al. 2001. Do infants segment words or recurring contiguous patterns? *Journal of experimental psychology, human perception and performance*, 27(3):644–655.

Bruna Pelucchi, Jessica F Hay, and Jenny R Saffran. 2009. Learning in reverse: Eight-month-old infants track backward transitional probabilities. *Cognition*, 113(2):244–247.

J. Pitman and M. Yor. 1997. The two-parameter Poisson-Dirichlet distribution derived from a stable subordinator. *Annals of Probability*, 25:855–900.

M. A. Pitt, L. Dilley, K. Johnson, S. Kiesling, W. Raymond, E. Hume, and Fosler-Lussier. 2007. Buckeye corpus of conversational speech.

J. Saffran, R. Aslin, and E. Newport. 1996. Statistical learning by 8-month-old infants. *Science*, 274:1926–1928.

Claude Shannon. 1948. A mathematical theory of communication. *Bell System Technical Journal*, 27(3):379–423.

Daniel Swingley. 2005. Statistical clustering and the contents of the infant vocabulary. *Cognitive Psychology*, 50:86–132.

A. Venkataraman. 2001. A statistical model for word discovery in transcribed speech. *Computational Linguistics*, 27(3):351–372.

Daniel J Weiss, Chip Gerfen, and Aaron D Mitchel. 2010. Colliding cues in word segmentation: the role of cue strength and general cognitive processes. *Language and Cognitive Processes*, 25(3):402–422.

Aris Xanthos. 2004. Combining utterance-boundary and predictability approaches to speech segmentation. In *First Workshop on Psycho-computational Models of Human Language Acquisition*, page 93.

A model of generalization in distributional learning of phonetic categories

Bozena Pajak
Brain & Cognitive Sciences
University of Rochester
Rochester, NY 14627-0268
bpajak@bcs.rochester.edu

Klinton Bicknell
Psychology
UC San Diego
La Jolla, CA 92093-0109
kbicknell@ucsd.edu

Roger Levy
Linguistics
UC San Diego
La Jolla, CA 92093-0108
rlevy@ucsd.edu

Abstract

Computational work in the past decade has produced several models accounting for phonetic category learning from distributional and lexical cues. However, there have been no computational proposals for how people might use another powerful learning mechanism: generalization from learned to analogous distinctions (e.g., from /b/–/p/ to /g/–/k/). Here, we present a new simple model of generalization in phonetic category learning, formalized in a hierarchical Bayesian framework. The model captures our proposal that linguistic knowledge includes the possibility that category types in a language (such as voiced and voiceless) can be shared across sound classes (such as labial and velar), thus naturally leading to generalization. We present two sets of simulations that reproduce key features of human performance in behavioral experiments, and we discuss the model's implications and directions for future research.

1 Introduction

One of the central problems in language acquisition is how phonetic categories are learned, an unsupervised learning problem involving mapping phonetic tokens that vary along continuous dimensions onto discrete categories. This task may be facilitated by languages' extensive re-use of a set of phonetic dimensions (Clements 2003), because learning one distinction (e.g., /b/–/p/ varying along the voice onset time (VOT) dimension) might help learn analogous distinctions (e.g., /d/–/t/, /g/–k/). Existing experimental evidence supports this view: both infants and adults generalize newly learned phonetic category distinctions to untrained sounds along the same dimension (McClaskey et al. 1983, Maye et al. 2008, Perfors & Dunbar 2010, Pajak & Levy 2011a). However, while many models have been proposed to account for learning of phonetic categories (de Boer & Kuhl 2003, Vallabha et al. 2007, McMurray et al. 2009, Feldman et al. 2009, Toscano & McMurray 2010, Dillon et al. 2013), there have been no computational proposals for how generalization to analogous distinctions may be accomplished. Here, we present a new simple model of generalization in phonetic category learning, formalized in a hierarchical Bayesian framework. The model captures our proposal that linguistic knowledge includes the possibility that category types in a language (such as voiced and voiceless) can be shared across sound classes (defined as previously learned category groupings, such as vowels, consonants, nasals, fricatives, etc.), thus naturally leading to generalization.

One difficulty for the view that learning one distinction might help learn analogous distinctions is that there is variability in how the same distinction type is implemented phonetically for different sound classes. For example, VOT values are consistently lower for labials (/b/–/p/) than for velars (/g/–/k/) (Lisker & Abramson 1970), and the durations of singleton and geminate consonants are shorter for nasals (such as /n/–/nn/) than for voiceless fricatives (such as /s/–/ss/) (Giovanardi & Di Benedetto 1998, Mattei & Di Benedetto 2000). Improving on our basic model, we implement a modification that deals with this difficulty by explicitly building in the possibility for analogous categories along the same dimension to have different absolute phonetic values along that dimension (e.g., shorter overall durations for nasals than for fricatives).

In Section 2 we discuss the relevant background on phonetic category learning, including previous modeling work. Section 3 describes our basic computational model, and Section 4 presents simulations demonstrating that the model can reproduce the qualitative patterns shown by adult learners in cases when there is no phonetic variability between sound classes. In Section 5 we describe the extended model that accommodates phonetic variability across sound classes, and in Section 6 we show that the improved model qualitatively matches adult learner performance both when the sound classes implement analogous distinction types in identical ways, and when they differ in the exact phonetic implementation. Section 7 concludes with discussion of future research.

2 Background

One important source of information for unsupervised learning of phonetic categories is the shape of the distribution of acoustic-phonetic cues. For example, under the assumption that each phonetic category has a unimodal distribution on a particular cue, the number of modes in the distribution of phonetic cues can provide information about the number of categories: a unimodal distribution along some continuous acoustic dimension, such as VOT, may indicate a single category (e.g., /p/, as in Hawaiian); a bimodal distribution may suggest a two-category distinction (e.g., /b/ vs. /p/, as in English); and a trimodal distribution implies a three-category distinction (e.g., /b/, /p/, and /p^{h}/, as in Thai). Infants extract this distributional information from the speech signal (Maye et al. 2002, 2008) and form category representations focused around the modal values of categories (Kuhl 1991, Kuhl et al. 1992, Lacerda 1995). Furthermore, information about some categories bootstraps learning of others: infants exposed to a novel bimodal distribution along the VOT dimension for one place of articulation (e.g., alveolar) not only learn that novel distinction, but also generalize it to an analogous contrast for another (e.g., velar) place of articulation (Maye et al. 2008). This ability is preserved beyond infancy, and is potentially used during second language learning, as adults are also able to both learn from distributional cues and use this information when making category judgments about untrained sounds along the same dimensions (Maye & Gerken 2000, 2001, Perfors & Dunbar 2010, Pajak & Levy 2011a,b).

The phonetic variability in how different sound classes implement the same distinction type might in principle hinder generalization across classes. However, there is evidence of generalization even in cases when sound classes differ in the exact phonetic implementation of a shared distinction type. For example, learning a singleton/geminate length contrast for the class of voiceless fricatives (e.g., /s/–/ss/, /f/–/ff/) generalizes to the class of sonorants (e.g., /n/–/nn/, /j/–/jj/) even when the absolute durations of sounds in the two classes are different – overall longer for fricatives than for sonorants (Pajak & Levy 2011a) – indicating that learners are able to accomodate the variability of phonetic cues across different sound classes.

Phonetic categorization from distributional cues has been modeled using Gaussian mixture models, where each category is represented as a Gaussian distribution with a mean and covariance matrix, and category learning involves estimating the parameters of each mixture component and – for some models – the number of components (de Boer & Kuhl 2003, Vallabha et al. 2007, McMurray et al. 2009, Feldman et al. 2009, Toscano & McMurray 2010, Dillon et al. 2013).[1] These models are successful at accounting for distributional learning, but do not model generalization. We build on this previous work (specifically, the model in Feldman et al. 2009) and implement generalization of phonetic distinctions across different sound classes.

3 Basic generalization model

The main question we are addressing here concerns the mechanisms underlying generalization. How do learners make use of information about some phonetic categories when learning other categories? Our proposal is that learners expect category types (such as singleton and geminate, or voiced and voiceless) to be shared among sound classes (such as sonorants and fricatives). We implement this proposal with a hierarchical Dirichlet process (Teh et al. 2006), which allows for sharing categories across data groups (here, sound classes). We build on previous computational work in this area that models phonetic categories as Gaussian distributions. Furthermore, we follow Feldman et al. (2009) in using Dirichlet processes (Ferguson 1973), which allow the model to learn the number of categories from the data, and implementing the process of learning from distributional cues via nonparametric Bayesian inference.

[1] In Dillon et al. (2013) each phoneme is modeled as a mixture of Gaussians, where each component is an allophone.

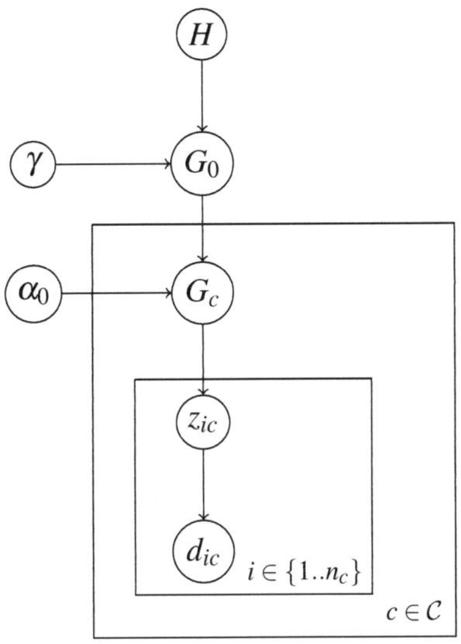

Figure 1: The graphical representation of the basic model.

$$
\begin{array}{llll}
H: & \mu & \sim & \mathcal{N}(\mu_0, \frac{\sigma^2}{\kappa_0}) \\
 & \sigma^2 & \sim & InvChiSq(\nu_0, \sigma_0^2) \\
G_0 & & \sim & DP(\gamma, H) \\
G_c & & \sim & DP(\alpha_0, G_0) \\
z_{ic} & & \sim & G_c \\
d_{ic} & & \sim & \mathcal{N}(\mu_{z_{ic}}, \sigma^2_{z_{ic}}) \\
\hdashline
f_c & & \sim & \mathcal{N}(0, \sigma_f^2) \\
d_{ic} & & \sim & \mathcal{N}(\mu_{z_{ic}}, \sigma^2_{z_{ic}}) + f_c
\end{array}
$$

Figure 2: Mathematical description of the model. The variables below the dotted line refer to the extended model in Figure 6.

3.1 Model details

As a first approach, we consider a simplified scenario of a language with a set of sound classes, each of which contains an unknown number of phonetic categories, with perceptual token defined as a value along a single phonetic dimension. The model learns the set of phonetic categories in each sound class, and the number of categories inferred for one class can inform the inferences about the other class. Here, we make the simplifying assumption that learners acquire a context-independent distribution over sounds, although the model could be extended to use linguistic context (such as coarticulatory or lexical information; Feldman et al. 2009).

Figure 1 provides the graphical representation of the model, and Figure 2 gives its mathematical description. Table 1 provides the key to the model variables. In the model, speech sounds are produced by selecting a phonetic category z_{ic}, which is defined as a mean $\mu_{z_{ic}}$ and variance $\sigma^2_{z_{ic}}$ along a single phonetic dimension,[2] and then sampling a phonetic value from a Gaussian with that mean and variance. We assume a weak prior over categories that does not reflect learners' prior language knowledge (but we return to the possible role of prior language knowledge in the discussion). Learners' beliefs about the sound inventory (distribution over categories and mean and variance of each category) are encoded through a hierarchical Dirichlet process. Each category is sampled from the distribution G_c, which is the distribution over categories in a single sound class. In order to allow sharing of categories across classes, the G_c distribution for each class is sampled from a Dirichlet process with base distribution G_0, which is shared across classes, and concentration parameter α_0 (which determines the sparsity of the distribution over categories). G_0, then, stores the full set of categories realized in any class, and it is sampled from a Dirichlet process with concentration parameter γ and base distribution H, which is a normal inverse chi-squared prior on category

Variable	Explanation
H	base distribution over means and variances of categories
G_0	distribution over possible categories
G_c	distribution over categories in class c
γ, α_0	concentration parameters
z_{ic}	category for datapoint d_{ic}
d_{ic}	datapoint (perceptual token)
n_c	number of datapoints in class c
$\mathcal{C}$	set of classes
f_c	offset parameter
σ_f	standard deviation of prior on f_c

Table 1: Key for the variables in Figures 1, 2, and 6. The variables below the dotted line refer to the extended model in Figure 6.

[2] Although we are modeling phonetic categories as having values along a single dimension, the model can be straightforwardly extended to multiple dimensions, in which case the variance would be replaced by a covariance matrix $\Sigma_{z_{ic}}$.

means and variances.[3] The parameters of the normal inverse chi-squared distribution are: ν_0 and κ_0, which can be thought of as pseudo-observations, as well as μ_0 and σ_0^2, which determine the prior distribution over means and variances, as in Figure 2.

3.2 Inference

The model takes as input the parameters of the base distribution H, the concentration parameters α_0 and γ, and the data, which is composed of a list of phonetic values. The model infers a posterior distribution over category labels for each datapoint via Gibbs sampling. Each iteration of Gibbs sampling resamples the assignments of each datapoint to a lower-level category (in G_c) and also resamples the assignments of lower-level categories to higher-level categories (in G_0). We marginalize over the category means and variances.

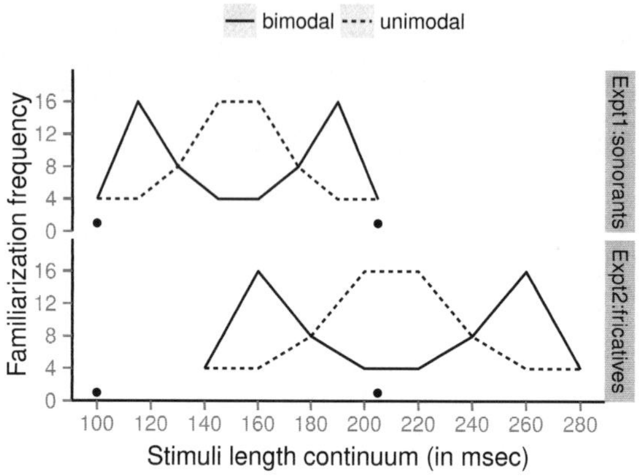

Figure 3: Experiment 1 & 2 training (Pajak and Levy 2011a). The y axis reflects the frequency of tokens from each training continuum. The four points indicate the values of the untrained datapoints.

4 Simulations: basic model

The first set of simulations has three goals: first, to establish that our model can successfully perform distributional learning and second, to show that it can use information about one type of class to influence judgements about another, in the case that there is no variability in category structure between classes. Finally, these simulations reveal a limitation of this basic model, showing that it cannot generalize in the presence of substantial between-class variability in category realizations. We address this limitation in Section 5.

4.1 The data

The data we use to evaluate the model come from the behavioral experiments in Pajak & Levy (2011a). Adult native English speakers were exposed to novel words, where the middle consonant varied along the length dimension from short (e.g., [ama]) to long (e.g., [amma]). The distributional information suggested either one category along the length dimension (unimodal distribution) or two categories (bimodal distribution), as illustrated in Figure 3. In Experiment 1, the training included sounds in the sonorant class (4 continua: [n]-...-[nn], [m]-...-[mm], [j]-...-[jj], [l]-...-[ll]) with the duration range of 100–205msec. In Experiment 2 the training included sounds in the voiceless fricative class (4 continua: [s]-...-[ss], [f]-...-[ff], [θ]-...-[θθ], [ʃ]-...-[ʃʃ]) with the duration range of 140–280msec. The difference in duration ranges between the two classes reflected the natural duration distributions of sounds in these classes: generally shorter for sonorants and longer for fricatives (Greenberg 1996, Giovanardi & Di Benedetto 1998, Mattei & Di Benedetto 2000).

Subsequently, participants' expectations about the number of categories in the trained class and another untrained class were probed by asking for judgments about tokens at the endpoints of the continua: participants were presented with pairs of words (e.g., sonorant [ama]–[amma] or fricative [asa]–[assa]) and asked whether these were two different words in this language or two repetitions of the same word. As illustrated in Table 2, in the test phase of Experiment 1 the durations of both the trained and the untrained class were identical (100msec for any short consonant and 205msec for any long consonant), whereas in the test phase of Experiment 2 the durations were class-specific: longer for trained fricatives (140msec for a short fricative and 280msec for a long fricative) and shorter for untrained sonorants (100msec for a short sonorant and 205msec for a long sonorant).

The experiment results are illustrated in Figure 4. The data from the 'trained' condition shows that learners were able to infer the number of categories from distributional cues: they were more

[3]In the case of categories defined along multiple dimensions, the base distribution would be a normal inverse-Wishart.

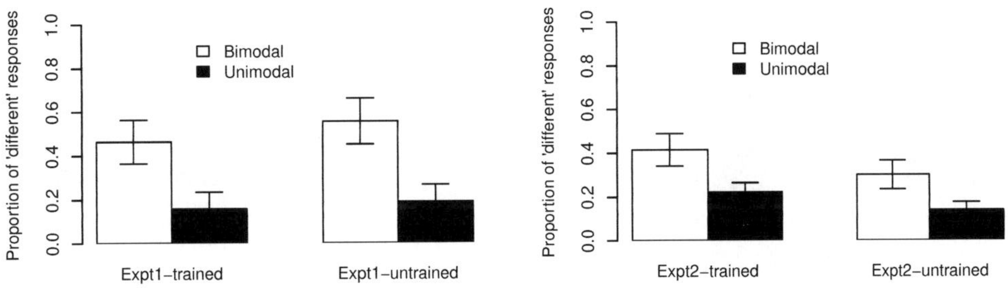

Figure 4: Experiment 1 & 2 results: proportion of 'different' responses on 'different' trials (Pajak and Levy, 2011a).

	Expt. 1	**Expt. 2**
trained	(sonorants) 100ms – 205ms	(fricatives) 140ms – 280ms
untrained	(fricatives) 100ms – 205ms	(sonorants) 100ms – 205ms

Table 2: Experiment 1 & 2 test (Pajak and Levy, 2011a).

likely to posit two categories (i.e., respond 'different' on 'different' trials) when the distribution was bimodal than when the distribution was unimodal. In addition, as demonstrated by the 'untrained' condition, learners used the information about the trained class to make inferences about the untrained class: they were more likely to accept length-based category distinctions for fricatives after learning the distinction for sonorants (Expt. 1), and vice versa (Expt. 2). This generalization occurred both (a) when each class implemented the distinction in exactly the same way (with the same absolute durations; Expt. 1), and (b) when the classes differed in how the shared distinction type was implemented (the absolute durations of the untrained class were shifted relative to the trained class; Expt. 2).

The model simulations described below attempt to replicate the key features of human performance: distributional learning and generalization. We model both experiments of Pajak & Levy (2011a): (a) 'same durations' across classes (Expt. 1), and (b) 'different durations' across classes (Expt. 2). Thus, the datasets we used were closely modeled after their experimental design: (1) Expt. 1 bimodal, (2) Expt. 1 unimodal, (3) Expt. 2 bimodal, and (4) Expt. 2 unimodal. In each dataset, the data consisted of a list of phonetic values (duration in msec), where each datapoint was tagged as belonging to either the sonorant or the fricative class. The frequencies of the 'trained' class were as listed in Figure 3 (simulating a single training continuum). In addition to the 'trained' class, each dataset included two datapoints from the 'untrained' class with the values as listed in Table 2 in the 'untrained' condition. These two datapoints were included in order to evaluate the model's categorization of sounds for which no distributional evidence is available, thus assessing the extent of generalization. We simulated weak perceptual noise by adding to each datapoint normally-distributed error with standard deviation of 0.3 times the distance between adjacent continuum steps.

4.2 Methodology

We ran the basic model on each of the four datasets. For each, we performed 1,000,000 iterations of Gibbs sampling, and analyzed the results for the second half. To assess convergence, we ran four Markov chains for each dataset, using two overdispersed initializations: (1) assigning one category label to all datapoints, and (2) assigning a different label to each datapoint. We used a weak prior base distribution H ($\kappa_0 = .001$; $\nu_0 = .001$; $\sigma_0^2 = 1$; μ_0 was set to the overall mean of the data), and set the concentration parameters $\gamma = \alpha_0 = 1$.

4.3 Results and discussion

The simulation results are illustrated in Figure 5,[4] plotting the proportion of samples on which the model assigned the datapoints to two different categories, as opposed to a single category.[5] Note that

[4] All variables we report in all simulations appear to have converged to the posterior, as assessed by $\hat{R}$ values of 1.1 or less, calculated across the 4 chains (Gelman & Rubin 1992).

[5] No models we report assign the trained category datapoints to more than two categories more than 1% of the time.

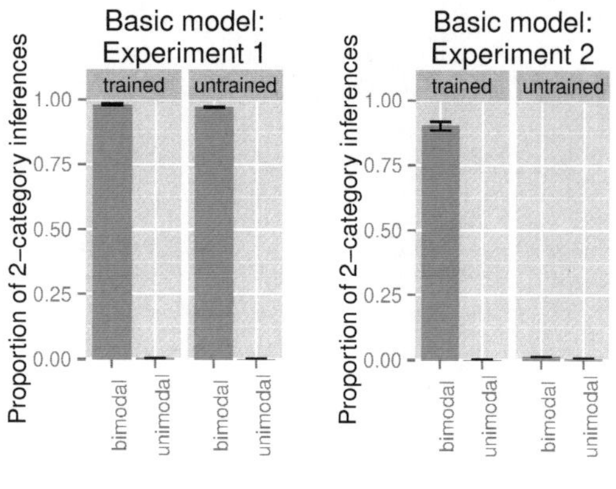

Figure 5: Simulation results for the basic model. Error bars give 95% binomial confidence intervals, computed using the estimated number of effectively independent samples in the Markov chains.

in the 'trained' condition, this means categorization of all datapoints along the continuum. In the 'untrained' condition, on the other hand, it is categorization of two datapoints: one from each endpoint of the continuum.

The results in the 'trained' conditions demonstrate that the model was able to learn from the distributional cues, thus replicating the success of previous phonetic category learning models.

Of most interest here are the results in the 'untrained' condition. The figure on the left shows the results modeling the 'same-durations' experiment (Expt. 1), demonstrating that the model categorizes the two datapoints in the untrained sound class in exactly the same way as it did for the trained sound class: two categories in the bimodal condition, and one category in the unimodal condition. Thus, these results suggest that we can successfully model generalization of distinction types across sound classes in phonetic category learning by assuming that learners have an expectation that category types (such as short and long, or voiceless and voiced) may be shared across classes.

The figure on the right shows the results modeling the 'different-durations' experiment (Expt. 2), revealing a limitation of the model: failure to generalize when the untrained class has the same category structure but different absolute phonetic values (overall shorter in the untrained class than in the trained class). Instead, the model categorizes both untrained datapoints as belonging to a single category. This result diverges from the experimental results, where learners generalize the learned distinction type in both cases, whether the absolute phonetic values of the analogous categories are identical or not. We address this problem in the next section by implementing a modification to the model that allows more flexibility in how each class implements the same category types.

5 Extended generalization model

The goal of the extended model is to explicitly allow for phonetic variability across sound classes. As a general approach, we could imagine functions that transform categories across classes so that the same categories can be "reused" by being translated around to different parts of the phonetic space. These functions would be specific operations representing any intrinsic differences between sound classes. Here, we use a very simple function that can account for one widely attested type of transformation: different absolute phonetic values for analogous categories in distinct sound classes (Ladefoged & Maddieson 1996), such as longer overall durations for voiceless fricatives than for sonorants. This type of transformation has been successfully used in prior modeling work to account for learning allophones of a single phoneme that systematically vary in phonetic values along certain dimensions (Dillon et al. 2013).

5.1 Model details

We implement the possibility for between-class variability by allowing for one specific type of idiosyncratic implementation of categories across classes: learnable class-specific 'offsets' by which the data in a class are shifted along the phonetic dimension, as illustrated in Figure 6 (the key for the variables is in Table 1).

5.2 Inference

Each iteration of MCMC now includes a Metropolis-Hastings step to resample the offset parameters f_c, which uses a zero-mean Gaussian proposal, with standard deviation $\sigma_p = \frac{\text{range of data}}{5}$.

6 Simulations: extended model

This second set of simulations has two goals: (1) to establish that the extended model can successfully replicate the performance of the basic model in both distributional learning and generalization in the no-variability case, and (2) to show that explicitly allowing for variability across classes lets the model generalize when there is between-class variability in category realizations.

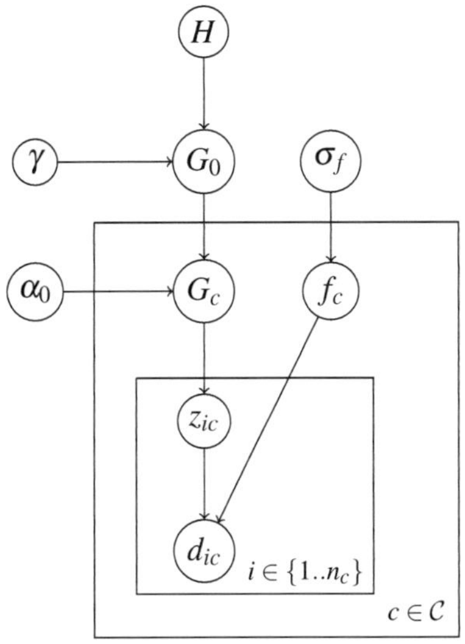

Figure 6: The graphical representation of the extended model.

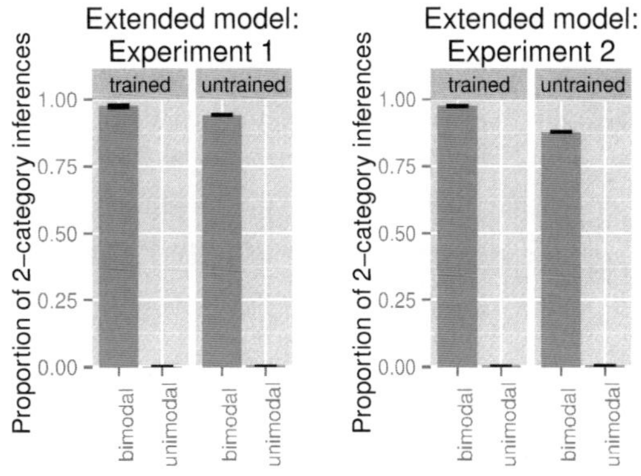

Figure 7: Simulation results for the extended model. Error bars give 95% binomial confidence intervals, computed using the estimated number of effectively independent samples in the Markov chains.

6.1 Methodology

We used the same prior as in the first set of simulations, and used a Gaussian prior on the offset parameter with standard deviation $\sigma_f = 1000$. Because only the relative values of offset parameters are important for category sharing across classes, we set the offset parameter for one of the classes to zero. The four Markov chains now crossed category initialization with two different initial values of the offset parameter.

6.2 Results and discussion

The simulation results are illustrated in Figure 7. The figure on the left demonstrates that the extended model performs similarly to the basic model in the case of no variability between classes. The figure on the right, on the other hand, shows that – unlike the basic model – the extended model succeeds in generalizing the learned distinction type to an untrained sound class when there is phonetic variability between classes. These results suggest that allowing for variability in category implementations across sound classes may be necessary to account for human learning. Taken together, these results are consistent with our proposal that language learners have an expectation that category types can be shared across sound classes. Furthermore, learners appear to have implicit knowledge of the ways that sound classes can vary in their exact phonetic implementations of different category types. This type of knowledge may include – as in our extended generalization model – the possibility that phonetic values of categories in one class can be systematically shifted relative to another.

7 General discussion

In this paper we presented the first model of generalization in phonetic category learning, in which learning a distinction type for one set of sounds (e.g., /m/–/mm/) immediately generalizes to another set of sounds (e.g., /s/–/ss/), thus reproducing the key features of adult learner performance in behavioral experiments. This extends previous computational work in phonetic category learning, which focused on modeling the process of learning from distributional cues, and did not address the question of generalization. The basic premise of the proposed model is that learners' knowledge of phonetic categories is represented hierarchically: individual sounds are grouped into categories, and individual categories are grouped into sound classes. Crucially, the category structure established for one sound class can be directly shared with another class, although different classes can implement the categories in idiosyncratic ways, thus mimicking natural variability in how analogous categories (e.g., short /m/ and /s/, or long /mm/ and /ss/) are phonetically implemented for different sound classes.

The simulation results we presented succeed in reproducing the human pattern of generalization performance, in which the proportion of two-category inferences about the untrained class is very similar to that for the trained class. Note, however, that there are clear quantitative differences between the two in learning performance: the model learns almost perfectly from the available distributional cues ('trained' condition), while adult learners are overall very conservative in accepting two categories along the length dimension, as indicated by the overall low number of 'different' responses. There are two main reasons why the model might be showing more extreme categorization preferences than humans in this particular task. First, humans have cognitive limitations that the current model does not, such as those related to memory or attention. In particular, imperfect memory makes it harder for humans to integrate the distributional information from all the trials in the exposure, and longer training would presumably improve performance. Second, adults have strong native-language biases that affect learning of a second language (Flege 1995). The population tested by Pajak & Levy (2011a) consisted of adult native speakers of American English, a language in which length is not used contrastively. Thus, the low number of 'different' responses in the experiments can be attributed to participants' prior bias against category distinctions based on length. The model, on the other hand, has only a weak prior that was meant to be easily overridden by data.

This last point is of direct relevance for the area of second language (L2) acquisition, where one of the main research foci is to investigate the effects of native-language knowledge on L2 learning. The model we proposed here can potentially be used to systematically investigate the role of native-language biases when learning category distinctions in a new language. In particular, an L2 learner, whose linguistic representations include two languages, could be implemented by adding a language-level node to the model's hierarchical structure (through an additional Dirichlet process). This extension will allow for category structures to be shared not just within a language for different sound classes, but also across languages, thus effectively acting as a native-language bias.

As a final note, we briefly discuss alternative ways of modeling generalization in phonetic category learning. In the model we described in this paper, whole categories are generalized from one class to another. However, one might imagine another approach to this problem where generalization is a byproduct of learners' attending more to the dimension that they find to be relevant for distinguishing between some categories in a language. That is, learners' knowledge would not include the expectation that whole categories may be shared across classes, as we argued here, but rather that a given phonetic dimension is likely to be reused to distinguish between categories in multiple sound classes.

This intuition could be implemented in different ways. In a Dirichlet process model of category learning, the concentration parameter α might be learned, and shared for all classes along a given phonetic dimension, thus producing a bias toward having a similar number of categories across classes. Alternatively, the variance of categories along a given dimension might be learned, and also shared for all classes. Under this scenario, learning category variance along a given dimension would help categorize novel sounds along that dimension. That is, two novel datapoints would be likely categorized into separate categories if the inferred variance along the relevant dimension was smaller than the distance between the datapoints, but into a single category if the inferred variance was comparable to that distance.

Finally, this model assumes that sound classes are given in advance, and that only the categories within each class are learned. While this assumption may seem warranted for some types of perceptually dissimilar sound classes (e.g., consonants and vowels), and also may be appropriate for L2 acquisition, it is not clear that it is true for all sound classes that allow for generalization in infancy. It remains for future work to determine how learners may generalize while simultaneously learning the sound classes.

We plan to pursue all these directions in future work with the ultimate goal of improving our understanding how human learners represent their linguistic knowledge and how they use it when acquiring a new language.

Acknowledgments

We thank Gabriel Doyle and three anonymous CMCL reviewers for useful feedback. This research was supported by NIH Training Grant T32-DC000041 from the Center for Research in Language at UC San Diego to B.P. and NIH Training Grant T32-DC000035 from the Center for Language Sciences at University of Rochester to B.P.

References

de Boer, Bart & Patricia K. Kuhl. 2003. Investigating the role of infant-directed speech with a computer model. *Acoustic Research Letters Online* 4(4). 129–134.

Clements, George N. 2003. Feature economy in sound systems. *Phonology* 20. 287–333.

Dillon, Brian, Ewan Dunbar & William Idsardi. 2013. A single-stage approach to learning phonological categories: Insights from Inuktitut. *Cognitive Science* 37. 344–377.

Feldman, Naomi H., Thomas L. Griffiths & James L. Morgan. 2009. Learning phonetic categories by learning a lexicon. In *Proceedings of the 31st Annual Conference of the Cognitive Science Society*, 2208–2213. Austin, TX: Cognitive Science Society.

Ferguson, Thomas S. 1973. A Bayesian analysis of some nonparametric problems. *Annals of Statistics* 1. 209–230.

Flege, James E. 1995. Second-language speech learning: theory, findings and problems. In Winifred Strange (ed.), *Speech perception and linguistic experience: issues in cross-language research*, 229–273. Timonium, MD: York Press.

Gelman, Andrew & Donald B. Rubin. 1992. Inference from iterative simulation using multiple sequences. *Statistical Science* 7. 457–511.

Giovanardi, Maurizio & Maria-Gabriella Di Benedetto. 1998. Acoustic analysis of singleton and geminate fricatives in Italian. *The European Journal of Language and Speech (EACL/ESCA/ELSNET)* 1998. 1–13.

Greenberg, Steven. 1996. The Switchboard transcription project. Report prepared for the 1996 CLSP/JHU Workshop on Innovative Techniques in Continuous Large Vocabulary Speech Recognition.

Kuhl, Patricia K. 1991. Human adults and human infants show a "perceptual magnet effect" for the prototypes of speech categories, monkeys do not. *Perception and Psychophysics* 50(2). 93–107.

Kuhl, Patricia K., Karen A. Williams, Francisco Lacerda, Kenneth N. Stevens & Björn Lindblom. 1992. Linguistic experience alters phonetic perception in infants by 6 months of age. *Science* 255. 606–608.

Lacerda, Francisco. 1995. The perceptual magnet-effect: An emergent consequence of exemplar-based phonetic memory. In K. Ellenius & P. Branderud (eds.), *Proceedings of the 13th International Congress of Phonetic Sciences*, 140–147. Stockholm: KTH and Stockholm University.

Ladefoged, Peter & Ian Maddieson. 1996. *The sounds of the world's languages*. Oxford, UK; Cambridge, MA: Blackwell.

Lisker, Leigh & Arthur S. Abramson. 1970. The voicing dimensions: Some experiments in comparative phonetics. In *Proceedings of the Sixth International Congress of Phonetic Sciences*, Prague: Academia.

Mattei, Marco & Maria-Gabriella Di Benedetto. 2000. Acoustic analysis of singleton and geminate nasals in Italian. *The European Journal of Language and Speech (EACL/ESCA/ELSNET)* 2000. 1–11.

Maye, Jessica & LouAnn Gerken. 2000. Learning phonemes without minimal pairs. In S. Catherine Howell, Sarah A. Fish & Thea Keith-Lucas (eds.), *Proceedings of the 24th Annual Boston University Conference on Language Development*, 522–533. Somerville, MA: Cascadilla Press.

Maye, Jessica & LouAnn Gerken. 2001. Learning phonemes: how far can the input take us? In A. H-J. Do, L. Domínguez & A. Johansen (eds.), *Proceedings of the 25th Annual Boston University Conference on Language Development*, 480–490. Somerville, MA: Cascadilla Press.

Maye, Jessica, Daniel J. Weiss & Richard N. Aslin. 2008. Statistical phonetic learning in infants: facilitation and feature generalization. *Developmental Science* 11(1). 122–134.

Maye, Jessica, Janet F. Werker & LouAnn Gerken. 2002. Infant sensitivity to distributional information can affect phonetic discrimination. *Cognition* 82. B101–B111.

McClaskey, Cynthia L., David B. Pisoni & Thomas D. Carrell. 1983. Transfer of training of a new linguistic contrast in voicing. *Perception and Psychophysics* 34(4). 323–330.

McMurray, Bob, Richard N. Aslin & Joseph C. Toscano. 2009. Statistical learning of phonetic categories: insights from a computational approach. *Developmental Science* 12(3). 369–378.

Pajak, Bozena & Roger Levy. 2011a. How abstract are phonological representations? Evidence from distributional perceptual learning.

In *Proceedings of the 47th Annual Meeting of the Chicago Linguistic Society*, Chicago, IL: University of Chicago.

Pajak, Bozena & Roger Levy. 2011b. Phonological generalization from distributional evidence. In L. Carlson, C. Hölscher & T. Shipley (eds.), *Proceedings of the 33rd Annual Conference of the Cognitive Science Society*, 2673–2678. Austin, TX: Cognitive Science Society.

Perfors, Amy & David Dunbar. 2010. Phonetic training makes word learning easier. In S. Ohlsson & R. Catrambone (eds.), *Proceedings of the 32nd Annual Conference of the Cognitive Science Society*, 1613–1618. Austin, TX: Cognitive Science Society.

Teh, Yee Whye, Michael I. Jordan, Matthew J. Beal & David M. Blei. 2006. Hierarchical Dirichlet processes. *Journal of the American Statistical Association* 101(476). 1566–1581.

Toscano, Joseph C. & Bob McMurray. 2010. Cue integration with categories: Weighting acoustic cues in speech using unsupervised learning and distributional statistics. *Cognitive Science* 34. 434–464.

Vallabha, Gautam K., James L. McClelland, Ferran Pons, Janet F. Werker & Shigeaki Amano. 2007. Unsupervised learning of vowel categories from infant-directed speech. *Proceedings of the National Academy of Sciences* 104(33). 13273–13278.

Learning non-concatenative morphology

Michelle A. Fullwood
Dept. of Linguistics and Philosophy
Massachusetts Institute of Technology
maf@mit.edu

Timothy J. O'Donnell
Dept. of Brain and Cognitive Sciences
Massachusetts Institute of Technology
timod@mit.edu

Abstract

Recent work in computational psycholinguistics shows that morpheme lexica can be acquired in an unsupervised manner from a corpus of words by selecting the lexicon that best balances productivity and reuse (e.g. Goldwater et al. (2009) and others). In this paper, we extend such work to the problem of acquiring non-concatenative morphology, proposing a simple model of morphology that can handle both concatenative and non-concatenative morphology and applying Bayesian inference on two datasets of Arabic and English verbs to acquire lexica. We show that our approach successfully extracts the non-contiguous triliteral root from Arabic verb stems.

1 Introduction

What are the basic structure-building operations that enable the creative use of language, and how do children exposed to a language acquire the inventory of primitive units which are used to form new expressions? In the case of word formation, recent work in computational psycholinguistics has shown how an inventory of morphemes can be acquired by selecting a lexicon that best balances the ability of individual sound sequences to combine productively against the reusability of those sequences (e.g., Brent (1999), Goldwater et al. (2009), Feldman et al. (2009), O'Donnell et al. (2011), Lee et al. (2011).) However, this work has focused almost exclusively on one kind of structure-building operation: concatenation. The languages of the world, however, exhibit a variety of other, non-concatenative word-formation processes (Spencer, 1991).

Famously, the predominant mode of Semitic word formation is non-concatenative. For example, the following Arabic words, all related to the concept of writing, share no contiguous sequences of segments (i.e., phones), but they do share a discontinuous subsequence $\sqrt{\text{ktb}}$, which has been traditionally analyzed as an independent morpheme, termed the "root".

kataba	"he wrote"
kutiba	"it was written"
yaktubu	"he writes"
ka:tib	"writer"
kita:b	"book"
kutub	"books"
maktab	"office"

Table 1: List of Arabic words with root $\sqrt{\text{ktb}}$

Many Arabic words appear to be constructed via a process of interleaving segments from different morphemes, as opposed to concatenation.

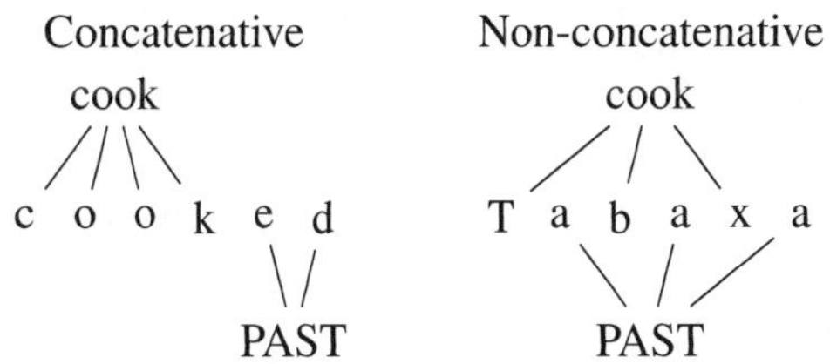

Figure 1: Schematic of concatenative vs non-concatenative morphology

Such non-concatenative morphology is pervasive in the world's languages. Even English, whose morphology is fundamentally concatenative, displays pockets of non-concatenative behavior, for example in the irregular past tenses (see Table 2).

In these words, the stem vowels undergo ablaut changing between tenses. This cannot be handled in a purely concatenative framework unless we consider these words listed exceptions. However, such irregulars do show limited productiv-

bite /bajt/	bit /bɪt/
sing /sɪŋ/	sang /sæŋ/
give /gɪv/	gave /gejv/
feel /fil/	felt /fɛlt/

Table 2: Examples of English irregular verbs

ity (see Albright and Hayes (2003), Prasada and Pinker (1993), Bybee and Slobin (1982), Bybee and Moder (1983), Ambridge (2010)), and in other languages such stem changing processes are fully productive.

In Semitic, it is clear that non-concatenative word formation is productive. Borrowings from other languages are modified to fit the available non-concatenative templates. This has also been tested psycholinguistically: Berman (2003), for instance, shows that Hebrew-speaking preschoolers can productively form novel verbs out of nouns and adjectives, a process that requires the ability to extract roots and apply them to existing verbal templates.

Any model of word formation, therefore, needs to be capable of generalizing to both concatenative and non-concatenative morphological systems. In this paper, we propose a computational model of word formation which is capable of capturing both types of morphology, and explore its ramifications for morphological segmentation.

We apply Bayesian inference on a small corpus of Arabic and English words to learn the morphemes that comprise them, successfully learning the Arabic root with great accuracy, but less successfully English verbal inflectional suffixes. We then examine the shortcomings of the model and propose further directions.

2 Arabic Verbal Morphology

In this paper, we focus on Arabic verbal stem morphology. The Arabic verbal stem is built from the interleaving of a consonantal root and a vocalism that conveys voice (active/passive) and aspect (perfect/imperfect). The stem can then undergo further derivational prefixation or infixation. To this stem inflectional affixes indicating the subject's person, number and gender are then added. In the present work, we focus on stem morphology, leaving inflectional morphology to future extensions of the model.

There are nine common forms of the Arabic verbal stem, also known by the Hebrew grammatical term *binyan*. In Table 3, $\sqrt{\text{fʕl}}$ represents the triconsonantal root. Only the perfect forms are given.

Form	Active	Passive
I	faʕal	fuʕil
II	faʕʕal	fuʕʕil
III	faaʕal	fuuʕil
IV	ʔafʕal	ʔufʕil
V	tafaʕʕal	tufuʕʕil
VI	tafaaʕal	tufuuʕil
VII	ʔinfaʕal	-
VIII	ʔiftaʕal	ʔiftiʕil
X	ʔistafʕal	ʔistufʕil

Table 3: List of common Arabic verbal binyanim

Each of these forms has traditionally been associated with a particular semantics. For example, Form II verbs are generally causatives of Form I verbs, as is *kattab* "to cause to write" (c.f. *katab* "to write"). However, as is commonly the case with derivational morphology, these semantic associations are not completely regular: many forms have been lexicalized with alternative or more specific meanings.

2.1 Theoretical accounts

The traditional Arab grammarians' account of the Arabic verb was as follows: each form was associated with a template with slots labelled C_1, C_2 and C_3, traditionally represented with the consonants $\sqrt{\text{fʕl}}$, as described above. The actual root consonants were slotted into these gaps. Thus the template of the Form VIII active perfect verb stem was $\text{taC}_1\text{aC}_2\text{C}_2\text{aC}_3$. This, combined with the triconsonantal root, made up the verbal stem.

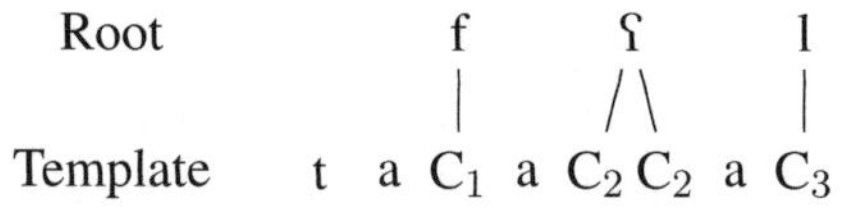

Figure 2: Traditional analysis of Arabic Form V verb

The first generative linguistic treatment of Arabic verbal morphology (McCarthy, 1979; McCarthy, 1981) adopted the notion of the root and template, but split off the derivational prefixes and infixes and vocalism from the template. Borrowing from the technology of autosegmental phonology (Goldsmith, 1976), the template was now comprised of C(onsonant) and V(owel) slots. Rules governing the spreading of segments ensured that consonants and vowels appeared in the correct positions within a template.

Under McCarthy's model, the analysis for [tafaʕʕal] would be as follows:

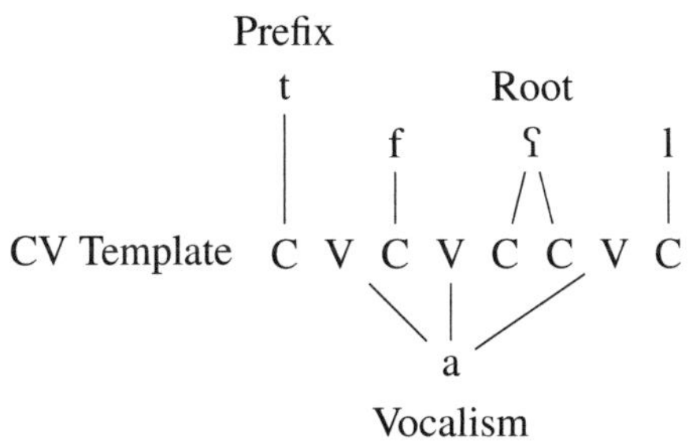

Figure 3: McCarthy analysis of Arabic Form V verb

While increasing the number of morphemes associated with each verb, the McCarthy approach economized on the variety of such units in the lexicon. The inventory of CV templates was limited; there were three vocalisms corresponding to active and passive voice intersecting with perfect and imperfect aspect; and only four derivational prefixes (/ʔ/,/n/,/t/,/st/), one of which became an infix via morphophonological rule in Form VIII.[1]

We adopt a middle ground between the traditional Arab grammarians' description of the verbal stem and McCarthy's analysis as our starting point. We describe this approach in the next section.

3 The Approach

Our initial model of morphology adopts McCarthy's notion of an abstract template, but coalesces the prefixes and infixes with the vocalism into what we term the "residue." Each stem is thus composed of two morphemes: the root and the residue, and their interleaving is dictated by a template with slots for root and residue segments.

For example, ʔiktatab = - - - r - - r - r (template) + ktb (root) + ʔitaa (residue), where r indicates a root segment and - a residue segment.

The residue may be of length 0, effectively making the word consist of a single morpheme. Concatenative morphology may be modelled in this framework by grouping all the root segments together, for example *cooked* [kukt] = r r r - (template) + kuk (root) + t (residue).

The template, root and residue are each drawn from a separate sub-lexicon, modeled using tools from Bayesian non-parametric statistics (see Section 4). These tools put a prior distribution on the lexica that biases them in favour of reusing existing frequent forms and small lexica by promoting maximal sharing of morphemes.

When applied to data, we derive a segmentation for each word into a root and a residue.

4 Model

Following earlier work on Bayesian lexicon learning (e.g. Goldwater et al. (2009), we use a distribution over lexical items known as the Pitman–Yor Process (PYP) (Pitman and Yor, 1995). Let G be a distribution over primitive phonological elements of the lexicon (e.g., words, roots, residues, templates, morphemes, etc.). The behavior of PYP process $\text{PYP}(a, b, G)$ with base measure G and parameters a and b can be described as follows. The first time we sample from $\text{PYP}(a, b, G)$ a new lexical item will be sampled using G. On subsequent samples from $\text{PYP}(a, b, G)$, we either reuse an existing lexical item i with probability $\frac{n_i - a}{N+b}$, where N is the number of lexical items sampled so far, n_i is the number of times that lexical item i has been used in the past, and $0 \leq a \leq 1$ and $b > -a$ are parameters of the model. Alternatively, we sample a new lexical item with probability $\frac{aK+b}{N+b}$, where K is the number of times a *new* lexical item was sampled in the past from the underlying distribution G. Notice that this process induces a rich-get-richer scheme for sampling from the process. The more a particular lexical item has been reused, the more likely it is to be reused in the future. The Pitman–Yor process also produces a bias towards smaller, more compact lexica.

In our model, we maintain three sublexica for templates (L_{Tp}), roots (L_{Rt}), and residues (L_{Rs}) each drawn from a Pitman–Yor process with its own hyperparameters.

$$L_X \sim \text{PYP}(a_X, b_X, G_X) \qquad (1)$$

where $X \in \{\text{Tp}, \text{Rt}, \text{Rs}\}$ Words are drawn by first drawing a template, then drawing a root and a residue (of the appropriate length) and inserting the segments from the root and residue in the appropriate positions in the word as indicated by the

[1]Other theories of Arabic morphology that reject the existence of the root are also extant in the literature; see e.g. (Bat-El, 1994) for a stem modification and vowel overwriting approach.

template. Our templates are strings in $\{\mathrm{Rt}, \mathrm{Rs}\}^*$ indicating for each position in a word whether that position is part of the word's root (Rt) or residue (Rs). These templates themselves are drawn from a base measure G_{Tp} which is defined as follows. To add a new template to the template lexicon first draw a length for that template, K, from a Poisson distribution.

$$K \sim \text{POISSON}(5) \tag{2}$$

We then sample a template of length K by drawing a Bernoulli random variable t_i for each position $i \in 1..K$ is a root or residue position.

$$t_i \sim \text{BERNOULLI}(\theta) \tag{3}$$

The base measure over templates, G_{Tp}, is defined as the concatenation of the t_i's.

The base distributions over roots and residues, G_{Rt} and G_{Rs}, are drawn in the following manner. Having drawn a template, T we know the lengths of the root, K_{Rt}, and residue K_{Rt}. For each position in the root or residue r_i where $i \in 1..K_{\mathrm{Rt/Rs}}$, we sample a phone from a uniform distribution over phones.

$$r_i \sim \text{UNIFORM}(|\text{alphabet}|) \tag{4}$$

5 Inference

Inference was performed via Metropolis–Hastings sampling. The sampler was initialized by assigning a random template to each word in the training corpus. The algorithm then sampled a new template, root, and residue for each word in the corpus in turn. The proposal distribution over templates for our sampler considered all templates currently in use by another word, as well as a randomly generated template from the prior. Samples from this proposal distribution were corrected into the true distribution using the Metropolis–Hastings criterion.

6 Related work

The approach of this paper builds on previous work on Bayesian lexicon learning starting with Goldwater et al. (2009). However, to our knowledge, this approach has not been applied to non-concatenative morphological segmentation. Where it has been applied to Arabic (e.g. Lee et al. (2011)), it has been applied to unvowelled text, since standard Arabic orthography drops short vowels. However, this has the effect of reducing the problem mostly to one of concatenative morphology.

Non-concatenative morphology has been approached computationally via other research, however. Kataja and Koskenniemi (1988) first showed that Semitic roots and patterns could be described using regular languages. This insight was subsequently computationally implemented using finite state methods by Beesley (1991) and others. Roark and Sproat (2007) present a model of both concatenative and non-concatenative morphology based on the operation of composition that is similar to the one we describe above.

The narrower problem of isolating roots from Semitic words, for instance as a precursor to information retrieval, has also received much attention. Existing approaches appear to be mostly rule-based or dictionary-based (see Al-Shawakfa et al. (2010) for a recent survey).

7 Experiments

We applied the morphological model and inference procedure described in Sections 4 and 5 to two datasets of Arabic and English.

7.1 Data

The Arabic corpus for this experiment consisted of verbal stems taken from the verb concordance of the Quranic Arabic Corpus (Dukes, 2011). All possible active, passive, perfect and imperfect fully-vowelled verbal stems for Forms I–X, excluding the relatively rare Form IX, were generated. We used this corpus rather than a lexicon as our starting point to obtain a list of relatively high frequency verbs.

This list of stems was then filtered in two ways: first, only triconsonantal "strong" roots were considered. The so-called "weak" roots of Arabic either include a vowel or semi-vowel, or a doubled consonant. These undergo segmental changes in various environments, which cannot be handled by our current generative model.

Secondly, the list was filtered through the Buckwalter stem lexicon (Buckwalter, 2002) to obtain only stems that were licit according to the Buckwalter morphological analyzer.

This process yielded 1563 verbal stems, comprising 427 unique roots, 26 residues, and 9 templates. The stems were supplied to the sampler in the Buckwalter transliteration.

The English corpus was constructed along similar lines. All verb forms related to the 299 most frequent lemmas in the Penn Treebank (Marcus et al., 1999) were used, excluding auxiliaries such as *might* or *should*. Each lemma thus had up to five verbal forms associated with it: the bare form (*forget*), the third person singular present (*forgets*), the gerund (*forgetting*), past tense (*forgot*), and past participle (*forgotten*).

This resulted in 1549 verbal forms, comprising 295 unique roots, 108 residues, and 55 templates. CELEX (Baayen et al., 1995) pronunciations for these words were supplied to the sampler in CELEX's DISC transliteration.

Deriving a gold standard analysis for English verbs was less straightforward than in the Arabic case. The following convention was used: The root was any subsequence of segments shared by all the forms related to the same lemma. Thus, for the example lemma of *forget*, the correct template, root and residue were deemed to be:

forget	f@gEt	r r r - r	f@gt	E
forgets	f@gEts	r r r - r -	f@gt	Es
forgot	f@gQt	r r r - r	f@gt	Q
forgetting	f@gEtIN	r r r - r - -	f@gt	EIN
forgotten	f@gQtH	r r r - r -	f@gt	QH

Table 4: Correct analyses under the root/residue model for the lemma *forget*

37 templates were concatenative, and 18 non-concatenative. The latter were necessary to accommodate 46 irregular lemmas associated with 254 forms.

7.2 Results and Discussion

We ran 10 instances of the sampler for 200 sweeps through the data. For the Arabic training set, this number of sweeps typically resulted in the sampler finding a local mode of the posterior, making few further changes to the state during longer runs. An identical experimental set-up was used for English. Evaluation was performed on the final state of each sampler instance.

The correctness of the sampler's output was measured in terms of the accuracy of the templates it predicted for each word. The word-level accuracy indicates the number of words that had their entire template correctly sampled, while the segment-level accuracy metric gives partial credit by considering the average number of correct bits

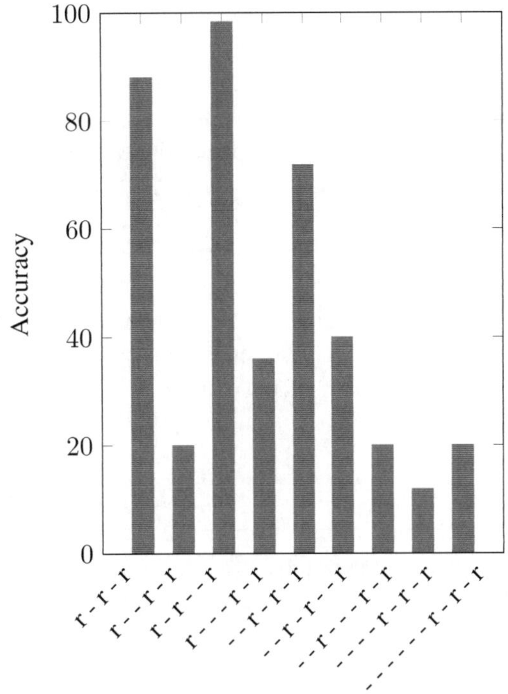

Figure 4: Unweighted accuracy with which each template was sampled

(r versus -) in each sampled template.

Table 5 shows the average accuracy of the 10 samples, weighted by each sample's joint probability.

Accuracy	Word-level	Segment-level
Arabic	92.3%	98.2%
English	43.9%	85.3%

Table 5: Average weighted accuracy of samples

Arabic Analyses Figure 4 shows the average unweighted accuracy with which each of the 9 Arabic templates was sampled.

Figure 4 reveals an effect of both the rarity and the length of each template. For instance, the performance on template r - - r - r (second bar from left) is exceptionally low, but this is the result of there being only one instance of this template in the training set: Euwqib, the passive form of the Form III verb of root Eqb, in the Buckwalter transliteration.[2] In addition, the longer the word,

[2]This is an artifact of Arabic orthography and the Buckwalter transliteration, which puts the active form EAqab with template r - r - r in correspondence with the passive template r - - r - r.

the poorer the performance of the model. This is likely the result of the difficulty of searching over the space of templates for longer forms. Since the number of potential templates increases exponentially with the length of the form, finding the correct template becomes increasingly difficult. This problem can likely be addressed in future models by adopting an analysis similar to McCarthy's whereby the residue is further subdivided into vocalism, prefixes and infixes. Note that even in such long forms, however, the letters belonging to the root were generally isolated in one of the two morphemes.

English Analyses The English experiment yielded poorer results than the Arabic dataset. The statistics of the datasets reveal the cause of the failure of the English model: the English dataset had several times more residues and templates than the Arabic dataset did, thus lacking as much uniform structure. Nevertheless, the relatively high segment-level accuracy shows that the model tended to find templates that were only incorrect in 1 or 2 positions.

The dominant pattern of errors was in the direction of overgeneralization of the concatenative templates to the irregular forms. Out of the 254 words related to a lemma with an irregular past form, 241 received incorrect templates, 232 of which were concatenative, often correctly splitting off the regular suffix where there was one. For example, *sing* and *singing* were parsed as *sing+∅* and *sing+ing*, while *sung* was parsed as a separate root. Note that under an analysis of English irregulars as separate memorized lexical items, the sampler behaved correctly in such cases.

However, out of 1295 words related to perfectly regular lemmas, the sampler determined 628 templates incorrectly. Out of these, 325 were given concatenative templates, but with too much or too little segmental material allocated to the suffix. For example, the word *invert* was analyzed as *inver+t*, with its other forms following suit as *inver+ted*, *inver+ting* and *inver+ts*. This is likely due to subregularities in the word corpus: with many words ending with -t, this analysis becomes more attractive.

The remaining 303 regular verbs were given non-concatenative templates. For instance, *identify* was split up into *dfy* and *ienti*. No consistent pattern could be discerned from these cases.

8 Conclusion

We have proposed a model of morpheme-lexicon learning that is capable of handling concatenative and non-concatenative morphology up to the level of two morphemes. We have seen that Bayesian inference on this model with an Arabic dataset of verbal stems successfully learns the non-contiguous root and residue as morphemes.

In future work, we intend to extend our simplified model of morphology to McCarthy's complete model by adding concatenative prefixation and suffixation processes and segment-spreading rules. Besides being capable of handling the inflectional aspects of Arabic morphology, we anticipate that this extension will improve the performance of the model on Arabic verbal stems as well, since the number of non-concatenative templates that have to be learned will decrease. For example, the template for the Form V verb [tafaʕʕal] can be reduced to that for the Form II verb [faʕʕal] plus an additional prefix.

We also anticipate that the performance on English will be vastly improved, since the dominant mode of word formation in English is concatenative, while the small number of irregular past tenses and plurals that undergo ablaut can be handled using the non-concatenative architecture of the model. This would also be more in line with native speakers' intuitions and linguistic analyses of English morphology.

Acknowledgments

Parts of the sampler code were written by Peter Graff. We would also like to thank Adam Albright and audiences at the MIT Phonology Circle and the Northeast Computational Phonology Workshop (NECPhon) for feedback on this project. This material is based upon work supported by the National Science Foundation Graduate Research Fellowship Program under Grant No. 1122374.

References

Emad Al-Shawakfa, Amer Al-Badarneh, Safwan Shatnawi, Khaleel Al-Rabab'ah, and Basel Bani-Ismail. 2010. A comparison study of some Arabic root finding algorithms. *Journal of the American Society for Information Science and Technology*, 61(5):1015–1024.

Adam Albright and Bruce Hayes. 2003. Rules vs. analogy in English past tenses: A computational/experimental study. *Cognition*, 90(2):119–161.

Ben Ambridge. 2010. Children's judgments of regular and irregular novel past–tense forms: New data on the English past–tense debate. *Developmental Psychology*, In Press.

Harald R. Baayen, Richard Piepenbrock, and Leon Gulikers. 1995. *The CELEX Lexical Database. Release 2 (CD-ROM).* Linguistic Data Consortium, University of Pennsylvania, Philadelphia, Pennsylvania.

Outi Bat-El. 1994. Stem modification and cluster transfer in Modern Hebrew. *Natural Language and Linguistic Theory*, 12:571–593.

Kenneth R. Beesley. 1991. Computer analysis of Arabic morphology: A two-level approach with detours. In Bernard Comrie and Mushira Eid, editors, *Perspectives on Arabic Linguistics III: Papers from the Third Annual Symposium on Arabic Linguistics*, pages 155–172. John Benjamins. Read originally at the Third Annual Symposium on Arabic Linguistics, University of Utah, Salt Lake City, Utah, 3-4 March 1989.

Ruth A. Berman. 2003. Children's lexical innovations. In Joseph Shimron, editor, *Language Processing and Acquisition in Languages of Semitic, Root-based, Morphology*, pages 243–292. John Benjamins.

Michael R. Brent. 1999. Speech segmentation and word discovery: A computational perspective. *Trends in Cognitive Sciences*, 3(8):294–301, August.

Tim Buckwalter. 2002. Buckwalter Arabic morphological analyzer version 1.0. Technical Report LDC2002L49, Linguistic Data Consortium.

Joan L. Bybee and Carol Lynn Moder. 1983. Morphological classes as natural categories. *Language*, 59(2):251–270, June.

Joan L. Bybee and Daniel I. Slobin. 1982. Rules and schemas in the development and use of the English past tense. *Language*, 58(2):265–289.

Kais Dukes. 2011. Quranic Arabic Corpus. http://corpus.quran.com/.

Naomi H. Feldman, Thomas L. Griffiths, and James L. Morgan. 2009. Learning phonetic categories by learning a lexicon. In *Proceedings of the 31st Annual Meeting of the Cognitive Science Society*.

John Anton Goldsmith. 1976. *Autosegmental Phonology*. Ph.D. thesis, Massachusetts Institute of Technology.

Sharon Goldwater, Thomas L. Griffiths, and Mark Johnson. 2009. A Bayesian framework for word segmentation: Exploring the effects of context. *Cognition*, 112:21–54.

Laura Kataja and Kimmo Koskenniemi. 1988. Finite-state description of Semitic morphology: a case study of Ancient Akkadian. In *Proceedings of the 12th conference on Computational linguistics - Volume 1*, COLING '88, pages 313–315, Stroudsburg, PA, USA. Association for Computational Linguistics.

Yoong Keok Lee, Aria Haghighi, and Regina Barzilay. 2011. Modeling syntactic context improves morphological segmentation. In *Proceedings of the Conference on Natural Language Learning*.

Mitchell P. Marcus, Beatrice Santorini, Mary Ann Marcinkiewicz, and Ann Taylor. 1999. Treebank 3 technical report. Technical report, Linguistic Data Consortium, Philadelphia.

John J. McCarthy. 1979. *Formal Problems in Semitic Phonology and Morphology*. Ph.D. thesis, Massachusetts Institute of Technology.

John J. McCarthy. 1981. A prosodic theory of nonconcatenative morphology. *Linguistic Inquiry*, 12:373–418.

Timothy J. O'Donnell, Jesse Snedeker, Joshua B. Tenenbaum, and Noah D. Goodman. 2011. Productivity and reuse in language. In *Proceedings of the 33rd Annual Conference of the Cognitive Science Society*.

Jim Pitman and Marc Yor. 1995. The two-parameter Poisson–Dirichlet distribution derived from a stable subordinator. Technical report, Department of Statistics University of California, Berkeley.

Sandeep Prasada and Steven Pinker. 1993. Generalisation of regular and irregular morphological patterns. *Language and Cognitive Processes*, 8(1):1–56.

Brian Roark and Richard Sproat. 2007. *Computational Approaches to Morphology and Syntax*. Oxford University Press.

Andrew Spencer. 1991. *Morphological Theory*. Blackwell.

Statistical Representation of Grammaticality Judgements: the Limits of N-Gram Models

Alexander Clark, Gianluca Giorgolo, and Shalom Lappin
Department of Philosophy, King's College London
`firstname.lastname@kcl.ac.uk`

Abstract

We use a set of enriched n-gram models to track grammaticality judgements for different sorts of passive sentences in English. We construct these models by specifying scoring functions to map the log probabilities (logprobs) of an n-gram model for a test set of sentences onto scores which depend on properties of the string related to the parameters of the model. We test our models on classification tasks for different kinds of passive sentences. Our experiments indicate that our n-gram models achieve high accuracy in identifying ill-formed passives in which ill-formedness depends on local relations within the n-gram frame, but they are far less successful in detecting non-local relations that produce unacceptability in other types of passive construction. We take these results to indicate some of the strengths and the limitations of word and lexical class n-gram models as candidate representations of speakers' grammatical knowledge.

1 Introduction

Most advocates (Pereira, 2000; Bod et al., 2003) and critics (Chomsky, 1957; Fong et al., 2013) of a probabilistic view of grammatical knowledge have assumed that this view identifies the grammatical status of a sentence directly with the probability of its occurrence. By contrast, we seek to characterize grammatical knowledge statistically, but without reducing grammaticality directly to probability. Instead we specify a set of scoring procedures for mapping the logprob value of a sentence into a relative grammaticality score, on the basis of the properties of the sentence and of the logprobs that an n-gram word model generates for the corpus containing the sentence. A scoring procedure in this set generates scores in terms of which we construct a grammaticality classifier, using a parameterized standard deviation from the mean value. The classifier provides a procedure for testing the accuracy of different scoring criteria in separating grammatical from ungrammatical passive sentences.

We evaluate this approach by applying it to the task of distinguishing well and ill-formed sentences with passive constructions headed by four different sorts of verbs: intransitives (*appear, last*), pseudo-transitives, which take a restricted set of notional objects (*laugh a hearty laugh, weigh 10 kg*), ambiguous transitives, which allow both agentive and thematic subjects (*the jeans / the tailor fitted John*), and robust transitives that passivize freely (*write, move*). Intransitives and pseudo-transitives generally yield ill-formed passives. Passives formed from ambiguous transitives tend to be well-formed only on the agentive reading. Robust transitives, for the most part, yield acceptable passives, even if they are semantically (or pragmatically) odd.

Experimenting with several scoring procedures and alternative values for our standard deviation parameter, we found that our classifier can distinguish pairwise between elements of the first two classes of passives and those of the latter two with a high degree of accuracy. However, its performance is far less reliable in identifying the difference between ambiguous and robust transitive passives. The first classification task relies on local lexical patterns that can be picked up by n-gram models, while the second requires identification of anomalous relations between passivized verbs and *by*-phrases, which are not generally accessible to measurement within the range of an n-gram.

We also observed that as we increased the size of the training corpus, the performance of our enriched models on the classification task also increased. This result suggests that better n-gram language models are more sensitive to the sorts of patterns that our scoring procedures rely on to generate accurate grammaticality classifications.

We note the important difference between

grammaticality and acceptability. Following standard assumptions, we take grammaticality to be a theoretical notion, and acceptability to be an empirically testable property. Acceptability is, in part, determined by grammaticality, but also by factors such as sentence length, processing limitations, semantic acceptability and many other elements. Teasing apart these two concepts, and explicating their precise relationship raises a host of subtle methodological issues that we will not address here. Oversimplifying somewhat, we are trying to reconstruct a gradient notion of grammaticality which is derived from probabilistic models, that can serve as a core component of a full model of acceptability.

We distinguish our task from the standard task of error detection in NLP (e.g. Post (2011)), that can be used in various language processing systems, such as machine translation (Pauls and Klein, 2012), language modeling and so on. In error detection, the problem is a supervised learning task. Given a corpus of examples labeled as grammatical or ungrammatical, the problem is to learn a classifier to distinguish them. We use supervised learning as well, but only to measure the upper bound of an unsupervised learning method. We assume that native speakers do not, in general, have access to systematic sets of ungrammatical sentences that they can use to calibrate their judgement of acceptability. Rather ungrammatical sentences are unusual or unlikely. However, we use some ungrammatical sentences to set an optimal threshold for our scoring procedures.

2 Enriched N-Gram Language Models

We assume that we have some high quality language model which defines a probability distribution over whole sentences. As has often been noted, it is not possible to reduce grammaticality directly to a probability of this type, for several reasons. First, if one merely specifies a fixed probability value as a threshold for grammaticality, where strings are deemed to be grammatical if and only if their probability is higher than the threshold, then one is committed to the existence of only a finite number of grammatical sentences. The probabilities of the possible strings of words in a language sum to 1, and so at most $1/\epsilon$ sentences can have a probability of at least ϵ. Second, probability can be affected by factors that do not influence grammaticality. For example, the word 'yak' is rarer (and therefore less probable) than the word 'horse', but this does not affect the relative grammaticality of 'I saw a horse' versus 'I saw a yak'. Third, a short ungrammatical sentence may have a higher probability than a long grammatical sentence with many rare words.

In spite of these arguments against a naive reduction of grammaticality, probabilistic inference does play a role in linguistic judgements, as indicated by the fact that they are often gradient. Probabilistic inference is pervasive throughout all domains of cognition (Chater et al., 2006), and therefore it is plausible to assume that knowledge of language is also probabilistic in nature. Moreover language models do seem to play a crucial role in speech recognition and sentence processing. Without them we would not be able to understand speech in a noisy environment.

We propose to accommodate these different considerations by using a scoring function to map probabilities to grammaticality rankings. This function does not apply directly to probabilities, but rather to the parameters of the language model. The probability of a particular sentence with respect to a log-linear language model will be the product of certain parameters: in log space, the sum. We define scores that operate on this collection of parameters.

2.1 Scores

We have experimented with scores of two different types that correlate with the grammaticality of a sentence. Those of the first type are different implementations of the idea of normalizing the logprob assigned by an n-gram model to a string by eliminating the significance of factors that do not influence the grammatical status of a sentence, such as sentence length and word frequency. Scores of the second type are based on the intuition that the (un)grammaticality of a sentence is largely determined by its problematic components. These scores are functions of the lowest scoring n-grams in the sentence.

Mean logprob (ML) This score is the logprob of the entire sentence divided by the length of the sentence, or equivalently the mean of the logprobs for the single trigrams:
$\mathsf{ML} = \frac{1}{n}\log P_{\text{TRIGRAM}}(\langle w_1, \ldots, w_n\rangle)$
By normalizing the logprob for the entire sentence by its length we eliminate the effect of sentence length on the acceptability score.

Weighted mean logprob (WML) This score is calculated by dividing the logprob of the entire sentence by the sum of the unigram probabilities of the lexical items that compose the sentence:
$\mathsf{WML} = \frac{\log P_{\text{TRIGRAM}}(\langle w_1,\ldots,w_n\rangle)}{\log P_{\text{UNIGRAM}}(\langle w_1,\ldots,w_n\rangle)}$
This score eliminates at the same time the effect of the length of the sentence and the lower probability assigned to sentences with rare lexical items.

Synctactic log odds ratio (SLOR) This score was first used by Pauls and Klein (2012) and performs a normalization very similar to WML (we will see below that in fact the two scores are basically equivalent):
$\mathsf{SLOR} = \frac{\log P_{\text{TRIGRAM}}(\langle w_1,\ldots,w_n\rangle) - \log P_{\text{UNIGRAM}}(\langle w_1,\ldots,w_n\rangle)}{n}$

Minimum (Min) This score is equal to the lowest logprob assigned by the model to the n-grams of the sentence divided by the unigram logprob of the lexical item heading the n-gram:
$\mathsf{Min} = \min_i \left[\frac{\log P(w_i|w_{i-2}w_{i-1})}{\log P(w_i)}\right]$
In this way, if a single n-gram is assigned a low probability (normalized for the frequency of its head lexical item), then this low score is in some sense propagated to the whole sentence.

Mean of the first quartile (MFQ) This score is a generalization of the Min score. We order the single n-gram logprobs from the lowest to the highest, and we consider the first (lowest) quartile. We then normalize the logprobs for these n-grams by the unigram probability of the head lexical item, and we take the mean of these scores. In this way we obtain a score that is more robust than the simple Min, as, in general, a grammatical anomaly influences the logprob of more than one n-gram.

2.2 N-Gram Models

We are using n-gram models on the understanding that they are fundamentally inadequate for describing natural languages in their full syntactic complexity. In spite of their limitations, they are a good starting point, as they perform well as language models across a wide range of language modeling tasks. They are easy to train, as they do not require annotated training data.

We do not expect that our n-gram based grammaticality scores will be able to idenitfy all of the cases of ungrammaticality that we encounter. Our working hypothesis is that they can capture cases of ill-formedness that depend on local factors, that can be identified within n-gram frames, as opposed to those which involve non-local relations. If these models can detect local grammaticality violations, then we will have a basis for thinking that richer, more structured language models can recognize non-local as well as local sources of ungrammaticality.

3 Experiments with Passives

Rather than trying to test the performance of these models over all types of ungrammaticality, we limit ourselves to a case study of the passive. By tightly controlling the verb types and grammatical construction to which we apply our models we are better able to study the power and the limits of these models as candidate representations of grammatical knowledge.

3.1 Types of Passives

Our controlled experiments on passives are, in part, inspired by speakers' judgments discussed in Ambridge et al. (2008). Their experimental work measures the acceptability of various passive sentences.

The active-passive alternation in English is exemplified by the pair of sentences

- John broke the window.
- The window was broken by John.

The acceptability of the passive sentence depends largely on lexical properties of the verb. Some verbs do not allow the formation of the passive, as in the case of pure intransitive verbs like *appear*, discussed below, which permit neither the active transitive, nor the passive.

We conducted some prelimiary experiments, not reported here, on modelling the data on passives from recent work in progress that Ben Ambridge and his colleagues are doing, and which he was kind enough to make available to us. We observed that the scores we obtained for our language models did not fully track these judgements, but we did notice that we obtained much better correlation at the low end of the judgment distribution. In Ambridge's current data this judgement range corresponds to passives constructed with intransitive verbs.

The Ambridge data indicates that the capacity of verbs to yield well-formed passive verb phrases forms a continuum. Studying the judgement patterns in this data we identified four reasonably salient points along this hierarchial continuum.

First, at the low end, we have intransitives like *appear*: (**John appeared the book. *The book was appeared*). Next we have what may be described as pseudo-transitives verbs like *laugh*, which permit only notional NP objects and do not easily passivize (*Mary laughed a hearty laugh/*a joke. ?A hearty laugh/*A joke was laughed by Mary*) above them. These are followed by cases of ambiguous transitives like *fit*, which, in active form, carry two distinct readings that correspond to an agentive and a thematic subject, respectively.

- The tailor fitted John for a new suit.
- The jeans fitted John

Only the agentive reading can be passivized.

- John was fitted by the tailor.
- *John was fitted by the jeans.

Finally, the most easily passivized verbs are robust transitives, which take the widest selection of NP subjects in passive form (*John wrote the book. The book was written by John*).

This continuum causes well-formedness in passivization to be a gradient property, as the Ambridge data illustrates. Passives tend to be more or less acceptable along this spectrum. The gradience of acceptability for passives implies the partial overlap of the score distributions for the different types of passives that our experiments show.

The experiments were designed to test our hypothesis that n-gram based language models are capable of detecting ungrammatical patterns only in cases where they do not depend on relations between words that cross the n-word boundary applied in training. Therefore we expect such a model to be capable of detecting the ungrammaticality of a sentence like *A horrible death was died by John*, because the trigrams *death was died*, *was died by* and *died by John* are unlikely to appear in any corpus of English. On the other hand, we do not expect a trigram model to store the information necessary to identify the relative anomaly of a sentence like *Two hundred people were held by the theater*, because all the trigrams (as well as the bigrams and the unigrams) that constitute the sentence are likely to appear with reasonable frequency in a large corpus of English.

The experiments generalize this observation and test the performance of n-gram models on a wider range of verb types. To quantify the performance of the different models we derive simple classifiers using the scores we have defined and testing them in a binary classification task. This task measures the ability of the classifier to distinguish between grammatical sentences, and sentences containing different types of grammatical errors.

The models are trained in an unsupervised manner using only corpus data, which we assume to be uniformly grammatical. In order to evaluate the scoring methods, we use some supervised data to set the optimal value of a simple threshold. This is not however a supervised classification task: we want to see how well the scores *could* be used to separate grammatical and ungrammatical data, and though unorthodox, this seems a more direct way of measuring this conditional property than stipulating some fixed threshold.

3.2 Training data

We used the British National Corpus (BNC) (BNC Consortium, 2007) to obtain our training data. We trained six different language models, using six different subcorpora of the BNC. The first model used the entire collection of written texts annotated in the BNC, for a total of approximately 100 million words. The other models were trained on increasingly smaller portions of the written texts collection: 40 million words, 30 million words, 15 million words, 7.6 million words, and 3.8 million words. We constructed these corpora by randomly sampling an appropriate number of complete sentences.

All models were trained on word sequences. For smoothing the n-gram probability distributions we used Kneser-Ney interpolation, as described in Goodman (2001).

3.3 Test data

We constructed the test data for our hypothesis in a controlled fashion. We first compiled a list of verbs for each of the four verb types that we consider (intransitives, pseudo-transitives, ambiguous transitives, and robust transitives). We selected verbs from the BNC that appeared at least 100 times in their past participle form in the entire corpus in order to ensure a sufficient number of passive uses in the training data.[1] We selected 40 intransitive verbs, 13 pseudo transitives, 23 ambiguous transitives and 40 transitive verbs. To classify the verbs we relied on our intuitions as native speakers of English.

Using these lists we automatically generated four corpora by selecting an agent and a patient from a predefined pool of NPs, randomly selecting a determiner (if necessary) and a number (if the NP allows plurals). The resulting corpora are of the following sizes:

- intransitive verbs – 24480 words, 3240 sentences,
- pseudo transitive verbs – 7956 words, 1053 sentences,
- ambiguous transitive verbs – 14076 words, 1863 sentences,
- robust transitive verbs – 24480 words, 3240 sentences.

Each corpus was evaluated by the six models. We computed our derived scores for each sentence on the basis of the logprobs that the language models assigns.

3.4 Binary classifiers

For each model and for each score we constructed a set of simple binary classifiers on the basis of the results obtained for the transitive verb corpus. We took the mean of each score assigned by the model to the transitive sentences, and we set different thresholds by subtracting from this value a number of standard deviations ranging from 0 to 2.75. The rationale behind these classifiers is that, assuming the passives of the robust transitives to be grammatical, the scores for the other cases should be comparatively lower. Therefore by setting a threshold "to the left" of the mean we should be able to distinguish between grammatical sentences, whose score is to the right of the threshold, and ungrammatical ones, expected to a have a score lower than the threshold. Formally the classifier is defined as follows:

$$c_s(w) = \begin{cases} + & \text{if } s(w) \geq m - S \cdot \sigma \\ - & \text{otherwise} \end{cases} \quad (1)$$

[1]Notice that in most cases the past participle form is the same as the simple past form, and for this reason we set the threshold to such a high value.

where s is one of our scores, w is the sentence to be classified, $s(w)$ represents the value assigned by the score to sentence w, m is the mean for the score in the transitive condition, σ is the standard deviation for the score again in the transitive condition, and S is a factor by which we move the threshold away from the mean. The classifier assigns the grammatical $(+)$ tag only to those sentences that are assigned values higher than the threshold $m - S \cdot \sigma$.

Alternatively in terms of the widely used z-score, defined as $z_s(w) = (s(w) - m)/\sigma$ we can say that w is classified as grammatical iff $z_s(w) \geq -S$.

4 Results

For reasons of space we will limit the presentation of our detailed results to the 100 million word model, as it offers the sharpest effects. We will, however, also report comparisons on the most important metrics for the complete set of models.

In Figure 1 we show the distribution of the five scores for the four different corpora (transitive, ambiguous, pseudo, and intransitive) obtained using the 100 million word model. In all cases we observe the same general pattern: the sentences in the corpus generated with robust transitives are assigned comparatively high scores, and these gradually decrease when we consider the ambiguous, the pseudo and the intransitive conditions. Interestingly, this order reflects the degree of "transitivity" that these verb types exhibit. Notice, however, that the four conditions seem to group into two different macro-distributions. On the right we have the transitive-ambiguous sentences and on the left the pseudo-intransitive cases. This partially confirms our hypothesis that n-gram models have problems recognizing lexical dependencies that determine the felicitousness of passives constructed using ambiguous transitive verbs, as these are, for the most part, non-local. Nevertheless, it is important to note that the overlap of the distributions for these two cases is also due to the fact that many cases in the ambiguous transitive corpus are indeed grammatical.

Figure 2 summarizes the (balanced) accuracies obtained by our classifiers for each comparison, by each model. These results confirm our hypothesis that the classifiers tend to perform better when distinguishing passive sentences constructed with a robust transitive verbs from those headed by

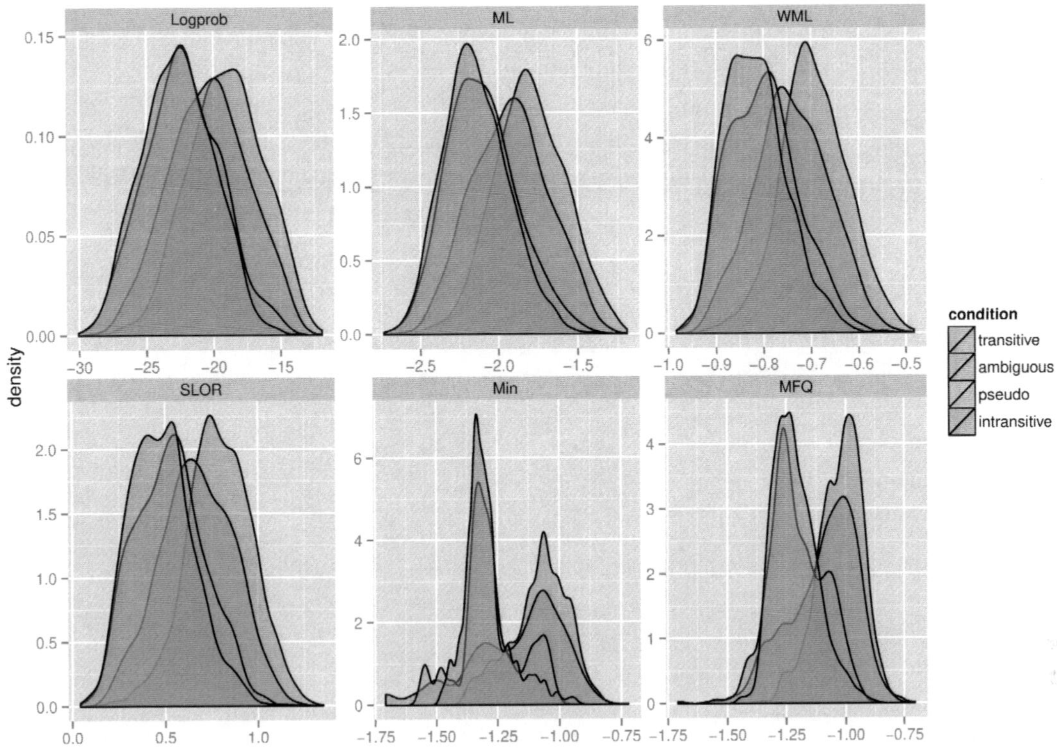

Figure 1: Distributions of the six scores Logprob, ML, WML, SLOR, Min and MFQ for the four different conditions (robust transitive passives, ambiguous transitive passives, pseudo transitive passives and intransitive passives) for the 100 million words language model.

pseudo-transitives and intransitives.

In the comparison between transitive and ambiguous transitive sentences, the classifiers are "stuck" at around 60% accuracy. Using larger training corpora produces only a marginal improvement. This contrasts with what we observe for the transitive/pseudo and transitive/intransitive classification tasks. In the transitive/pseudo task, we already obtain reasonable accuracy with the model trained with the smallest BNC subset. Oddly, the overall best result is achieved with 30 million words, although the result obtained with the model trained on the full BNC corpus is not much lower. For the transitive/intransitive classification task we observe a much steadier and larger growth in accuracy, reaching the overall best result of 85.1%. Table 1 reports the best results for each comparison by each language model. For each condition we report the best accuracy obtained, the corresponding F1 score, the score that achieves the best result, and the best accuracy obtained by just using the logprobs. These results are obtained using different values for the S parameter. However, in general the best results are obtained when the S parameter is set to a value in the interval $[0.5, 1.5]$.

In comparing the performance of the individual scores, we first notice that, while for the transitive/ambiguous comparison all scores perform pretty much at the same level, there is a clear hierarchy between scores for the other comparisons.

We observe that the baseline raw logprob assigned by the n-grams models performs much worse than the scores, resulting in roughly 10% less accuracy than the best performing score in every condition. ML performs slightly better, obtaining around 5% greater accuracy than logprob as a predictor. This shows that even though the length of the sentences in our test data is relatively constant (between 9 and 11 words), there is still an improvement if we take this structural factor into account. The two scores WML and SLOR display the same pattern, showing that they are effectively equivalent. This is not surprising given that they are designed to modify the raw logprob by tak-

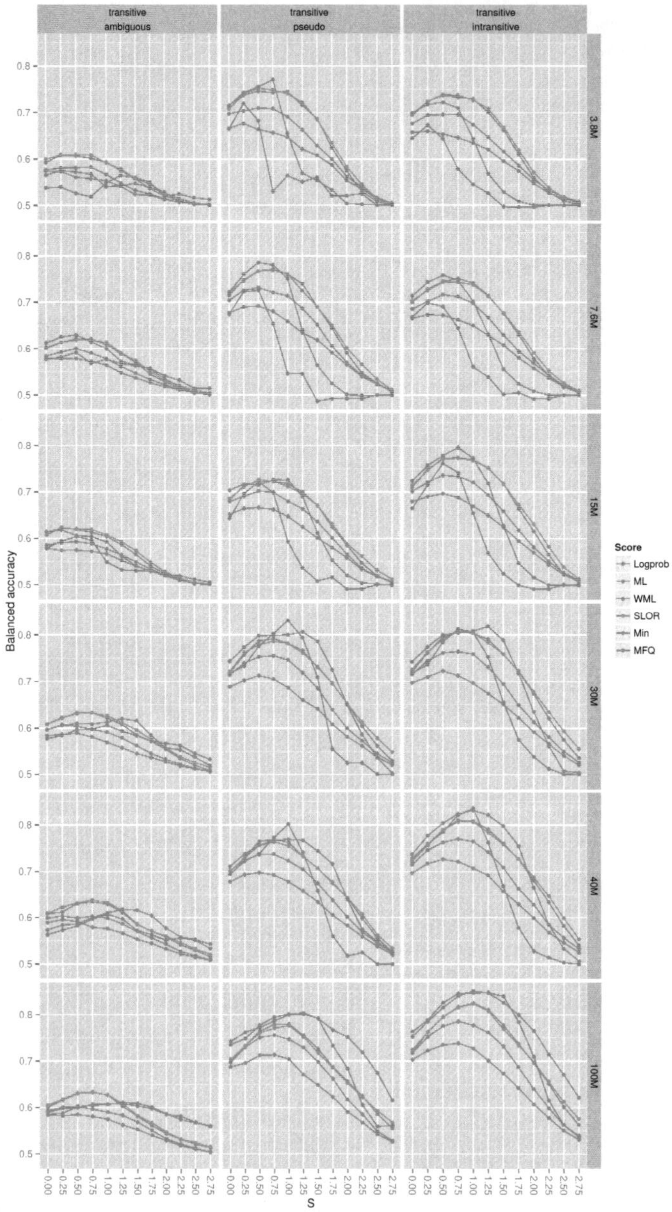

Figure 2: Accuracies for the classifiers for each model. S represents the number of standard deviations "to the left" of the mean of the transitive condition score, used to set the threshold.

ing into account exactly the same factors (length of the sentence and frequency of the unigrams that compose the sentence). These two scores perform generally better in the transitive/ambiguous comparison, and they achieve good performance when the size of the training model is small. However, for the most part, the two scores derived from the logprobs of the least probable n-grams in the sentence, Min and MFQ, get the best results. Min exhibits erratic behavior (mainly due to its non-normal distribution for each condition, as shown in figure 1), and it seems to be more stable only in the presence of a large training set. MFQ has a much more robust contour, as it is significantly less dependent on the choice of S.

5 Conclusions and Future Work

In Clark and Lappin (2011) we propose a model of negative evidence that uses probability of occurrence in primary linguistic data as the basis for estimating non-grammaticality through relatively

Model	Comparison	Best accuracy	F1	Best performing score	Logprob accuracy
	transitive/ambiguous	60.9%	0.7	SLOR	57.3%
3.8M	transitive/pseudo	77%	0.81	MFQ	67.6%
	transitive/intransitive	73.8%	0.72	SLOR	65.6%
	transitive/ambiguous	62.9%	0.68	MFQ	57.8%
7.6M	transitive/pseudo	78.5%	0.76	MFQ	69.1%
	transitive/intransitive	75.8%	0.72	MFQ	67.3%
	transitive/ambiguous	62.3%	0.66	WML	57.8%
15M	transitive/pseudo	72.6%	0.78	SLOR	66.5%
	transitive/intransitive	79.5%	78.3	MFQ	69.5%
	transitive/ambiguous	63.3%	0.75	WML	58.9%
30M	transitive/pseudo	83.1%	0.88	Min	71.2%
	transitive/intransitive	81.8%	0.82	MFQ	72.2%
	transitive/ambiguous	63.8%	0.75	SLOR	59.5%
40M	transitive/pseudo	80.1%	0.86	Min	69.7%
	transitive/intransitive	83.5%	0.83	SLOR	72.6%
	transitive/ambiguous	63.3%	0.75	SLOR	58.4%
100M	transitive/pseudo	80.3%	0.9	MFQ	71.3%
	transitive/intransitive	85.1%	0.85	SLOR	73.8%

Table 1: Best accuracies

low frequency in a sample of this data. Here we follow Clark et al. (2013) in effectively inverting this strategy.

We identify a set of scoring functions based on parameters of probabilistic models that we use to define a grammaticality threshold, which we use to classify strings as grammatical or ill-formed. This model offers a stochastic characterisation of grammaticality without reducing grammaticality to probability.

We expect enriched lexical n-gram models of the kind that we use here to be capable of recognizing the distinction between grammatical and ungrammatical sentences when it depends on local factors within the frame of the n-grams on which they are trained. We further expect them not to be able to identify this distinction when it depends on non-local relations that fall outside of the n-gram frame.

It might be thought that this hypothesis concerning the capacities and limitations of n-gram models is too obvious to require experimental support. In fact, this is not the case. Reali and Christiansen (2005) show that n-gram models can be used to distinguish grammatical from ungrammatical auxiliary fronted polar questions with a high degree of success. More recently Frank et al. (2012) argue for the view that a purely sequential, non-hierarchical view of linguistic structure is adequate to account for most aspects of linguistic knowledge and processing.

We have constructed an experiment with different (pre-identified) passive structures that provides significant support for our hypothesis that lexical n-gram models are very good at capturing local syntactic relations, but cannot handle more distant dependencies.

In future work we will be experimenting with more expressive language models that can represent non-local syntactic relations. We will proceed conservatively by first extending our enriched lexical n-gram models to chunking models, and then to dependency grammar models, using only as much syntactic structure as is required to identify the judgement patterns that we are studying.

To the extent that this research is successful it will provide motivation for the view that syntactic knowledge is inherently probabilistic in nature.

Acknowledgments

The research described in this paper was done in the framework of the Statistical Models of Grammaticality (SMOG) project at King's College London, funded by grant ES/J022969/1 from the Economic and Social Research Council of the UK. We are grateful to Ben Ambridge for providing us with the data from his experiments and for helpful discussion of the issues that we address in this paper. We also thank the three anonymous CMCL 2013 reviewers for useful comments and suggestions, that we have taken account of in preparing the final version of the paper.

References

Ben Ambridge, Julian M Pine, Caroline F Rowland, and Chris R Young. 2008. The effect of verb semantic class and verb frequency (entrenchment) on childrens and adults graded judgements of argument-structure overgeneralization errors. *Cognition*, 106(1):87–129.

BNC Consortium. 2007. The British National Corpus, version 3 (BNC XML Edition). Distributed by Oxford University Computing Services on behalf of the BNC Consortium.

R. Bod, J. Hay, and S. Jannedy. 2003. *Probabilistic linguistics*. MIT Press.

N. Chater, J.B. Tenenbaum, and A. Yuille. 2006. Probabilistic models of cognition: Conceptual foundations. *Trends in Cognitive Sciences*, 10(7):287–291.

N. Chomsky. 1957. *Syntactic Structures*. Mouton, The Hague.

A. Clark and S. Lappin. 2011. *Linguistic Nativism and the Poverty of the Stimulus*. Wiley-Blackwell, Malden, MA.

A. Clark, G. Giorgolo, and S. Lappin. 2013. Towards a statistical model of grammaticality. In *Proceedings of the 35th Annual Conference of the Cognitive Science Society*.

Sandiway Fong, Igor Malioutov, Beracah Yankama, and Robert C. Berwick. 2013. Treebank parsing and knowledge of language. In Aline Villavicencio, Thierry Poibeau, Anna Korhonen, and Afra Alishahi, editors, *Cognitive Aspects of Computational Language Acquisition*, Theory and Applications of Natural Language Processing, pages 133–172. Springer Berlin Heidelberg.

Stefan Frank, Rens Bod, and Morten Christiansen. 2012. How hierarchical is language use? In *Proceedings of the Royal Society B*, number doi: 10.1098/rspb.2012.1741.

J.T. Goodman. 2001. A bit of progress in language modeling. *Computer Speech & Language*, 15(4):403–434.

A. Pauls and D. Klein. 2012. Large-scale syntactic language modeling with treelets. In *Proceedings of the 50th Annual Meeting of the Association for Computational Linguistics*, pages 959–968. Jeju, Korea.

F. Pereira. 2000. Formal grammar and information theory: together again? *Philosophical Transactions of the Royal Society of London. Series A: Mathematical, Physical and Engineering Sciences*, 358(1769):1239–1253.

M. Post. 2011. Judging grammaticality with tree substitution grammar derivations. In *Proceedings of the 49th Annual Meeting of the Association for Computational Linguistics: Human Language Technologies*, pages 217–222.

F. Reali and M.H. Christiansen. 2005. Uncovering the richness of the stimulus: Structure dependence and indirect statistical evidence. *Cognitive Science*, 29(6):1007–1028.

An Analysis of Memory-based Processing Costs using Incremental Deep Syntactic Dependency Parsing*

Marten van Schijndel
The Ohio State University
vanschm@ling.osu.edu

Luan Nguyen
University of Minnesota
lnguyen@cs.umn.edu

William Schuler
The Ohio State University
schuler@ling.osu.edu

Abstract

Reading experiments using naturalistic stimuli have shown unanticipated facilitations for completing center embeddings when frequency effects are factored out. To eliminate possible confounds due to surface structure, this paper introduces a processing model based on deep syntactic dependencies. Results on eye-tracking data indicate that completing deep syntactic embeddings yields significantly more facilitation than completing surface embeddings.

1 Introduction

Self-paced reading and eye-tracking experiments have often been used to support theories about inhibitory effects of working memory operations in sentence processing (Just and Carpenter, 1992; Gibson, 2000; Lewis and Vasishth, 2005), but it is possible that many of these effects can be explained by frequency (Jurafsky, 1996; Hale, 2001; Karlsson, 2007). Experiments on large naturalistic text corpora (Demberg and Keller, 2008; Wu et al., 2010; van Schijndel and Schuler, 2013) have shown significant memory effects at the ends of center embeddings when frequency measures have been included as separate factors, but these memory effects have been facilitatory rather than inhibitory.

Some of the memory-based measures that produce these facilitatory effects (Wu et al., 2010; van Schijndel and Schuler, 2013) are defined in terms of initiation and integration of *connected components* of syntactic structure,[1] with the presumption that referents that belong to the same connected component may cue one another using content-based features, while those that do not must rely on noisier temporal features that just encode how recently a referent was accessed. These measures, based on left-corner parsing processes (Johnson-Laird, 1983; Abney and Johnson, 1991), abstract counts of unsatisfied dependencies from noun or verb referents (Gibson, 2000) to cover all syntactic dependencies, motivated by observations of Demberg and Keller (2008) and Kwon et al. (2010) of the inadequacies of Gibson's narrower measure.

But these experiments use naturalistic stimuli without constrained manipulations and therefore might be susceptible to confounds. It is possible that the purely phrase-structure-based connected components used previously may ignore some integration costs associated with filler-gap constructions, making them an unsuitable generalization of Gibson-style dependencies. It is also possible that the facilitatory effect for integration operations in naturally-occurring stimuli may be driven by syntactic center embeddings that arise from modifiers (e.g. *The CEO sold [[the shares] of the company]*), which do not require any dependencies to be deferred, but which might be systematically under-predicted by frequency measures, producing a confound with memory measures when frequency measures are residualized out.

In order to eliminate possible confounds due to exclusion of unbounded dependencies in filler-gap constructions, this paper evaluates a processing model that calculates connected components on deep syntactic dependency structures rather than surface phrase structure trees. This model accounts unattached fillers and gaps as belonging to separate connected components, and therefore performs additional initiation and integration op-

*Thanks to Micha Elsner and three anonymous reviewers for their feedback. This work was funded by an Ohio State University Department of Linguistics Targeted Investment for Excellence (TIE) grant for collaborative interdisciplinary projects conducted during the academic year 2012–13.

[1]Graph theoretically, the set of connected components of a graph $\langle V, E\rangle$ is the set of maximal subsets of it $\{\langle V_1, E_1\rangle, \langle V_2, E_2\rangle, ...\}$ such that any pair of vertices in each V_i can be connected by edges in the corresponding E_i.

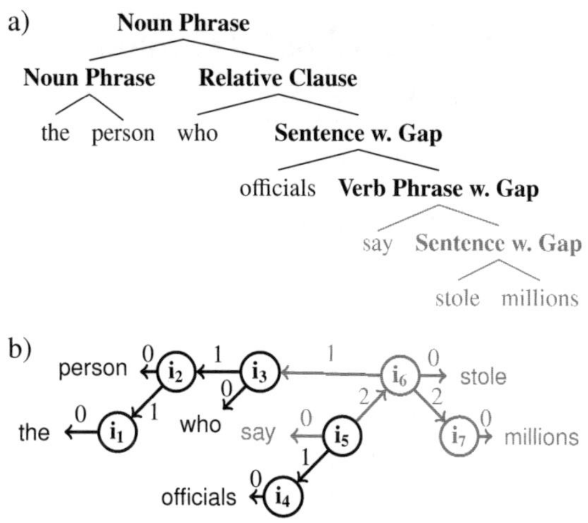

Figure 1: Graphical representation of (a) a single connected component of surface syntactic phrase structure corresponding to (b) two connected components of deep syntactic dependency structure for the noun phrase *the person who officials say stole millions*, prior to the word *say*. Connections established prior to the word *say* are shown in black; subsequent connections are shown in gray.

erations in filler-gap constructions as hypothesized by Gibson (2000) and others. Then, in order to control for possible confounds due to modifier-induced center embedding, this refined model is applied to two partitions of an eye-tracking corpus (Kennedy et al., 2003): one consisting of sentences containing only non-modifier center embeddings, in which dependencies are deferred, and the other consisting of sentences containing no center embeddings or containing center embeddings arising from attachment of final modifiers, in which no dependencies are deferred. Processing this partitioned corpus with deep syntactic connected components reveals a significant increase in facilitation in the non-modifier partition, which lends credibility to the observation of negative integration cost in processing naturally-occurring sentences.

2 Connected Components

The experiments described in this paper evaluate whether inhibition and facilitation in reading correlate with operations in a hierarchic sequential prediction model that initiate and integrate connected components of hypothesized syntactic structure during incremental parsing. The model used in these experiments refines previous connected component models by allowing fillers and gaps to occur in separate connected components of a deep syntactic dependency graph (Mel'čuk, 1988; Kintsch, 1988), even when they belong to the same connected component when defined on surface structure.

For example, the surface syntactic phrase structure and deep syntactic dependency structure for the noun phrase *the person who officials say stole millions* are shown in Figure 1.[2] Notice that after the word *officials*, there is only one connected component of surface syntactic phrase structure (from the root noun phrase to the verb phrase with gap), but two disjoint connected components of deep syntactic dependency structure (one ending at $\mathbf{i}_3$, and another at $\mathbf{i}_5$). Only the deep syntactic dependency structure corresponds to familiar (Just and Carpenter, 1992; Gibson, 1998) notions of how memory is used to store deferred dependencies in filler-gap constructions. The next section will describe a generalized categorial grammar, which (i) can be viewed as context-free, to seed a latent-variable probabilistic context-free grammar to accurately derive parses of filler-gap constructions, and (ii) can be viewed as a deep syntactic dependency grammar, defining dependencies for connected components in terms of function applications.

3 Generalized Categorial Grammar

In order to evaluate memory effects for hypothesizing unbounded dependencies between referents of fillers and referents of clauses containing gaps, a memory-based processor must define connected components in terms of deep syntactic dependencies (including unbounded dependencies) rather than in terms of surface syntactic phrase structure trees. To do this, at least some phrase structure edges must be removed from the set of connections that define a connected component.

Because these unbounded dependencies are not represented locally in the original Treebank format, probabilities for operations on these modified

[2]Following Mel'čuk (1988) and Kintsch (1988), the graphical dependency structure adopted here uses positionally-defined labels ('0' for the predicate label, '1' for the first argument ahead of a predicate, '2' for the last argument behind, etc.) but includes unbounded dependencies between referents of fillers and referents of clauses containing gaps. It is assumed that semantically-labeled structures would be isomorphic to the structures defined here, but would generalize across alternations such as active and passive constructions, for example.

connected components are trained on a corpus annotated with generalized categorial grammar dependencies for 'gap' arguments at all categories that subsume a gap (Nguyen et al., 2012). This representation is similar to the HPSG-like representation used by Hale (2001) and Lewis and Vasishth (2005), but has a naturally-defined dependency structure on which to calculate connected components. This generalized categorial grammar is then used to identify the first sign that introduces a gap, at which point a deep syntactic connected component containing the filler can be encoded (stored), and a separate deep syntactic connected component for a clause containing a gap can be initiated.

A generalized categorial grammar (Bach, 1981) consists of a set U of primitive category types; a set O of type-constructing operators allowing a recursive definition of a set of categories $C =_{\text{def}} U \cup (C \times O \times C)$; a set X of vocabulary items; a mapping M from vocabulary items in X to semantic functions with category types in C; and a set R of inference rules for deriving functions with category types in C from other functions with category types in C. Nguyen et al. (2012) use primitive category types for clause types (e.g. **V** for finite verb-headed clause, **N** for noun phrase or nominal clause, **D** for determiners and possessive clauses, etc.), and use the generalized set of type-constructing operators to characterize not only function application dependencies between arguments immediately ahead of and behind a functor (**-a** and **-b**, corresponding to '\' and '/' in Ajdukiewicz-Bar-Hillel categorial grammars), but also long-distance dependencies between fillers and categories subsuming gaps (**-g**), dependencies between relative pronouns and antecedent modificands of relative clauses (**-r**), and dependencies between interrogative pronouns and their arguments (**-i**), which remain unsatisfied in derivations but function to distinguish categories for content and polar questions. A lexicon can then be defined in M to introduce lexical dependencies and obligatory pronominal dependencies using numbered functions for predicates and deep syntactic arguments, for example:

$$\text{the} \Rightarrow (\lambda_i\ (0\,i)\text{=the}) : \mathbf{D}$$
$$\text{person} \Rightarrow (\lambda_i\ (0\,i)\text{=person}) : \mathbf{N\text{-}aD}$$
$$\text{who} \Rightarrow (\lambda_{k\,i}\ (0\,i)\text{=who} \wedge (1\,i)\text{=}k) : \mathbf{N\text{-}rN}$$
$$\text{officials} \Rightarrow (\lambda_i\ (0\,i)\text{=officials}) : \mathbf{N}$$

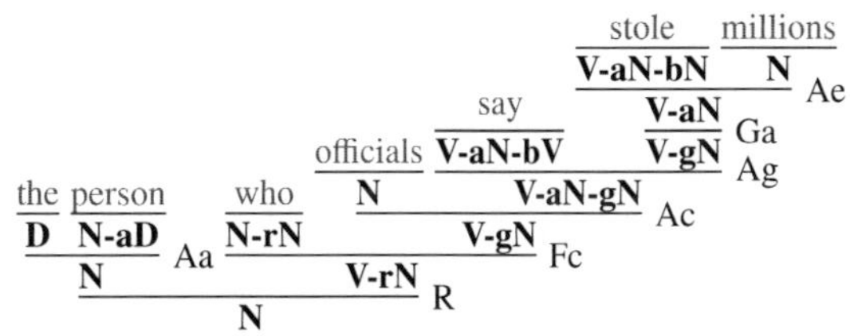

Figure 2: Example categorization of the noun phrase *the person who officials say stole millions.*

$$\text{say} \Rightarrow (\lambda_i\ (0\,i)\text{=say}) : \mathbf{V\text{-}aN\text{-}bV}$$
$$\text{stole} \Rightarrow (\lambda_i\ (0\,i)\text{=stole}) : \mathbf{V\text{-}aN\text{-}bN}$$
$$\text{millions} \Rightarrow (\lambda_i\ (0\,i)\text{=millions}) : \mathbf{N}$$

Inference rules in R are then defined to compose arguments and modifiers and propagate gaps. Arguments g of type d ahead of functors h of type c-**a**d are composed by passing non-local dependencies $\psi \in \{\textbf{-g}, \textbf{-i}, \textbf{-r}\} \times C$ from premises to conclusion in all combinations:

$$g{:}d \quad h{:}\, c\text{-}\mathbf{a}d \Rightarrow (f_{c\text{-}\mathbf{a}d}\, g\, h){:}\, c \qquad \text{(Aa)}$$
$$g{:}d\psi \quad h{:}\, c\text{-}\mathbf{a}d \Rightarrow \lambda_k\, (f_{c\text{-}\mathbf{a}d}\, (g\,k)\, h){:}\, c\psi \qquad \text{(Ab)}$$
$$g{:}d \quad h{:}\, c\text{-}\mathbf{a}d\psi \Rightarrow \lambda_k\, (f_{c\text{-}\mathbf{a}d}\, g\, (h\,k)){:}\, c\psi \qquad \text{(Ac)}$$
$$g{:}d\psi \quad h{:}\, c\text{-}\mathbf{a}d\psi \Rightarrow \lambda_k\, (f_{c\text{-}\mathbf{a}d}\, (g\,k)\, (h\,k)){:}\, c\psi \qquad \text{(Ad)}$$

Similar rules compose arguments behind functors:

$$g{:}\, c\text{-}\mathbf{b}d \quad h{:}d \Rightarrow (f_{c\text{-}\mathbf{b}d}\, g\, h){:}\, c \qquad \text{(Ae)}$$
$$g{:}\, c\text{-}\mathbf{b}d\psi \quad h{:}d \Rightarrow \lambda_k\, (f_{c\text{-}\mathbf{b}d}\, (g\,k)\, h){:}\, c\psi \qquad \text{(Af)}$$
$$g{:}\, c\text{-}\mathbf{b}d \quad h{:}d\psi \Rightarrow \lambda_k\, (f_{c\text{-}\mathbf{b}d}\, g\, (h\,k)){:}\, c\psi \qquad \text{(Ag)}$$
$$g{:}\, c\text{-}\mathbf{b}d\psi \quad h{:}d\psi \Rightarrow \lambda_k\, (f_{c\text{-}\mathbf{b}d}\, (g\,k)\, (h\,k)){:}\, c\psi \qquad \text{(Ah)}$$

These rules use composition functions $f_{c\text{-}\mathbf{a}d}$ and $f_{c\text{-}\mathbf{b}d}$ for initial and final arguments, which define dependency edges numbered v from referents of predicate functors i to referents of arguments j, where v is the number of unsatisfied arguments $\varphi_1 ... \varphi_v \in \{\textbf{-a}, \textbf{-b}\} \times C$ in a category label:

$$f_{u\varphi_{1..v-1}\text{-}\mathbf{a}c} \stackrel{\text{def}}{=} \lambda_{g\,h\,i}\, \exists_j\, (v\,i)\text{=}j \wedge (g\,j) \wedge (h\,i) \qquad \text{(1a)}$$
$$f_{u\varphi_{1..v-1}\text{-}\mathbf{b}c} \stackrel{\text{def}}{=} \lambda_{g\,h\,i}\, \exists_j\, (v\,i)\text{=}j \wedge (g\,i) \wedge (h\,j) \qquad \text{(1b)}$$

R also contains inference rules to compose modifier functors g of type u-**a**d ahead of modificands h of type d:

$$g{:}\, u\text{-}\mathbf{a}d \quad h{:}c \Rightarrow (f_{\text{IM}}\, g\, h){:}c \qquad \text{(Ma)}$$
$$g{:}\, u\text{-}\mathbf{a}d\psi \quad h{:}c \Rightarrow \lambda_k\, (f_{\text{IM}}\, (g\,k)\, h){:}c\psi \qquad \text{(Mb)}$$
$$g{:}\, u\text{-}\mathbf{a}d \quad h{:}c\psi \Rightarrow \lambda_k\, (f_{\text{IM}}\, g\, (h\,k)){:}c\psi \qquad \text{(Mc)}$$

$$\frac{\exists_{i^1 j^1 .. i^\ell j^\ell} \ldots \wedge (g^\ell{:}c/d\{j^\ell\}\, i^\ell) \quad x_t}{\exists_{i^1 j^1 .. i^\ell} \ldots \wedge ((g^\ell f){:}c\, i^\ell)} \; x_t \Rightarrow f{:}d \tag{–Fa}$$

$$\frac{\exists_{i^1 j^1 .. i^\ell j^\ell} \ldots \wedge (g^\ell{:}c/d\{j^\ell\}\, i^\ell) \quad x_t}{\exists_{i^1 j^1 .. i^\ell j^\ell i^{\ell+1}} \ldots \wedge (g^\ell{:}c/d\{j^\ell\}\, i^\ell) \wedge (f{:}e\, i^{\ell+1})} \; x_t \Rightarrow f{:}e \tag{+Fa}$$

$$\frac{\exists_{i^1 j^1 .. i^{\ell-1} j^{\ell-1} i^\ell} \ldots \wedge (g^\ell{:}d\, i^\ell)}{\exists_{i^1 j^1 .. i^\ell j^\ell} \ldots \wedge ((f\, g^\ell){:}c/e\{j^\ell\}\, i^\ell)} \; \begin{cases} g{:}d\; h{:}e \Rightarrow (f\, g\, h){:}c & \text{or} \\ g{:}d\; h{:}e \Rightarrow \lambda_k (f\, (g\, k)\, h){:}c & \text{or} \\ g{:}d\; h{:}e \Rightarrow \lambda_k (f\, g\, (h\, k)){:}c & \text{or} \\ g{:}d\; h{:}e \Rightarrow \lambda_k (f\, (g\, k)\, (h\, k)){:}c \end{cases} \tag{–La}$$

$$\frac{\exists_{i^1 j^1 .. i^{\ell-1} j^{\ell-1} i^\ell} \ldots \wedge (g^{\ell-1}{:}a/c\{j^{\ell-1}\}\, i^{\ell-1}) \wedge (g^\ell{:}d\, i^\ell)}{\exists_{i^1 j^1 .. i^{\ell-1} j^{\ell-1}} \ldots \wedge (g^{\ell-1} \circ (f\, g^\ell){:}a/e\{j^{\ell-1}\}\, i^{\ell-1})} \; \begin{cases} g{:}d\; h{:}e \Rightarrow (f\, g\, h){:}c & \text{or} \\ g{:}d\; h{:}e \Rightarrow \lambda_k (f\, (g\, k)\, h){:}c & \text{or} \\ g{:}d\; h{:}e \Rightarrow \lambda_k (f\, g\, (h\, k)){:}c & \text{or} \\ g{:}d\; h{:}e \Rightarrow \lambda_k (f\, (g\, k)\, (h\, k)){:}c \end{cases} \tag{+La}$$

Figure 3: Basic processing productions of a right-corner parser.

$$g{:}\, u\text{-}\mathbf{a}d\psi \;\; h{:}c\psi \Rightarrow \lambda_k\, (f_{\mathrm{IM}}\, (g\, k)\, (h\, k)){:}c\psi \tag{Md}$$

or for modifier functors behind a modificand:

$$g{:}c \;\; h{:}\, u\text{-}\mathbf{a}d \Rightarrow (f_{\mathrm{FM}}\, g\, h){:}c \tag{Me}$$

$$g{:}c\psi \;\; h{:}\, u\text{-}\mathbf{a}d \Rightarrow \lambda_k\, (f_{\mathrm{FM}}\, (g\, k)\, h){:}c\psi \tag{Mf}$$

$$g{:}c \;\; h{:}\, u\text{-}\mathbf{a}d\psi \Rightarrow \lambda_k\, (f_{\mathrm{FM}}\, g\, (h\, k)){:}c\psi \tag{Mg}$$

$$g{:}c\psi \;\; h{:}\, u\text{-}\mathbf{a}d\psi \Rightarrow \lambda_k\, (f_{\mathrm{FM}}\, (g\, k)\, (h\, k)){:}c\psi \tag{Mh}$$

These rules use composition functions f_{IM} and f_{FM} for initial and final modifiers, which define dependency edges numbered '1' from referents of modifier functors i to referents of modificands j:

$$f_{\mathrm{IM}} \stackrel{\text{def}}{=} \lambda_{g\, h\, j}\, \exists_i\, (1\, i){=}j \wedge (g\, i) \wedge (h\, j) \tag{2a}$$

$$f_{\mathrm{FM}} \stackrel{\text{def}}{=} \lambda_{g\, h\, j}\, \exists_i\, (1\, i){=}j \wedge (g\, j) \wedge (h\, i) \tag{2b}$$

R also contains inference rules for hypothesizing gaps $\mathbf{-g}d$ for arguments and modifiers:[3]

$$g{:}\, c\text{-}\mathbf{a}d \Rightarrow \lambda_k\, (f_{c\text{-}\mathbf{a}d}\, \{k\}\, g){:}\, c\text{-}\mathbf{g}d \tag{Ga}$$

$$g{:}\, c\text{-}\mathbf{b}d \Rightarrow \lambda_k\, (f_{c\text{-}\mathbf{a}d}\, \{k\}\, g){:}\, c\text{-}\mathbf{g}d \tag{Gb}$$

$$g{:}c \Rightarrow \lambda_k\, (f_{\mathrm{IM}}\, \{k\}\, g){:}c\text{-}\mathbf{g}d \tag{Gc}$$

and for attaching fillers e, d-**re**, d-**ie** as gaps **-g**d:

$$g{:}e \;\; h{:}\, c\text{-}\mathbf{g}d \Rightarrow \lambda_i\, \exists_j\, (g\, i) \wedge (h\, i\, j){:}e \tag{Fa}$$

$$g{:}d\text{-}\mathbf{re} \;\; h{:}\, c\text{-}\mathbf{g}d \Rightarrow \lambda_{k\, j}\, \exists_i\, (g\, k\, i) \wedge (h\, i\, j){:}\, c\text{-}\mathbf{re} \tag{Fb}$$

$$g{:}d\text{-}\mathbf{ie} \;\; h{:}\, c\text{-}\mathbf{g}d \Rightarrow \lambda_{k\, j}\, \exists_i\, (g\, k\, i) \wedge (h\, i\, j){:}\, c\text{-}\mathbf{ie} \tag{Fc}$$

[3]Since these unary inferences perform no explicit composition, they are defined to use only initial versions composition functions $f_{c\text{-}\mathbf{a}d}$ and f_{IM}.

and for attaching modificands as antecedents of relative pronouns:

$$g{:}e \;\; h{:}c\text{-}\mathbf{r}d \Rightarrow \lambda_i\, \exists_j\, (g\, i) \wedge (h\, i\, j){:}e \tag{R}$$

An example derivation of the noun phrase *the person who officials say stole millions* using these rules is shown in Figure 2. The semantic expression produced by this derivation consists of a conjunction of terms defining the edges in the graph shown in Figure 1b.

This GCG formulation captures many of the insights of the HPSG-like context-free filler-gap notation used by Hale (2001) or Lewis and Vasishth (2005): inference rules with adjacent premises can be cast as context-free grammars and weighted using probabilities, which allow experiments to calculate frequency measures for syntactic constructions. Applying a latent variable PCFG trainer (Petrov et al., 2006) to this formulation was shown to yield state-of-the-art accuracy for recovery of unbounded dependencies (Nguyen et al., 2012). Moreover, the functor-argument dependencies in a GCG define deep syntactic dependency graphs for all derivations, which can be used in incremental parsing to calculate connected components for memory-based measures.

4 Incremental Processing

In order to obtain measures of memory operations used in incremental processing, these GCG inference rules are combined into a set of parser

$$\frac{\exists_{i^1 j^1 .. i^n j^n .. i^\ell j^\ell} \ldots \wedge (g^n{:}y/z\psi \{j^n\}\, i^n) \wedge \ldots \wedge (g^\ell{:}c/d \{j^\ell\}\, i^\ell) \quad x_t}{\exists_{i^1 j^1 .. i^n j^n .. i^\ell} \ldots \wedge (g^n{:}y/z\psi \{j^n\}\, i^n) \wedge \ldots \wedge ((g^\ell(f'\{j^n\} f)){:}c\, i^\ell)} \; x_t \Rightarrow \lambda_k(f'\{k\}\, f){:}d \tag{–Fb}$$

$$\frac{\exists_{i^1 j^1 .. i^n j^n .. i^\ell j^\ell} \ldots \wedge (g^n{:}y/z\psi \{j^n\}\, i^n) \wedge \ldots \wedge (g^\ell{:}c/d \{j^\ell\}\, i^\ell) \quad x_t}{\exists_{i^1 j^1 .. i^n j^n .. i^\ell j^\ell i^{\ell+1}} \ldots \wedge (g^n{:}y/z\psi \{j^n\}\, i^n) \wedge \ldots \wedge (g^\ell{:}c/d \{j^\ell\}\, i^\ell) \wedge ((f'\{j^n\} f){:}e\, i^{\ell+1})} \; x_t \Rightarrow \lambda_k(f'\{k\}\, f){:}e \tag{+Fb}$$

$$\frac{\exists_{i^1 j^1 .. i^n j^n .. i^{\ell-1} j^{\ell-1} i^\ell} \ldots \wedge (g^n{:}y/z\psi \{j^n\}\, i^n) \wedge \ldots \wedge (g^\ell{:}d\, i^\ell)}{\exists_{i^1 j^1 .. i^n j^n .. i^\ell j^\ell} \ldots \wedge (g^n{:}y/z\psi \{j^n\}\, i^n) \wedge \ldots \wedge ((f g^\ell) \circ (f'\{j^n\}){:}c\psi/e \{j^\ell\}\, i^\ell)}$$

$$g{:}d \;\; h{:}e \Rightarrow \lambda_k(f g\, (f'\{k\}\, h)){:}c\psi \tag{–Lb}$$

$$\frac{\exists_{i^1 j^1 .. i^n j^n .. i^{\ell-1} j^{\ell-1} i^\ell} \ldots \wedge (g^n{:}y/z\psi \{j^n\}\, i^n) \wedge \ldots \wedge (g^{\ell-1}{:}a/c\psi \{j^{\ell-1}\}\, i^{\ell-1}) \wedge (g^\ell{:}d\, i^\ell)}{\exists_{i^1 j^1 .. i^n j^n .. i^{\ell-1} j^{\ell-1}} \ldots \wedge (g^n{:}y/z\psi \{j^n\}\, i^n) \wedge \ldots \wedge (g^{\ell-1} \circ (f g^\ell) \circ (f'\{j^n\}){:}a/e \{j^{\ell-1}\}\, i^{\ell-1})}$$

$$g{:}d \;\; h{:}e \Rightarrow \lambda_k(f g\, (f'\{k\}\, h)){:}c\psi \tag{+Lb}$$

Figure 4: Additional processing productions for attaching a referent of a filler j^n as the referent of a gap.

productions, similar to those of the 'right corner' parser of van Schijndel and Schuler (2013), except that instead of recognizing shallow hierarchical sequences of connected components of surface structure, the parser recognizes shallow hierarchical sequences of connected components of deep syntactic dependencies. This parser exploits the observation (van Schijndel et al., in press) that left-corner parsers and their variants do not need to initiate or integrate more than one connected component at each word. These two operations are then augmented with rules to introduce fillers and attach fillers as gaps.

This parser is defined on *incomplete connected component states* which consist of an *active sign* (with a semantic referent and syntactic form or category) lacking an *awaited sign* (also with a referent and category) yet to come. Semantic functions of active and awaited signs are simplified to denote only sets of referents, with gap arguments (λ_k) stripped off and handled by separate connected components. Incomplete connected components, therefore, always denote semantic functions from sets of referents to sets of referents.

This paper will notate semantic functions of connected components using variables g and h, incomplete connected component categories as c/d (consisting of an active sign of category c and an awaited sign of category d), and associations between them as $g{:}c/d$. The semantic representation used here is simply a deep syntactic dependency structure, so a connected component function is satisfied if it holds for some output referent i given input referent j. This can be notated $\exists_{i\,j}\, (g{:}c/d \{j\}\, i)$, where the set $\{j\}$ is equivalent to $(\lambda_{j'}\; j'{=}j)$. Connected component functions that have a common referent j can then be composed into larger connected components:[4]

$$\exists_{ijk}\, (g \{j\}\, i) \wedge (h \{k\}\, j) \;\Leftrightarrow\; \exists_{ij}\, (g{\circ}h \{k\}\, i) \tag{3}$$

Hierarchies of ℓ connected components can be represented as conjunctions: $\exists_{i^1 j^1 ... i^\ell j^\ell}\, (g^1{:}c^1/d^1 \{j^1\}\, i^1) \wedge \ldots \wedge (g^\ell{:}c^\ell/d^\ell \{j^\ell\}\, i^\ell)$. This allows constraints such as unbounded dependencies between referents of fillers and referents of clauses containing gaps to be specified across connected components by simply plugging variables for filler referents into argument positions for gaps.

A nondeterministic incremental parser can now be defined as a deductive system, given an input sequence consisting of an initial connected component state of category $\mathbf{T}/\mathbf{T}$, corresponding to an existing discourse context, followed by a sequence of observations $x_1, x_2, \ldots,$ processed in time order. As each x_t is encountered, it is connected to an existing connected component or it introduces a new disjoint component using the productions shown in Figures 3, 4, and 5.

[4]These are connected components of dependency structure resulting from one or more composition functions being composed, with each function's output as the previous function's second argument. This uses a standard definition of function composition: $((f \circ g)\, x) = (f\, (g\, x))$.

$$\frac{\exists_{i^1 j^1 .. i^{\ell-1} j^{\ell-1} i^\ell} \ldots \wedge (g^\ell{:}d\, i^\ell)}{\exists_{i^1 j^1 .. i^\ell j^\ell} \ldots \wedge ((f\, g^\ell) \circ (\lambda_{h\,k\,i}\, (h\, k)){:}a/e\psi\, \{j^\ell\}\, i^\ell)}\; g{:}d\;\, h{:}e\psi \Rightarrow (f\, g\, h){:}c \qquad (\text{–Lc})$$

$$\frac{\exists_{i^1 j^1 .. i^{\ell-1} j^{\ell-1} i^\ell} \ldots \wedge (g^{\ell-1}{:}a/c\, \{j^{\ell-1}\}\, i^{\ell-1}) \wedge (g^\ell{:}d\, i^\ell)}{\exists_{i^1 j^1 .. i^{\ell-1} j^{\ell-1}} \ldots \wedge (g^{\ell-1} \circ (f\, g^\ell) \circ (\lambda_{h\,k\,i}\, (h\, k)){:}a/e\psi\, \{j^{\ell-1}\}\, i^{\ell-1})}\; g{:}d\;\, h{:}e\psi \Rightarrow (f\, g\, h){:}c \qquad (\text{+Lc})$$

$$\frac{\exists_{i^1 j^1 .. i^\ell j^\ell} \ldots \wedge (g^{\ell-1}{:}c/d\psi\, \{j^{\ell-1}\}\, i^{\ell-1}) \wedge (g^\ell{:}d\psi/e\, \{j^\ell\}\, i^\ell)}{\exists_{i^1 j^1 .. i^{\ell-1} j^{\ell-1}} \ldots \wedge (g^{\ell-1} \circ (\lambda_{h\,i} \exists_j (h\, j)) \circ g^\ell{:}c/e\, \{j^{\ell-1}\}\, i^{\ell-1})} \qquad (\text{+N})$$

Figure 5: Additional processing productions for hypothesizing filler-gap attachment.

Operations on dependencies that can be derived from surface structure (see Figure 3) are taken directly from van Schijndel and Schuler (2013). First, if an observation x_t can immediately fill the awaited sign of the last connected component $g^\ell{:}c/d$, it is hypothesized to do so, turning this incomplete connected component into a complete connected component $(g^\ell f){:}c$ (Production –Fa); or if the observation can serve as an initial sub-sign of this awaited sign, it is hypothesized to form a new complete sign $f{:}e$ in a new component with x_t as its first observation (Production +Fa). Then, if either of these resulting complete signs $g^\ell{:}d$ can immediately attach as an initial child of the awaited sign of the most recent connected component $g^{\ell-1}{:}a/c$, it is hypothesized to merge and extend this connected component, with x_t as the last observation of the completed connected component (Production +La); or if it can serve as an initial sub-sign of this awaited sign, it is hypothesized to remain disjoint and form its own connected component (Production –La). The side conditions of La productions are defined to unpack gap propagation (instances of λ_k that distinguish rules Aa–h and Ma–h) from the inference rules in Section 3, because this functionality will be replaced with direct substitution of referent variables into subordinate semantic functions, below.

The Nguyen et al. (2012) GCG was defined to pass up unbounded dependencies, but in incremental deep syntactic dependency processing, unbounded dependencies are accounted as separate connected components. When hypothesizing an unbounded dependency, the processing model simply cues the active sign of a previous connected component containing a filler without completing the current connected component. The four +F, –F, +L, and –L operations are therefore combined with applications of unary rules Ga–c for hypothesizing referents as fillers for gaps (providing f' in the equations in Figure 4). Productions –Fb and +Fb fill gaps in initial children, and Productions –Lb and +Lb fill gaps in final children. Note that the Fb and Lb productions apply to the same types of antecedents as Fa and La productions respectively, so members of these two sets of productions cannot be applied together.

Applications of rules Fa–c and R for introducing fillers are applied to store fillers as existentially quantified variable values in Lc productions (see Figure 5). These Lc productions apply to the same type of antecedent as La and Lb productions, so these also cannot be applied together.

Finally, connected components separated by gaps which are no longer hypothesized (ψ) are reattached by a +N production. This +N production may then be paired with a –N production which yields its antecedent unchanged as a consequent. These N productions apply to antecedents and consequents of the same type, so they may be applied together with one F and one L production, but since the +N production removes in its consequent a ψ argument required in its antecedent, it may not apply more than once in succession (and applying the –N production more than once in succession has no effect).

An incremental derivation of the noun phrase *the person who officials say stole millions,* using these productions, is shown in Figure 6.

5 Evaluation

The F, L, and N productions defined in the previous section can be made probabilistic by first computing a probabilistic context-free grammar (PCFG) from a tree-annotated corpus, then transforming that PCFG model into a model of probabilities over incremental parsing operations using a grammar transform (Schuler, 2009). This allows the intermediate PCFG to be optimized using an existing PCFG-based latent variable trainer

$$\exists_{\mathbf{i}_0}\ (..:\mathbf{T/T}\,\{\mathbf{i}_0\}\,\mathbf{i}_0) \quad \text{the} \qquad {+}\text{Fa},{-}\text{La},{-}\text{N}$$

$$\exists_{\mathbf{i}_0\,\mathbf{i}_2}\ (..:\mathbf{T/T}\,\{\mathbf{i}_0\}\,\mathbf{i}_0) \wedge (..:\mathbf{N/N\text{-}aD}\,\{\mathbf{i}_2\}\,\mathbf{i}_2) \quad \text{person} \qquad {-}\text{Fa},{-}\text{La},{-}\text{N}$$

$$\exists_{\mathbf{i}_0\,\mathbf{i}_2}\ (..:\mathbf{T/T}\,\{\mathbf{i}_0\}\,\mathbf{i}_0) \wedge (..:\mathbf{N/V\text{-}rN}\,\{\mathbf{i}_2\}\,\mathbf{i}_2) \quad \text{who} \qquad {+}\text{Fa},{+}\text{Lc},{-}\text{N}$$

$$\exists_{\mathbf{i}_0\,\mathbf{i}_2\,\mathbf{i}_3}\ (..:\mathbf{T/T}\,\{\mathbf{i}_0\}\,\mathbf{i}_0) \wedge (..:\mathbf{N/V\text{-}gN}\,\{\mathbf{i}_3\}\,\mathbf{i}_2) \quad \text{officials} \qquad {+}\text{Fa},{-}\text{La},{-}\text{N}$$

$$\exists_{\mathbf{i}_0\,\mathbf{i}_2\,\mathbf{i}_3\,\mathbf{i}_5}\ (..:\mathbf{T/T}\,\{\mathbf{i}_0\}\,\mathbf{i}_0) \wedge (..:\mathbf{N/V\text{-}gN}\,\{\mathbf{i}_3\}\,\mathbf{i}_2) \wedge (..:\mathbf{V\text{-}gN/V\text{-}aN\text{-}gN}\,\{\mathbf{i}_5\}\,\mathbf{i}_5) \quad \text{say} \qquad {+}\text{Fb},{+}\text{La},{+}\text{N}$$

$$\exists_{\mathbf{i}_0\,\mathbf{i}_2\,\mathbf{i}_6}\ (..:\mathbf{T/T}\,\{\mathbf{i}_0\}\,\mathbf{i}_0) \wedge (..:\mathbf{N/V\text{-}aN}\,\{\mathbf{i}_6\}\,\mathbf{i}_2) \quad \text{stole} \qquad {+}\text{Fa},{+}\text{La},{-}\text{N}$$

$$\exists_{\mathbf{i}_0\,\mathbf{i}_2\,\mathbf{i}_7}\ (..:\mathbf{T/T}\,\{\mathbf{i}_0\}\,\mathbf{i}_0) \wedge (..:\mathbf{N/N}\,\{\mathbf{i}_7\}\,\mathbf{i}_2) \quad \text{millions} \qquad {-}\text{Fa},{+}\text{La},{-}\text{N}$$

$$\exists_{\mathbf{i}_0}\ (..:\mathbf{T/T}\,\{\mathbf{i}_0\}\,\mathbf{i}_0)$$

Figure 6: Derivation of *the person who officials say stole millions*, showing connected components with unique referent variables (calculated according to the equations in Section 4). Semantic functions are abbreviated to '..' for readability. This derivation yields the following lexical relations: $(0\,\mathbf{i}_1)$=the, $(0\,\mathbf{i}_2)$=person, $(0\,\mathbf{i}_3)$=who, $(0\,\mathbf{i}_4)$=officials, $(0\,\mathbf{i}_5)$=say, $(0\,\mathbf{i}_6)$=stole, $(0\,\mathbf{i}_7)$=millions, and the following argument relations: $(1\,\mathbf{i}_2)=\mathbf{i}_1$, $(1\,\mathbf{i}_3)=\mathbf{i}_2$, $(1\,\mathbf{i}_5)=\mathbf{i}_4$, $(2\,\mathbf{i}_5)=\mathbf{i}_6$, $(1\,\mathbf{i}_6)=\mathbf{i}_3$, $(2\,\mathbf{i}_6)=\mathbf{i}_7$.

(Petrov et al., 2006). When applied to the output of this trainer, this transform has been shown to produce comparable accuracy to that of the original Petrov et al. (2006) CKY parser (van Schijndel et al., 2012). The transform used in these experiments diverges from that of Schuler (2009), in that the probability associated with introducing a gap in a filler-gap construction is reallocated from a –F–L operation to a +F–L operation (to encode the previously most subordinate connected component with the filler as its awaited sign and begin a new disjoint connected component), and the probability associated with resolving such a gap is reallocated from an implicit –N operation to a +N operation (to integrate the connected component containing the gap with that containing the filler).

In order to verify that the modifications to the transform correctly reallocate probability mass for gap operations, the goodness of fit to reading times of a model using this modified transform is compared against the publicly-available baseline model from van Schijndel and Schuler (2013), which uses the original Schuler (2009) transform.[5]

To ensure a valid comparison, both parsers are trained on a GCG-reannotated version of the Wall Street Journal portion of the Penn Treebank (Marcus et al., 1993) before being fit to reading times using linear mixed-effects models (Baayen et al., 2008).[6] This evaluation focuses on the processing that can be done up to a given point in a sentence. In human subjects, this processing includes both immediate lexical access and regressions that aid in the integration of new information, so the reading times of interest in this evaluation are log-transformed go-past durations.[7]

The first and last word of each line in the Dundee corpus, words not observed at least 5 times in the WSJ training corpus, and fixations after long saccades (>4 words) are omitted from the evaluation to filter out wrap-up effects, parser inaccuracies, and inattention and track loss of the eyetracker. The following predictors are centered and used in each baseline model: sentence position, word length, whether or not the previous or next word were fixated upon, and unigram and bigram probabilities.[8] Then each of the following predictors is residualized off each baseline before being centered and added to it to help residualize the next factor: length of the go-past region, cumulative total surprisal, total surprisal (Hale, 2001), and cumulative entropy reduction (Hale, 2003).[9] All 2-way interactions between these effects are

[5]The models used here also use random slopes to reduce their variance, which makes them less anticonservative.

[6]The models are built using *lmer* from the *lme4* R package (Bates et al., 2011; R Development Core Team, 2010).

[7]Go-past durations are calculated by summing all fixations in a region of text, including regressions, until a new region is fixated, which accounts for additional processing that may take place after initial lexical access, but before the next region is processed. For example, if one region ends at word 5 in a sentence, and the next fixation lands on word 8, then the go-past region consists of words 6-8 while go-past duration sums all fixations until a fixation occurs after word 8. Log-transforming eye movements and fixations may make their distributions more normal (Stephen and Mirman, 2010) and does not substantially affect the results of this paper.

[8]For the n-gram model, this study uses the Brown corpus (Francis and Kucera, 1979), the WSJ Sections 02-21 (Marcus et al., 1993), the written portion of the British National Corpus (BNC Consortium, 2007), and the Dundee corpus (Kennedy et al., 2003) smoothed with modified Kneser-Ney (Chen and Goodman, 1998) in SRILM (Stolcke, 2002).

[9]Non-cumulative metrics are calculated from the final word of the go-past region; cumulative metrics are summed over the go-past region.

included as predictors along with the predictors from the previous go-past region (to account for spillover effects). Finally, each model has subject and item random intercepts added in addition to by-subject random slopes (cumulative total surprisal, whether the previous word was fixated, and length of the go-past region) and is fit to centered log-transformed go-past durations.[10]

The Akaike Information Criterion (AIC) indicates that the gap-reallocating model (AIC = 128,605) provides a better fit to reading times than the original model (AIC = 128,619).[11]

As described in Section 1, previous findings of negative integration cost may be due to a confound whereby center-embedded constructions caused by modifiers, which do not require deep syntactic dependencies to be deferred, may be driving the effect. Under this hypothesis, embeddings that do not arise from final adjunction of modifiers (henceforth *canonical* embeddings) should yield a positive integration cost as found by Gibson (2000).

To investigate this potential confound, the Dundee corpus is partitioned into two parts. First, the model described in this paper is used to annotate the Dundee corpus. From this annotated corpus, all sentences are collected that contain canonical embeddings and lack modifier-induced embeddings.[12] This produces two corpora: one consisting entirely of canonical center-embeddings such as those used in self-paced reading experiments with findings of positive integration cost (e.g. Gibson 2000), the other consisting of the remainder of the Dundee corpus, which contains sentences with canonical embeddings but also includes modifier-caused embeddings.

The coefficient estimates for integration operations (–F+L and +N) on each of these corpora are then calculated using the baseline described above. To ensure embeddings are driving any observed effect rather than sentence wrap-up effects, the first and last words of each sentence are excluded from both data sets. Integration cost is measured by the amount of probability mass the parser allocates to –F+L and +N operations, accumulated over each go-past region, and this cost is added as a fixed effect and as a random slope by subject to the mixed model described earlier.[13]

Model	coeff	std err	t-score
Canonical	-0.040	0.010	-4.05
Other	-0.017	0.004	-4.20

Table 1: Fixed effect estimates for integration cost when used to fit reading times over two partitions of the Dundee corpus: one containing only canonical center embeddings and the other composed of the rest of the sentences in the corpus.

The fixed effect estimate for cumulative integration cost from fitting each corpus is shown in Table 1. Application of Welch's t-test shows that the difference between the estimated distributions of these two parameters is highly significant ($p < 0.0001$).[14] The strong negative correlation of integration cost to reading times in the purely canonical corpus suggests canonical (non-modifier) integrations contribute to the finding of negative integration cost.

6 Conclusion

This paper has introduced an incremental parser capable of using GCG dependencies to distinguish between surface syntactic embeddings and deep syntactic embeddings. This parser was shown to obtain a better fit to reading times than a surface-syntactic parser and was used to parse the Dundee eye-tracking corpus in two partitions: one consisting of canonical embeddings that require deferred dependencies and the other consisting of sentences containing no center embeddings or center embeddings arising from the attachment of clause-final modifiers, in which no dependencies are deferred. Using linear mixed effects models, completion (integration) of canonical center embeddings was found to be significantly more negatively correlated with reading times than completion of non-canonical embeddings. These results suggest that the negative integration cost observed in eye-tracking studies is at least partially due to deep syntactic dependencies and not due to confounds related to surface forms.

[10] Each fixed effect that has an absolute t-value greater than 10 when included in a random-intercepts only model is added as a random slope by-subject.

[11] The relative likelihood of the original model to the gap-sensitive model is 0.0009 (n = 151,331), which suggests the improvement is significant.

[12] Modifier-induced embeddings are found by looking for embeddings that arise from inference rules Ma-h in Section 3.

[13] Integration cost is residualized off the baseline before being centered and added as a fixed effect.

[14] Integration cost is significant as a fixed effect ($p = 0.001$) in both partitions: canonical (n = 16,174 durations) and non-canonical (n = 131,297 durations).

References

Steven P. Abney and Mark Johnson. 1991. Memory requirements and local ambiguities of parsing strategies. *J. Psycholinguistic Research*, 20(3):233–250.

R. Harald Baayen, D. J. Davidson, and Douglas M. Bates. 2008. Mixed-effects modeling with crossed random effects for subjects and items. *Journal of Memory and Language*, 59:390–412.

Emmon Bach. 1981. Discontinuous constituents in generalized categorial grammars. *Proceedings of the Annual Meeting of the Northeast Linguistic Society (NELS)*, 11:1–12.

Douglas Bates, Martin Maechler, and Ben Bolker, 2011. *lme4: Linear mixed-effects models using S4 classes*.

BNC Consortium. 2007. The british national corpus.

Stanley F. Chen and Joshua Goodman. 1998. An empirical study of smoothing techniques for language modeling. Technical report, Harvard University.

Vera Demberg and Frank Keller. 2008. Data from eye-tracking corpora as evidence for theories of syntactic processing complexity. *Cognition*, 109(2):193–210.

W. Nelson Francis and Henry Kucera. 1979. The brown corpus: A standard corpus of present-day edited american english.

Edward Gibson. 1998. Linguistic complexity: Locality of syntactic dependencies. *Cognition*, 68(1):1–76.

Edward Gibson. 2000. The dependency locality theory: A distance-based theory of linguistic complexity. In *Image, language, brain: Papers from the first mind articulation project symposium*, pages 95–126, Cambridge, MA. MIT Press.

John Hale. 2001. A probabilistic earley parser as a psycholinguistic model. In *Proceedings of the second meeting of the North American chapter of the Association for Computational Linguistics*, pages 159–166, Pittsburgh, PA.

John Hale. 2003. *Grammar, Uncertainty and Sentence Processing*. Ph.D. thesis, Cognitive Science, The Johns Hopkins University.

Philip N. Johnson-Laird. 1983. *Mental models: towards a cognitive science of language, inference, and consciousness*. Harvard University Press, Cambridge, MA, USA.

Daniel Jurafsky. 1996. A probabilistic model of lexical and syntactic access and disambiguation. *Cognitive Science: A Multidisciplinary Journal*, 20(2):137–194.

Marcel Adam Just and Patricia A. Carpenter. 1992. A capacity theory of comprehension: Individual differences in working memory. *Psychological Review*, 99:122–149.

Fred Karlsson. 2007. Constraints on multiple center-embedding of clauses. *Journal of Linguistics*, 43:365–392.

Alan Kennedy, James Pynte, and Robin Hill. 2003. The Dundee corpus. In *Proceedings of the 12th European conference on eye movement*.

Walter Kintsch. 1988. The role of knowledge in discourse comprehension: A construction-integration model. *Psychological review*, 95(2):163–182.

Nayoung Kwon, Yoonhyoung Lee, Peter C. Gordon, Robert Kluender, and Maria Polinsky. 2010. Cognitive and linguistic factors affecting subject/object asymmetry: An eye-tracking study of pre-nominal relative clauses in korean. *Language*, 86(3):561.

Richard L. Lewis and Shravan Vasishth. 2005. An activation-based model of sentence processing as skilled memory retrieval. *Cognitive Science*, 29(3):375–419.

Mitchell P. Marcus, Beatrice Santorini, and Mary Ann Marcinkiewicz. 1993. Building a large annotated corpus of English: the Penn Treebank. *Computational Linguistics*, 19(2):313–330.

Igor Mel'čuk. 1988. *Dependency syntax: theory and practice*. State University of NY Press, Albany.

Luan Nguyen, Marten van Schijndel, and William Schuler. 2012. Accurate unbounded dependency recovery using generalized categorial grammars. In *Proceedings of the 24th International Conference on Computational Linguistics (COLING '12)*, Mumbai, India.

Slav Petrov, Leon Barrett, Romain Thibaux, and Dan Klein. 2006. Learning accurate, compact, and interpretable tree annotation. In *Proceedings of the 44th Annual Meeting of the Association for Computational Linguistics (COLING/ACL'06)*.

R Development Core Team, 2010. *R: A Language and Environment for Statistical Computing*. R Foundation for Statistical Computing, Vienna, Austria. ISBN 3-900051-07-0.

William Schuler. 2009. Parsing with a bounded stack using a model-based right-corner transform. In *Proceedings of NAACL/HLT 2009*, NAACL '09, pages 344–352, Boulder, Colorado. Association for Computational Linguistics.

Damian G. Stephen and Daniel Mirman. 2010. Interactions dominate the dynamics of visual cognition. *Cognition*, 115(1):154–165.

Andreas Stolcke. 2002. Srilm – an extensible language modeling toolkit. In *Seventh International Conference on Spoken Language Processing*.

Marten van Schijndel and William Schuler. 2013. An analysis of frequency- and recency-based processing costs. In *Proceedings of NAACL-HLT 2013*. Association for Computational Linguistics.

Marten van Schijndel, Andy Exley, and William Schuler. 2012. Connectionist-inspired incremental PCFG parsing. In *Proceedings of CMCL 2012*. Association for Computational Linguistics.

Marten van Schijndel, Andy Exley, and William Schuler. in press. A model of language processing as hierarchic sequential prediction. *Topics in Cognitive Science*.

Stephen Wu, Asaf Bachrach, Carlos Cardenas, and William Schuler. 2010. Complexity metrics in an incremental right-corner parser. In *Proceedings of the 48th Annual Meeting of the Association for Computational Linguistics (ACL'10)*, pages 1189–1198.

Computational simulations of second language construction learning

Yevgen Matusevych
Department of
Culture Studies

Afra Alishahi
Department of Communication
and Information Sciences

Ad Backus
Department of
Culture Studies

Tilburg University, PO Box 90153, 5000 LE Tilburg, the Netherlands

Y.Matusevych@uvt.nl A.Alishahi@uvt.nl A.M.Backus@uvt.nl

Abstract

There are few computational models of second language acquisition (SLA). At the same time, many questions in the field of SLA remain unanswered. In particular, SLA patterns are difficult to study due to the large amount of variation between human learners. We present a computational model of second language construction learning that allows manipulating specific parameters such as age of onset and amount of exposure. We use the model to study general developmental patterns of SLA and two specific effects sometimes found in empirical studies: construction priming and a facilitatory effect of skewed frequencies in the input. Our simulations replicate the expected SLA patterns as well as the two effects. Our model can be used in further studies of various SLA phenomena.

1 Introduction

Computational models have been widely used for investigating how humans learn and process their native language. Various models of child language acquisition have been applied to studies of speech segmentation (e.g., ten Bosch, Hamme, & Boves, 2008), word learning (e.g., Frank, Goodman, & Tenenbaum, 2009; Fazly, Alishahi, & Stevenson, 2010), induction of linguistic structure (e.g., Elman, 1990), etc. In comparison, the acquisition of second language has received little attention from the modeling community. Most of the child language acquisition models cannot be directly used for investigating how humans process and acquire foreign languages. In order to do so, we have to model the existing knowledge of first language—i.e., bilingualism.

Li (2013) provides a state-of-the-art overview of models of bilingualism. One of his claims is that most existing models account for mature adult speaker's knowledge and do not explain how foreign language develops in learners. In other words, there are several computational models of second language *processing* (e.g., Shook & Marian, 2013; Roelofs, Dijkstra, & Gerakaki, 2013; Yang, Shu, McCandliss, & Zevin, 2013, etc.), but only few of Second Language *Acquisition* (SLA). The latter mostly simulate lexis and semantics acquisition (e.g., Li & Farkas, 2002; Li, 2009; Cuppini, Magosso, & Ursino, 2013, etc.), and those that address a higher level of language structure usually do not model the existing L1 knowledge (e.g., N. C. Ellis & Larsen-Freeman, 2009; Rappoport & Sheinman, 2005; but see Monner, Vatz, Morini, Hwang, & DeKeyser, 2013).

At the same time, a number of theoretical SLA issues are not well explained yet, including general questions such as how existing knowledge of the first language influences the acquisition of second language. To give a specific example, it is not clear yet when L1 structures lead to interference and when they do not.

In this paper, we use an existing model of early acquisition of argument structure constructions (Alishahi & Stevenson, 2008) and adapt it to bilingual input data, which allows us to investigate the acquisition process in second language learners. We demonstrate in a number of computational simulations that our model replicates natural L2 developmental patterns and two specific effects observed in human L2 learners, thus allowing us to make certain predictions about the issues under investigation.

2 Description of the model

A usage-based approach to language claims that humans learn abstract linguistic regularities from instances of language use. Specifically, general argument structure constructions are predicted to emerge over time from individual verb usages which share syntactic and semantic properties. Argument structure constructions, according to Goldberg, Casenhiser, and White (2007), are "pairings of form and meaning that provide the means of expressing simple propositions in a language" (p. 74). Since nearly all human utterances contain propositions, the learner's knowledge of argument structure constructions must reflect the level of his grammatical competence.

The model of Alishahi and Stevenson (2008) is based on this approach: the building block of the model is an *argument structure frame*, a collection of syntactic and semantic features which represents a verb usage. Abstract constructions are formed by detecting and clustering similar frames, and various linguistic tasks are simulated by having the model predict the most suitable values for the missing features in a frame. These components are described in the following sections.

2.1 Argument structure frames

In our SLA model, each frame contains the following features:

- **Head verb** in its infinitive form.
- **Number of arguments** that the verb takes.
- **Semantic primitives of the verb** representing the conceptual characteristics of the event that the verb describes.
- **Semantic properties of each argument** representing its conceptual meaning, independently of the event that it participates in.
- **Event-based properties of each argument** representing the characteristics each argument takes on in the particular event it is participating in.
- **Syntactic pattern** of the utterance.

A sample frame is shown in Table 1. In Section 3.3 we will further explain how values for each frame feature are selected.

Table 1: An example frame extracted from a verb usage *Bill went through the maze.*

Head verb (V.)	*go*
No. of arguments	2
V. sem. primitives	act, move, walk
Arg.1 sem. prop-s	name, male, person, ...
Arg.2 sem. prop-s	system, instrumentality, ...
Arg.1 event prop-s	volitional, sentient, ...
Arg.2 event prop-s	location, path, destination
Syntactic pattern	AGENT V. through LOC.

2.2 Learning Constructions

Alishahi and Stevenson (2008) use an incremental Bayesian algorithm for clustering similar frames into constructions. Each input frame is compared to all the existing constructions and a potentially new one, and is added to the best matching construction:

$$\text{BestConstruction}(F) = \underset{k}{\text{argmax}}\, P(k|F) \quad (1)$$

where k ranges over the indices of all constructions (index 0 represents the new construction). Using Bayes rule and dropping $P(F)$ which is constant for all k:

$$P(k|F) = \frac{P(k)P(F|k)}{P(F)} \sim P(k)P(F|k) \quad (2)$$

The prior probability $P(k)$ indicates the degree of entrenchment of construction k:

$$P(k) = \frac{N_k}{N+1}, P(0) = \frac{1}{N+1} \quad (3)$$

where N_k is the number of frames already clustered in construction k, and N is the total number of frames observed so far. The posterior probability of a frame F is expressed in terms of the (supposedly independent) probabilities of its features:

$$P(F|k) = \prod_{i \in Features(F)} P_i(j|k) \quad (4)$$

where j is the value of the ith feature of F, and $P_i(j|k)$ is the probability of displaying value j on feature i within construction k. This probability is estimated using a smoothed maximum likelihood formula.[1]

2.3 Bilingual acquisition

We accept the view that L1 and L2 learning have more commonalities than differences (see, e.g., MacWhinney, 2013), thus we do not explicitly encode the difference between the two languages. As the learner perceives a frame, he is not aware of which language the frame belongs to. All the input data are processed equally, so that constructions are formed in the same space and can contain frames from both languages. Such approach allows us to investigate how the existing L1 knowledge influences L2 acquisition.

[1]For single-valued features such as the head verb, likelihood is calculated by simply counting those members of construction k whose value for feature i exactly matches value j. For features with a set value such as the semantic properties of the verb and the arguments, the likelihood is calculated by comparing sets.

2.4 Sentence production

We use sentence production as our main evaluation task for SLA. Given a frame which represents an intended meaning through the semantic properties of an event (or verb) and its participants (or arguments), we want to predict the most probable values for the syntactic pattern feature. Following Alishahi and Stevenson (2008), we estimate the probability that feature i (in our case, the syntactic pattern) displays value j given other observed feature values in a partial frame F as

$$\begin{aligned} P_i(j|F) &= \sum_k P_i(j|k)P(k|F) \\ &= \sum_k P_i(j|k)P(k)P(F|k) \end{aligned} \tag{5}$$

The probabilities $P(k)$, $P(F|k)$ and $P_i(j|k)$ are estimated as before (see Equations 3 and 4). Ranging over the possible values j of feature i, the value of an unobserved feature can be predicted by maximizing $P_i(j|F)^2$:

$$\text{BestValue}_i(F) = \underset{j}{\text{argmax}}\, P_i(j|F) \tag{6}$$

3 Data

For cognitively plausible computational simulations we had to prepare naturalistic input based on the suitable corpora. While there are available corpora that contain recordings of child-directed speech (MacWhinney, 2000), the resources containing speech addressed to L2 learners appear to be very limited. Therefore, our choice of languages (German as a L1, and English as a L2) was motivated first of all by the data availability. We extracted naturalistic L1 and L2 data from two different sources.

3.1 Data sources

L2 English data were extracted from the Flensburg classroom corpus (Jäkel, 2010) that contains transcripts of lessons of English (as a foreign language) taught to children in German schools that cover all school age groups. We estimated the total number of occurrences of different verbs in the corpus. From 20 most frequent verbs we selected 6 that represented syntactically and semantically different linguistic constructions, since constructional variability was one of the crucial factors for the model. The verbs are: *go*, *come*, *read*, *show*, *look* and *put*. For each verb, we extracted all its occurrences from the corpus.

For L1 we used German data extracted from the CHILDES database (MacWhinney, 2000), namely from adults' speech directed to three children: Caroline (age from 0;10 to 4;3; von Stutterheim, 2004), Kerstin (from 1;3 to 3;4; M. Miller, 1979) and Leo (from 1;11 to 4;11; Behrens, 2006). In the same manner as for the English data, we selected six verbs—*machen 'to make'*, *kommen 'to come'*, *gucken 'to look'*, *gehen 'to go'*, *sehen 'to see'* and *geben 'to give'*— and extracted all their occurrences from the three corpora. Since the corpora were of different size, the number of occurrences for some verbs were incomparable between the corpora, thus we balanced the size of the samples used for further analysis by taking equal numbers of random verb uses from each corpus.

3.2 Data annotation

Since the basic input unit for our computational model was a frame, we manually annotated all the verb occurrences in order to extract frames. Approximately 100 instances per verb were annotated using the following general guidelines.

1. Instance grouping is based on the semantics of the main verb and its arguments as well as on the syntactic pattern.
2. We consider only arguments (both obligatory and optional), but not adjuncts, since there is evidence that the two are processed differently (see, e.g., Kennison, 2002).
3. We discard all instances where the main verb was represented by a compound form or by an infinitive, or appeared in a subordinate clause, since in all these cases the "core" frame of the argument structure construction might obtain additional structural or semantic characteristics.
4. We do consider imperatives and questions whose form does not contradict the previous point.
5. We treat German prefixed/particle verbs (e.g., *zumachen 'to close'*) and English compound verbs as an instance of the base verb (in this case, *machen 'to make'*), given that the prefixed/particle verb meaning is compositional and the prefix/particle is actually separated.
6. Considering the previous point, each particle/prefix in our instances represents an in-

[2] A non-deterministic alternative that we have to consider in the future is to sample the feature value from the estimated distribution.

dependent semantic component (see, e.g., Dewell, 2011, for detailed explanation), and we treat them as separate arguments.

7. We discard all the instances in which the verb is used in a formulaic sequence (e.g.,, *Wie geht's? 'How are you?'*), because formulaic sequences are believed to be processed and acquired as a whole (e.g., Wray, 2005; Bannard & Lieven, 2012).
8. Finally, we eliminate the case marking in German and use the Nominative case for all the arguments, because this feature is not crucial for our model, and there is evidence that German children before the age of 7 mostly rely on other features such as word order (Dittmar, Abbot-Smith, Lieven, & Tomasello, 2008).

3.3 Frame extraction

From the annotated data samples, for each verb we extracted frames and their respective frequencies of occurrence. Following Alishahi and Stevenson (2010), the semantic primitives of verbs and their arguments were semi-automatically extracted from WordNet (G. A. Miller, 1995), and the event-based properties of the arguments were manually compiled.

The syntactic pattern of the frame not only shows the order of the arguments, but also implicitly includes information about their semantic roles, i.e., AGENT, THEME, LOCATION, etc. Note that these semantic labels are used only for distinguishing between similar syntactic patterns with the verb in the same position but swapped arguments (cf. *[so] schnell geht es* vs. *es geht [so] schnell* 'it goes [so] fast'—both patterns occur rather frequently in German).[3]

Based on the manually extracted frames, an input corpus of verb uses was automatically generated for each set of experiments. The frequency of occurrence of each frame determined the probability of selecting this frame, and the same method was used for selecting specific arguments.

[3] Although the inclusion of semantic labels into syntactic pattern makes the learning task easier, there is, in fact, no agreement yet on how exactly children acquire the non-canonical word order. They must rely on pragmatics, and this phenomenon most thoroughly has been studied in the generative tradition under the name of scrambling, but still various explanations were proposed (see, e.g., Mykhaylyk & Ko, 2011). Due to this uncertainty, we found it acceptable to provide the learner with the means to distinguish between the patterns like in the example above, since it was highly important for German with its partially free word order.

4 Simulations and results

In this section we report on computational simulations that we ran using our model and the described input data. We investigate general L2 developmental patterns, priming effects in SLA, and the impact of skewed input on the learner's L2 proficiency. Although the latter two are not SLA phenomena per se and can be observed in L1 learners as well, they have been discussed in SLA domain and suit well our methodological framework.

4.1 L2 general development

Despite numerous attempts to capture and describe the dynamics of SLA, scholars admit that there is no 'typical' profile of general L2 development (for an overview, see Hasko, 2013). This is because many variables are involved, such as the learner's L1, the age of L2 onset, amount of input, type of instruction (if any), etc. They cause significant differences between individual learners and specific linguistic phenomena.

Generally, L2 develops gradually, and second language learners rarely achieve native-like L2 proficiency. To demonstrate that our model follows these patterns, we ran a number of simulations to compare how L1 and L2 proficiency changes over time. In our scenario, the learner was first presented 500 L1 verb uses in small steps (25 times 20 frames). After each step his L1 proficiency was tested in the following way. The learner was presented with 20 test frames in which the syntactic pattern was removed, and had to predict the most suitable syntactic pattern, relying on his current knowledge. We should note that because German has partially free word order, our German data contained a substantial number of frame groups consisting of two or more frames that were almost identical and differed only in the order of arguments in their syntactic patterns (i.e., AGENT *verb* THEME and THEME *verb* AGENT). These patterns are very close both linguistically (i.e., they carry very similar meanings) and algorithmically (i.e., the learner's preference for one of them is determined only by their respective frequencies of occurrence in the input). Therefore, asking the learner to predict the exact pattern would not be a fair task. For this reason, during the evaluation we only checked whether the pattern produced by the learner contained exactly the same set of arguments (and, possibly, the same preposition) as the target pattern. Thus, AGENT *kommen* THEME, *kommen* AGENT THEME, and THEME *kommen* AGENT were considered equal for the purpose of evaluation.

After the initial 25 steps of L1 training and testing, the learner was presented 500 more frames (25 times 20) which could be either from L1 or from L2 data in proportion 3 (L1) to 1 (L2). This way we simulated a common situation when a child starts learning a foreign language at school, thus being exposed to input from both languages, but L1 input prevails. The results averaged over 10 simulations (Figure 1) demonstrate that the L2 proficiency does not achieve that of L1.[4]

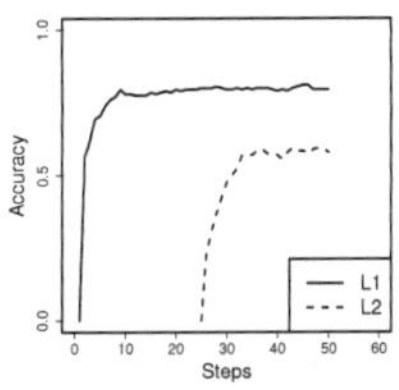

Figure 1: L1 and L2 development over time

We explain the lower L2 proficiency by two factors. First, by the moment when the learner started receiving L2 input, L1 constructions were already formed in his memory, so the L1 entrenchment prevented L2 constructions to fully emerge. Second, even within the period of SLA the amount of L2 input was 3 times smaller compared to that of L1. To investigate whether both factors were indeed important, we tried to eliminate each of them separately, i.e., to present both L1 and L2 from the very beginning keeping the ratio 3:1 (Figure 2, left), or to set an equal ratio while keeping the late age of L2 onset (Figure 2, right). As we can see, in neither case does the L2 proficiency reach that of L1. However, when both factors are eliminated—that is, from the very beginning the learner receives mixed L1/L2 input in equal proportion—he reaches comparable levels of L1 and L2 proficiency (Figure 3).

Additionally, we tried to separately manipulate each of the two parameters keeping the other one constant. We expected that (1) the lower the L2 age of onset, the higher the learner's proficiency at each moment of time with the L1/L2 ratio set at 3:1, and (2) the smaller the L1/L2 ratio (down to 1, when the amount of input is equal), the higher

[4]After presenting 4,000 more L2 frames to the learner this pattern was still observed, and neither L1 nor L2 proficiency converged to 1.

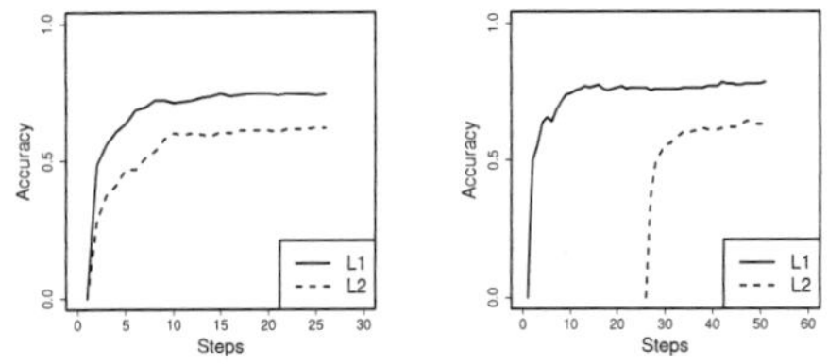

Figure 2: L1 and L2 proficiency provided equal age of onset (left) or input ratio (right)

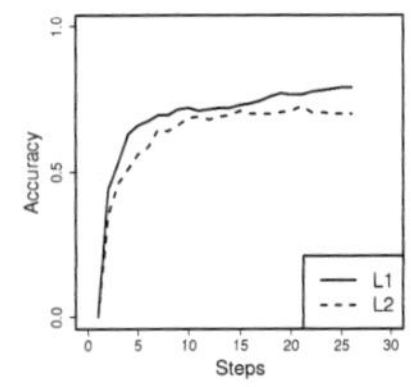

Figure 3: L1 and L2 proficiency provided equal learning conditions

the learner's proficiency at each moment of time with the age of onset set at 500 frames. We found no evidence for either effect. Part of the explanation might be that there was a substantial overlap between L1 and L2 syntactic patterns (especially considering we treated patterns as sets of elements irrespective of word order). Therefore the learner's existing L1 knowledge may indirectly have contributed to the L2 proficiency, in a pattern known as "positive transfer" (see, e.g., Benson, 2002). This can be demonstrated by comparing the initial slopes of L2 development lines in Figure 1 and Figure 2a. In the former case, representing L2 exposure after L1 constructions have already been entrenched, L2 acquisition goes faster in its initial stages, because the learner has, in fact, already acquired a number of syntactic patterns that are shared by the two languages. Monner et al. (2013), who computationally studied the effect of French L1 entrenchment on Spanish L2 grammatical gender learning, explain an exception in their results in similar fashion. However, this requires further investigation, possibly in simulations involving two languages that are typologically more distant.

4.2 Priming effects in L2

Structural priming effects, when speakers tend to recreate a recently encountered linguistic structure in further language use, have been demonstrated both in first (e.g., Bock, Dell, Chang, & Onishi, 2007; Potter & Lombardi, 1998, etc.) and in second language (e.g., McDonough, 2006; Gries &

Wulff, 2005) as well as across the two (e.g., Loebell & Bock, 2003; Vasilyeva et al., 2010). Some of these effects are explained in terms of construction grammar—primes can activate the respective constructions (see Goldberg & Bencini, 2005).

To give a specific example, Gries and Wulff (2005) asked L1 German learners of English to complete sentence fragments after being exposed to a prime sentence, which contained either a prepositional dative (*The racing driver showed the torn overall to the team manager.*) or a ditransitive construction (*The racing driver showed the helpful mechanic the damaged tyre*). The sentences produced by the learners demonstrated the constructional priming effect in L2 acquisition, which was also supported by corpus and sorting evidence (see Gries & Wulff, 2005, for details).

Since in our model we explicitly assume the existence of constructions in learner's memory, we should be able to observe constructional priming effects in L2. To investigate this, we partially simulated the experiment of Gries and Wulff (2005) computationally. First the model was presented with 250 L1 verb uses[5], after which, like in the previous experiment, L2 was introduced in parallel with L1 in small steps (25 times 10 frames). After each step, the learner was additionally presented with one of two primes. Priming frames, which we took from the actual dataset, were uses of the verb *show* with variable arguments, and the only difference between the two primes was the syntactic pattern—a prepositional dative or a ditransitive (see Table 2).

Table 2: The two primes used.

Head verb (V.)	*show*
No. of arg.	3
V. sem. prim.	act, cause, perceive
Arg.1 sem. prop.	*vary*
Arg.2 sem. prop.	*vary*
Arg.3 sem. prop.	*vary*
Arg.1 ev. prop.	volitional, sentient, ...
Arg.2 ev. prop.	sentient, animate, ...
Arg.3 ev. prop.	perceivable, ...
Synt. pattern	AG. *show* BENEF. THEME or AG. *show* THEME *to* BENEF.

[5]Since the impact of a single priming frame on the learner could be insignificant, we used a smaller step size in these simulations.

In the experiment by Gries and Wulff (2005) learners, after seeing a prime, were presented with a test fragment consisting of an agent and a verb (*The racing driver showed ...*), and were required to continue the sentence. In terms of our model, the test frame consisted of the head verb (*show*) and its semantic primitives, total number of arguments, the first argument (pronoun *you*) and its semantic and event properties. The other features (i.e., syntactic patterns and all the properties of the other two arguments) were missing, and the learner had to predict the best syntactic pattern for the test frame. After the prediction was made, both prime and test frame were discarded in order not to influence further results, and the learning continued.

Since we investigated priming effects in ditransitive (D) and prepositional dative (P) constructions, in the further analysis we only looked at the two respective syntactic patterns in the learner's production. That is, we calculated how many patterns of each type were produced after each prime (i.e., D-patterns after D-prime, P-patterns after D-prime, P-patterns after P-prime, and D-patterns after P-prime). Additionally, we ran an identical baseline simulation where the learner was not primed, being presented a test frame immediately after each learning step. Figure 4 shows how many P- and D-patterns were produced in each of the three conditions (*P-prime*, *D-prime* and *no prime*; the results are averaged over 100 simulations).

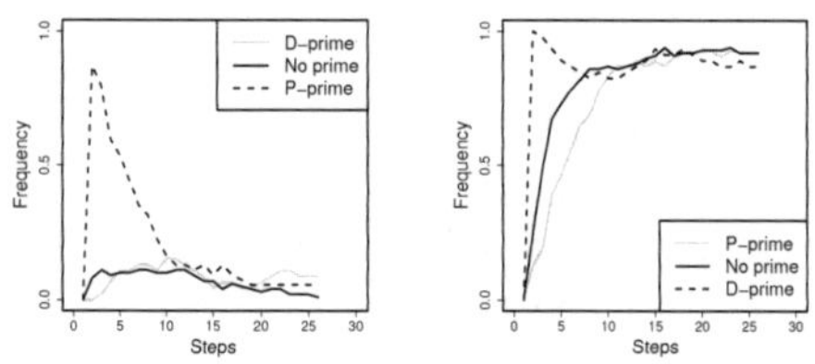

Figure 4: Frequency of prepositional (left) and ditransitive (right) pattern production

As we can see, on the initial 5-10 steps of development both P- and D-patterns were produced substantially more often after the respective matching prime (the jump of the dotted line on each plot) than after the non-matching prime or after no prime. After some time, however, the priming effect was leveled off, presumably because of the exposure to large amounts of training data, and the frequency of production of each of the two patterns aligned with the actual frequency of occurrence of the respective pattern in the training data (31 for D-pattern, 3 for P-pattern).

On the one hand, the presence of the priming effect in our results is in line with the findings of Gries and Wulff (2005). On the other hand, their participants were advanced foreign learners of English who must have achieved rather high proficiency in L2 by the moment of study, but they were still sensitive to the priming effect—a result that we could not replicate computationally.

4.3 Skewed vs. balanced L2 input

There is an ongoing discussion in the literature on the supposed facilitatory effect of skewed input on constructional acquisition, summarized by Boyd and Goldberg (2009). In monolingual contexts, it has been demonstrated that children (Casenhiser & Goldberg, 2005) and adults (Goldberg, Casenhiser, & Sethuraman, 2004) acquire a novel construction with artificial verbs faster if one verb has higher token frequency in the input compared to the other verbs, and slower in case of balanced input, with all the verbs having equal token frequencies.

As for SLA, N. C. Ellis and Ferreira-Junior (2009) showed that the distribution of verbs/constructions in input to L2 learners is Zipfian, and that the most frequent verb in each construction is acquired first. However, they do not provide evidence for a facilitatory effect of skewed distribution on construction learning. At the same time, there is experimental evidence that high type frequency facilitates the acquisition of *wh*-questions in L2 (McDonough & Kim, 2009).

Year and Gordon (2009) experimentally studied the facilitatory effect of skewed verb frequency in the input on L2 constructional learning. In their study, L1 Korean learners of English were presented with 5 English verbs in the ditransitive construction, where either all the verbs appeared equally often (balanced input), or one verb appeared 6 times more often than the other (skewed input). The learners' knowledge of the construction was assessed in the elicited production and acceptability judgement task. The exposure and testing procedures were distributed over 8 weeks, or over 4 weeks, or over 4 days, depending on the group. Surprisingly, in no group they found the evidence for the facilitatory effect of skewed input. These findings contrast with those in the other studies that we mentioned.

In order to address this issue computationally, we ran simulations using our model. Unlike Year and Gordon (2009) who investigated the acquisition of one construction only, we assessed the general L2 knowledge of all constructions that the learner was exposed to, since our model is perfectly suited for this.

The frequency distribution of verbs in our naturalistic L2 input was not uniform (79-81-61-58-48-29), however the most frequent verb appeared approximately 3 times more often than the least frequent, which was not comparable to the ratio of 1:6 in the study by Year and Gordon (2009). Thus, in addition to the natural data we introduced two more conditions. First, we estimated the distribution of verbs over different constructions in our data and concluded that two verbs—*go* and *show*—accounted for most syntactic patterns in the input. Therefore, to prepare truly skewed input data, we set the frequencies for these two verbs to 30 and for the other verbs to 1[6]. Second, we prepared the balanced input data by setting the frequency of each verb to 1.

Using the three types of input, we ran the exact same simulations as for investigating the general developmental pattern, and compared the learner's L2 proficiency over time in the three conditions. The results are shown in Figure 5.

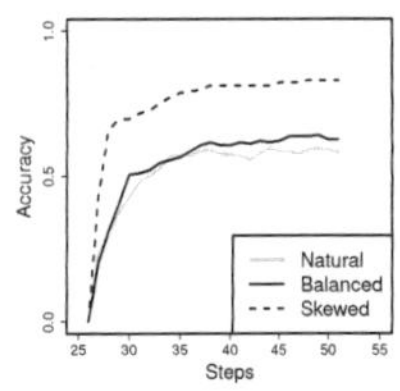

Figure 5: L2 proficiency over time on skewed vs. balanced input

As we can see, the learner's proficiencies with the natural and balanced input data do not differ much. However, the facilitatory effect of the skewed frequencies in the input is very evident. Thus, our findings contrast with the results of Year and Gordon (2009), but are in line with the general trend as summarized by Boyd and

[6]Although the ratio of 30:1 is much higher than that in the experiment being simulated, we had to account for the fact that individual frames within each verb were assigned their own frequencies, so a high-frequency frame of a low-frequency verb could still appear more often in the input than a low-frequency frame of a high-frequency verb. We excluded this possibility by setting the ratio to the high value.

Goldberg (2009). We agree with Year and Gordon's (2009) explanation that the lack of facilitatory effect that they found can be explained by the presentation order of the high-frequency verbs. Goldberg et al. (2007) demonstrated the effect of the presentation order of high- and low-frequency stimuli on the learners' performance. We believe that due to the rather large ratio 30:1 that we set in the skewed data, the two high-frequency verbs prevailed in the L2 input from the very initial stage of L2 learning, therefore our simulations were closer to the "skewed first" condition of Goldberg et al. (2007) than to the "skewed random" condition.

We have to note, however, that the facilitatory effect observed in our experiment could also be due to the fact that the distribution of the verbs in the test frames was also different for each of the three conditions, since the test data were sampled from the same distribution as the training data. We will further investigate this issue in the future.

5 Discussion

Patterns of second language development have been studied for decades, starting from the morpheme learning studies in 1970s (e.g., Wode, 1976). Although some classroom studies allow SLA theorists to make inferences about general L2 developmental patterns (e.g., R. Ellis, 1994; VanPatten & Benati, 2010), scholars agree that a typical pattern of L2 development can hardly exist due to the inherent complexity of the SLA process. The enormous variability of L2 learning conditions makes it difficult to provide general conclusions about SLA development. Partly for this reason, most longitudinal studies have been focusing on the development of specific linguistic features in small number of individuals (see an overview by Ortega & Iberri-Shea, 2005). DeKeyser (2013) emphasizes the methodological difficulties in this domain, especially when it comes to studying age effects in the second language of immigrant population. The inherent problems of documenting the individuals' language experience and sampling those learners who match a number of specific criteria make the research in this field very laborious and time-consuming.

In contrast, a computational framework can be effectively used for studying the complexities of learning a second language, specifically in relation to the characteristics of the first language. We present a computational model of second language acquisition which investigates grammatical L2 development in connection with the existing L1 knowledge, a setup that has not been properly addressed by the existing computational models of SLA (but see Monner et al., 2013).

We evaluate the model's acquired grammatical knowledge (in the form of emergent argument structure constructions) through sentence production. Our simulations replicate the expected patterns of L2 development, such as gradual emergence of constructions and increased proficiency in sentence production. Moreover, we investigate two specific SLA phenomena: construction priming and the facilitative effect of skewed frequencies in the input.

Priming effects have been demonstrated in second language learners (Gries & Wulff, 2005), although sometimes inconsistently (McDonough, 2006). We replicate a priming effect at the early stages of learning in our simulations, but this effect diminishes as the model receives more input. Systematic manipulation of various (potentially relevant) factors via computational simulation will shed more light on the nature of priming in SLA.

The facilitative effect of skewed input on construction learning has been subject of much debate (Boyd & Goldberg, 2009). Our experiments show that skewed frequencies in the input can improve the performance of the model in sentence production, but more careful investigation of this pattern is needed for a clear picture of the interaction between different parameters.

Although some of our results are inconclusive, we believe that our preliminary experiments clearly demonstrate the opportunities of the model for SLA research. In the future we plan investigating the described and other phenomena more thoroughly. Applying additional methods such as analysis of the frame categorization structure under different conditions, or quantitative comparison of the production data obtained in computational simulations and in the natural learner corpora (Gries & Wulff, 2005), could help us to draw specific implications for the SLA theory.

References

Alishahi, A., & Stevenson, S. (2008). A computational model of early argument structure acquisition. *Cognitive Science*, *32*(5), 789–834.

Alishahi, A., & Stevenson, S. (2010). A computational model of learning semantic roles from child-directed language. *Language and Cognitive Processes*, *25*(1), 50–93.

Bannard, C., & Lieven, E. (2012). Formulaic language in L1 acquisition. *Annual Review of Applied Linguistics*, *32*, 3–16.

Behrens, H. (2006). The input-output relationship in first language acquisition. *Language and Cognitive Processes*, *21*(1-3), 2–24.

Benson, C. (2002). Transfer/cross-linguistic influence. *ELT Journal*, *56*(1), 68–70.

Bock, K., Dell, G. S., Chang, F., & Onishi, K. H. (2007). Persistent structural priming from language comprehension to language production. *Cognition*, *104*(3), 437–458.

Boyd, J. K., & Goldberg, A. E. (2009). Input effects within a constructionist framework. *The Modern Language Journal*, *93*(3), 418–429.

Casenhiser, D., & Goldberg, A. E. (2005). Fast mapping between a phrasal form and meaning. *Developmental Science*, *8*(6), 500–508.

Cuppini, C., Magosso, E., & Ursino, M. (2013). Learning the lexical aspects of a second language at different proficiencies: A neural computational study. *Bilingualism: Language and Cognition*, *16*, 266–287.

DeKeyser, R. M. (2013). Age effects in second language learning: Stepping stones toward better understanding. *Language Learning*, *63*, 52–67.

Dewell, R. (2011). *The Meaning of Particle / Prefix Constructions in German*. John Benjamins.

Dittmar, M., Abbot-Smith, K., Lieven, E., & Tomasello, M. (2008). German children's comprehension of word order and case marking in causative sentences. *Child Development*, *79*(4), 1152–1167.

Ellis, N. C., & Ferreira-Junior, F. (2009). Constructions and their acquisition: Islands and the distinctiveness of their occupancy. *Annual Review of Cognitive Linguistics*, *7*(1), 187–220.

Ellis, N. C., & Larsen-Freeman, D. (2009). Constructing a second language: Analyses and computational simulations of the emergence of linguistic constructions from usage. *Language Learning*, *59*, 90–125.

Ellis, R. (1994). *The Study of Second Language Acquisition*. Oxford University Press.

Elman, J. L. (1990). Finding structure in time. *Cognitive Science*, *14*(2), 179–211.

Fazly, A., Alishahi, A., & Stevenson, S. (2010). A probabilistic computational model of cross-situational word learning. *Cognitive Science*, *34*(6), 1017–1063.

Frank, M. C., Goodman, N. D., & Tenenbaum, J. B. (2009). Using speakers referential intentions to model early cross-situational word learning. *Psychological Science*, *20*(5).

Goldberg, A. E., & Bencini, G. M. L. (2005). Support from language processing for a constructional approach to grammar. In A. Tyler (Ed.), *Language in Use: Cognitive and Discourse Perspectives on Language and Language Learning*. Georgetown University Press.

Goldberg, A. E., Casenhiser, D., & White, T. (2007). Constructions as categories of language. *New Ideas in Psychology*, *25*(2), 70–86.

Goldberg, A. E., Casenhiser, D. M., & Sethuraman, N. (2004). Learning argument structure generalizations. *Cognitive Linguistics*, *15*(3), 289–316.

Gries, S. T., & Wulff, S. (2005). Do foreign language learners also have constructions? *Annual Review of Cognitive Linguistics*, *3*(1), 182–200.

Hasko, V. (2013). Capturing the dynamics of second language development via learner corpus research: A very long engagement. *The Modern Language Journal*, *97*(S1), 1–10.

Jäkel, O. (2010). Working with authentic ELT discourse data: The Flensburg English Classroom Corpus. In R. Vogel & S. Sahel (Eds.), *NLK Proceedings 2010* (pp. 65–76). Universität Bielefeld.

Kennison, S. M. (2002). Comprehending noun phrase arguments and adjuncts. *Journal of Psycholinguistic Research*, *31*(1), 65–81.

Li, P. (2009). Lexical organization and competition in first and second languages: computational and neural mechanisms. *Cognitive Science*, *33*(4), 629–664.

Li, P. (2013). Computational modeling of bilingualism: How can models tell us more about the bilingual mind? *Bilingualism: Language and Cognition*, *16*, 241–245.

Li, P., & Farkas, I. (2002). A self-organizing connectionist model of bilingual processing. In R. R. Heredia & J. Altarriba (Eds.), *Bilingual Sentence Processing* (Vol. 134, pp. 59–85). Elsevier Science.

Loebell, H., & Bock, K. (2003). Structural priming across languages. *Linguistics*, *41*, 791–824.

MacWhinney, B. (2000). *The CHILDES project: Tools for analyzing talk* (3rd ed.). Lawrence Erlbaum Associates.

MacWhinney, B. (2013). The logic of the unified model. In S. Gass & A. Mackey (Eds.), *The Routledge Handbook of Second Language Acquisition* (pp. 211–227). Taylor & Francis Group.

McDonough, K. (2006). Interaction and syntactic priming: English L2 speakers' production of dative constructions. *Studies in Second Language Acquisition*, *28*(2), 179–207.

McDonough, K., & Kim, Y. (2009). Syntactic priming, type frequency, and EFL learners' production of wh-questions. *The Modern Language Journal*, *93*(3), 386–398.

Miller, G. A. (1995). WordNet: A lexical database for English. *Communications of the ACM*, *38*(11), 39–41.

Miller, M. (1979). *The Logic of Language Development in Early Childhood*. Springer-Verlag.

Monner, D., Vatz, K., Morini, G., Hwang, S.-O., & DeKeyser, R. M. (2013). A neural network model of the effects of entrenchment and memory development on grammatical gender learning. *Bilingualism: Language and Cognition*, *16*, 246–265.

Mykhaylyk, R., & Ko, H. (2011). Optional scrambling is not random: Evidence from English-Ukrainian acquisition. In M. Anderssen, K. Bentzen, & M. Westergaard (Eds.), *Variation in the Input* (Vol. 39, pp. 207–240). Springer.

Ortega, L., & Iberri-Shea, G. (2005). Longitudinal research in second language acquisition: Recent trends and future directions. *Annual Review of Applied Linguistics*, *25*, 26–45.

Potter, M. C., & Lombardi, L. (1998). Syntactic priming in immediate recall of sentences. *Journal of Memory and Language*, *38*(3), 265–282.

Rappoport, A., & Sheinman, V. (2005). A second language acquisition model using example generalization and concept categories. In *Proceedings of the Second Workshop on Psychocomputational Models of Human Language Acquisition* (pp. 45–52). Omnipress Inc.

Roelofs, A., Dijkstra, T., & Gerakaki, S. (2013). Modeling of word translation: Activation flow from concepts to lexical items. *Bilingualism: Language and Cognition*, *16*, 343–353.

Shook, A., & Marian, V. (2013). The bilingual language interaction network for comprehension of speech. *Bilingualism: Language and Cognition*, *16*, 304–324.

ten Bosch, L., Hamme, H. V., & Boves, L. (2008). A computational model of language acquisition: Focus on word discovery. In *Proceedings of Interspeech 2008* (pp. 2570–2573). ISCA.

VanPatten, B., & Benati, A. (2010). *Key Terms in Second Language Acquisition*. Bloomsbury.

Vasilyeva, M., Waterfall, H., Gámez, P. B., Gómez, L. E., Bowers, E., & Shimpi, P. (2010). Cross-linguistic syntactic priming in bilingual children. *Journal of Child Language*, *37*(5), 1047–1064.

von Stutterheim, C. (2004). *German Caroline Corpus [Electronic database]*. Retrieved from http://childes.psy.cmu.edu/data-xml/Germanic/German/Caroline.zip.

Wode, H. (1976). Developmental sequences in naturalistic L2 acquisition. *Working Papers on Bilingualism*, *11*, 1–31.

Wray, A. (2005). *Formulaic Language and the Lexicon*. Cambridge University Press.

Yang, J., Shu, H., McCandliss, B. D., & Zevin, J. D. (2013). Orthographic influences on division of labor in learning to read Chinese and English: Insights from computational modeling. *Bilingualism: Language and Cognition*, *16*, 354–366.

Year, J., & Gordon, P. (2009). Korean speakers' acquisition of the English ditransitive construction: The role of verb prototype, input distribution, and frequency. *The Modern Language Journal*, *93*(3), 399–417.

The semantic augmentation of a psycholinguistically-motivated syntactic formalism

Asad Sayeed and Vera Demberg
Computational Linguistics and Phonetics / M[2]CI Cluster of Excellence
Saarland University
66123 Saarbrücken, Germany
{asayeed,vera}@coli.uni-saarland.de

Abstract

We augment an existing TAG-based incremental syntactic formalism, PLTAG, with a semantic component designed to support the simultaneous modeling effects of thematic fit as well as syntactic and semantic predictions. PLTAG is a psycholinguistically-motivated formalism which extends the standard TAG operations with a prediction and verification mechanism and has experimental support as a model of syntactic processing difficulty. We focus on the problem of formally modelling semantic role prediction in the context of an incremental parse and describe a flexible neo-Davidsonian formalism and composition procedure to accompany a PLTAG parse. To this end, we also provide a means of augmenting the PLTAG lexicon with semantic annotation. To illustrate this, we run through an experimentally-relevant model case, wherein the resolution of semantic role ambiguities influences the resolution of syntactic ambiguities and vice versa.

1 Introduction

PLTAG (PsychoLinguistically-motivated TAG, Demberg and Keller, 2008; Demberg et al., 2014) is a variant of Tree-Adjoining Grammar (TAG) which is designed to allow the construction of TAG parsers that enforce strict incrementality and full connectedness through (1) constraints on the order of operations, (2) a new type of unlexicalized tree, so-called prediction trees, and (3) a verification mechanism that matches up and extends predicted structures with later evidence. Psycholinguistic evaluation has shown that PLTAG operations can be used to predict data from eye-tracking experiments, lending this syntactic formalism greater psycholinguistic support.

Syntax, however, may not just be the skeleton of a linguistic construction that bears semantic content: there is some evidence that syntactic structure and semantic plausibility interact with each other. In a strongly interactive view, we would expect that semantic plausibility could directly affect the syntactic expectations. Consider the sentences:

(1) a. The woman slid the butter to the man.
b. The woman slid the man the butter.

The ditransitive verb "to slide" provides three roles for participants in the predicate: agent, patient, and recipient. In both cases, "the woman" fills the agent role, "the butter" the patient, and "the man" the recipient. However, they do not generally fill all roles equally well. English-speakers have the intuition that "the butter" should neither be an agent nor a recipient under normal circumstances. Likewise, "the man" is not a typical patient in this situation. If there is a psycholinguistic effect of semantic plausibility, we would expect that an incomplete sentence like "The woman slid the butter" would generate an expectation in the listener of a PO construction (rather than DO) with preposition "to", as well as an expectation of a noun phrase and an expectation that that noun phrase would belong to the class of entities that are plausible recipients for entities that are slid.

If this is the case, then there is not only a syntactic expectation at this point but a semantic expectation that is in turn informed by the syntactic structure and semantic content up to that point. Constructing a model that is formally rich, psycholinguistically plausible, and empirically robust requires making design decisions about the specific relationship between syntax and semantics and the overall level of formal articulation on which the statistical model rests. For PLTAG, we are interested in preserving as many of its syntactic characteristics as are necessary to model the phenomena that it already does (Demberg and Keller, 2009).

In the rest of this paper, we therefore present a semantic augmentation of PLTAG that is based on neo-Davidsonian event semantics and is capable of supporting incrementality and prediction.

2 Psycholinguistic background

Does thematic fit dynamically influence the choice of preferred syntactic structures, does it shape predictions of upcoming semantic sorts, and can we measure this experimentally?

A classic study (Altmann and Kamide, 1999) about the influence of thematic fit on predictions showed that listeners can predict the complement of a verb based on its selectional restrictions. Participants heard sentences such as:

(2) a. The boy will *eat* the cake.
b. The boy will *move* the cake.

while viewing images that depicted sets of relevant objects, in this example, a cake, a train set, a ball, and a model car. Altmann and Kamide (1999) monitored participants' eye-movements while they heard the sentences and found an increased number of looks to the cake during the word *eat* compared the control condition, i.e., during the word *move* (only the cake is edible, but all depicted objects are movable). This indicates that selectional preference information provided by the verb is not only used as soon as it is available (i.e., incremental processing takes place), but this information also triggers the prediction of upcoming arguments of the verb. Subsequent work has demonstrated that this is not a simple association effect of *eat* and the edible item *cake*, but that people assign syntactic roles rapidly based on case marking and that missing obligatory thematic role fillers are predicted; in a German visual world study, Kamide et al. (2003a) presented participants with a scene containing a cabbage, a hare, a fox and a distractor object while they heard sentences like

(3) a. Der Hase frisst gleich den Kohl.
(*The hare*$_{nom}$ *will eat soon the cabbage*$_{acc}$.)
b. Den Hasen frisst gleich der Fuchs."
(*The hare*$_{acc}$ *will eat soon the fox*$_{nom}$.)

They found that, during the verb-adverb region, people looked more to the cabbage in the first condition and correctly anticipated the fox in the second condition. This means that they were able to correctly anticipate the filler of the missing thematic role. Kamide et al. (2003b) furthermore showed that role prediction is not only restricted to the immediately-following grammatical object, but that goals as in *The woman slid the butter to the man* are also anticipated.

Thematic fit furthermore seems to interact with syntactic structure. Consider the sentences in (4), which are locally ambiguous with respect to a main clause interpretation or a reduced relative clause.

(4) a. The doctor *sent* for the patient arrived.
b. The flowers *sent* for the patient arrived.

Comprehenders incur decreased processing difficulty in sentences like (4-b) compared to (4-a), due to flowers not being a good thematic fit for the agent role of sending (Steedman, 2000).

Taken together, the experimental evidence suggests that semantic information in the form of thematic fit can influence the syntactic structures maintained by the comprehender and that people do generate anticipations not only based on the syntactic requirements of a sentence, but also in terms of thematic roles. While there is evidence that both syntactic and semantic processing is rapid and incremental, there remain, however, some open questions on how closely syntactic and semantic processing are integrated with each other. The architecture suggested here models the parallel, highly incremental construction of syntactic and semantic structure, but leaves open to exploration the question of how quickly and strongly they interact with each other. Note that with the present architecture, thematic fit would only be calculated for word pairs which stand in a possible syntactic relation. The syntax thus exerts strong constraints on which plausibilities are considered. Our example in section 6.2 illustrates how even a tight form of direct interaction between syntax and semantics can be modelled.

3 Relation to previous work on joint syntactic-semantic models

Previous attempts have been made to combine the likelihood of syntactic structure and semantic plausibility estimates into one model for predicting human processing difficulty (Padó et al., 2009; Jurafsky, 2002). Padó et al. (2009) predict increased difficulty when the preferred syntactic analysis is incompatible with the analysis that would have the best thematic fit. They integrate syntactic and semantic models as a weighted combination of plausibility scores. The syntactic and semantic models are computed to some extent independently of one another, and then the result is adjusted by a set of functions that take into account conflicts between the models. In relation to the approach proposed here, it is also important to note that the semantic components in (Padó et al., 2009; Jurafsky, 2002) are limited to semantic role information, while the architecture proposed in this paper can build complete semantic expressions for a sentence. Furthermore, these models do not model the prediction and verification process (in particular, they do not make any semantic role predictions of upcoming input) which has been observed in human language processing.

Mitchell et al. (2010) propose an integrated measure of syntactic and semantic surprisal as a model of processing difficulty, and show that the semantic component improves modelling results over a syntax-only model. However, the syntactic and semantic surprisal components are only very loosely integrated with one another, as the semantic model is a distributional bag-of-words model which does not take syntax into account.

Finally, the syntactic model underlying (Padó et al., 2009; Mitchell et al., 2010) is an incremental top-down PCFG parser (Roark, 2001), which due to its parsing strategy fails to predict human processing difficulty that arises in certain cases, such as for center embedding (Thompson et al., 1991; Resnik, 1992). Using the PLTAG parsing model is thus more psycholinguistically adequate.

3.1 Towards a broad-coverage integration of syntax and semantics

The current paper does not propose a new model of sentence processing difficulty, but rather explores the formal architecture and mechanism necessary to enable the future implementation of an integrated syntactic-semantic model. A syntax-informed semantic surprisal component implemented using distributional semantics could use the semantic expressions generated during the PLTAG semantics construction to determine what words (in which relationships to the current word) from the previous context to condition on for calculating semantic surprisal.

4 PLTAG syntax

PLTAG uses the standard operations of TAG: substitution and adjunction. The order in which they are applied during a parse is constrained by incrementality. This also implies that, in addition to the standard operations, there are reverse `Up` versions of these operations where the prefix tree is substituted or adjoined into a new elementary tree (see figure 4). In order to achieve strict incrementality and full connectedness at the same time while still using linguistically motivated elementary trees, PLTAG has an additional type of (usually) unlexicalized elementary tree called prediction trees. Each node in a prediction tree is marked with upper and/or lower indices ^k_k to indicate its predictive status. Examples for prediction trees are given at the right hand side of figure 5b. The availability of prediction trees enable a sentence starting with "The thief quickly" to integrate both the NP ("The thief") and the ADVP ("quickly") into the derivation even though neither type of elementary tree can be substituted or adjoined to the other—the system predicts an S tree to which both can be attached, but no specific verb head. Prediction markers can be removed from nodes via the verification operation, which makes sure that predicted structure is matched against actually observed evidence from the input string. For the example above, the verb *ran* in "The thief quickly ran" verifies the predicted verb structure. In figures 5c through 5e, we also provide an example of prediction and verification as part of the demonstration of our semantic framework. Other foundational work on PLTAG (Demberg-Winterfors, 2010) contains more detailed description.

5 Neo-Davidsonian semantics

Davidsonian semantics organizes the representation of predicates around existentially-quantified event variables (e). Sentences are therefore treated as descriptions of these events, leading to a less recursive representation where predicates are not deeply embedded inside one another. Highly recursive representations can be incrementality-unfriendly, potentially requiring complex inference rules to "undo" recursive structures if relevant information arrives later in the sentence.

Neo-Davidsonian semantics (Parsons, 1990; Hunter, 2009) is an extension of Davidsonian semantics wherein the semantic roles are also separated out into their own first-order predicates, rather than being fixed arguments of the main predicate of the verb. This enables a single verb predicate to correspond to multiple possible arrangements of role predicates, also an incrementality-friendly characteristic[1]. The Neo-Davidsonian representation allows us separate the semantic prediction of a role from its syntactic fulfillment, permitting the type of flexible framework we are proposing in this paper.

We adopt a neo-Davidsonian approach to semantics by a formalism that bears similarity to existing frameworks such as (R)MRS (Robust Minimal Recursion Semantics) (Copestake, 2007). However, this paper is intended to explore what architecture is minimally required to augment the PLTAG syntactic framework, so we do not adopt these existing frameworks wholesale. Our examples such as figures 4, 5d, and several others demonstrate how this looks in practice.

6 Semantics for PLTAG

6.1 Semantic augmentation for the lexicon

Constructing the lexicon for a semantically augmented PLTAG uses a process based on the one for "purely syntactic" PLTAG. The PLTAG lexicon is extracted automatically from the PLTAG treebank, which has been derived from the Penn Treebank using heuristics for binarizing flat structures as well as additional noun phrase annotations (Vadas and Curran, 2007), PropBank (Palmer et al., 2003), and a slightly modified version of the head percolation table of Magerman (1994). PLTAG trees in the treebank are annotated with syntactic headedness information as well as information that allows one to distinguish arguments and modifiers.

Given the PLTAG treebank, we extract the canonical lexicon using well-established approaches from the LTAG literature (in particular (Xia et al., 2000): we traverse the converted tree from each leaf up towards the root, as long as the parental node is the head child of its parent. If a subtree is not the head child of its parent, we extract it as an elementary tree and proceed in this way for each word of the converted tree. Given the argument/modifier distinction, we then create substitution nodes in the parent tree for arguments or a root and foot node in the child tree for modifiers. Prediction trees are extracted automatically by calculating the minimal amount of structure needed to connect each word into a structure including all previous words of the sentence[2]. The parts of this minimally-needed connecting syntactic structure which belong to heads to the right of the current word are stored in the lexicon as prediction trees, c.f. right hand side of figure 5b.

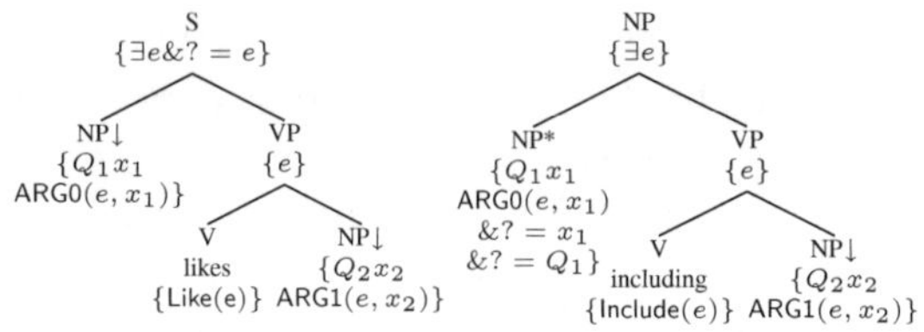

Figure 1: Verbal elementary trees extracted from example sentence *Pete likes sugary drinks including alcoholic ones.*

Since Propbank is used in the construction process of the PLTAG treebank, we can straightforwardly display the semantic role annotation on the tree and the extracted lexicon, with the exception that we display role annotations for PPs on their NP child. For arguments, annotations are retained on the substitution node in the parental tree, while for modifiers, the role annotation is displayed on the foot node of the auxiliary tree, as shown for the verbal trees extracted from the sentence *Pete likes sugary drinks including alcoholic ones* in Figure 1. PropBank assigns two roles to the NP node above *sugary drinks* (it is the ARG1 of *likes* and the ARG0 of *including*), but we can correctly tease apart these annotations in the lexical extraction process using the syntactic annotation and argument/modifier distinction.

Using the same procedure, prediction trees are annotated with semantic roles. It can then happen that one form of a prediction tree is annotated with different syntactic roles, hence introducing some additional ambiguity into the lexicon. For example, the NP substitution node in subject position of the prediction tree rooted in S_k in figure 5b could be an ARG0 for some verbs which can verify this tree and an ARG1 for others.

PLTAG elementary trees can contain one or more lexemes, where the first lexeme is the elementary tree's main anchor, and all further lexemes are predicted. In earlier PLTAG extractions, elementary trees with several lexemes were used for particle verbs like *show up* and some hand-coded constructions in which the first part is predictive of the second part, such as *either ... or* or *both ... and.* Here we extend this set of trees with

[1]Consider the optionality of the agent role in passive sentences, where the "by-phrase" may or may not appear.

[2]The reader is referred to (Demberg-Winterfors, 2010; Demberg et al., 2014) for full details of the PLTAG conversion and syntactic part of the lexicon extraction process.

more than one lexeme to verbs with subcategorized PPs, as shown, for example, in the second lexicon entry of *slid* in figure 5a. Note the difference to the lexicon entry of optional PPs in figure 5b as in *on Sunday*. Furthermore,

- All elementary trees which have a role annotation in PropBank also have a corresponding annotation $\exists e$ on their root node that represents the existentially-quantified neo-Davidsonian event variable for that predicate, see fig. 1.
- The event variables and entity variables on an elementary tree are available for binding on the path from the anchor[3] of the elementary tree to the root node.
- Every role annotation on a node is in the form of a predicate $\mathsf{ARG}n(e, x)$, where e is the event variable, and x is an entity variable to which the role is conferred.
- Every role annotation is prefixed with a variable binding Qx, where Q is a higher-order variable that represents an unknown quantifier. This ensures that all variables are bound if a role appears before its filler.
- Every elementary tree for an open-class word has a head with corresponding predicate. For example, "butter" has a predicate $\mathsf{Butter}(x)$.
- Prediction trees for open lexical classes (such as NPs) have a head with a $\_\_(x)$ predicate.
- Every nominal elementary tree has a Qx at the root node so that the entity variable that is the argument to the predicate on the head is bound. The Qx is on the root node so that our semantic processing procedure for substitutions and adjunctions (described in the next section) can unify the entity variable x with variables on higher trees.

For PPs, we obtain role annotations from PropBank and NomBank. Other closed-class syntactic types such as pronouns have appropriately-selected quantifier constants and predicates (e.g. "someone" would be represented as $\exists x \mathsf{Person}(x) \& ? = \exists \& ? = x$, see next paragraph for the use of question marks). Determiners are merely annotated with a quantifier "constant" symbol and no variables or predicates.

Then we require a type of additional annotation to which we refer as a "variable assignment statement", which we use in our syntactic combination process. These statements are written $? = v$, where v is either a quantifier variable (Q) or constant (e.g. $\exists$) or an entity variable (x). These statements represent the possibility that an incoming tree might have a variable v that could have the same binding as one already in the prefix tree. Variable assignment statements occur on root nodes or foot nodes, except where there is a descendent DT subsitution node, which receives an additional $? = Q$ statement. The type of variable assignment statement (event, entity or quantifier) depends on the root node type (entity type like NP or N vs. event type like S or VP), as shown in figure 1. The next section describes the use of these statements in semantic parsing. Note that variable assignment statements need not be represented explicitly in an implementation, as reassigning variables can be done via references or other data structures. We use them as a representational and illustrative convenience here.

6.2 Semantic parsing procedure

We integrate semantics into the overall process of PLTAG parsing by the rules in figures 2 and 3. In addition, we provide a more procedural description here. At the highest level, a step in an incremental parse follows this pattern:

1. On scanning a new word or doing a prediction step, the PLTAG statistical model selects a tree from the lexicon, an operation (substition, adjunction, verification), and a position in the prefix tree at which to insert the tree (or none, if this is the first word).
2. All the nodes of the incoming tree are visited by the visit operation, and their semantic content is appended as conjuncts to the output semantic expression.
3. The operation of attaching the new tree into the derived tree is performed (pltagOp):
   (a) Variable assignment statements are emitted and appended to the semantic output expression according to the rules in figure 3, as well as to the semantic expression at the syntactic node at which the integration occurs. For verification, the Verify rule has to be applied to all nodes that are verified.
   (b) The syntactic integration of merging the nodes at the substitution or adjunction site is performed. The rules in 3 also make sure that the semantic expressions

[3]Lowest node on the path to where the anchor would be in a prediction tree which does not have a lexical anchor.

$$\frac{D : \{\Psi\} \qquad T}{\text{pltagOp}(D, T) : \{\Psi \& \text{visit}(T)\}}\ \textsf{PltagStep} \qquad\qquad \frac{D : \{\Psi\}}{D : \text{resolveEqns}(\Psi)}\ \textsf{Resolve}$$

Figure 2: Overall rules for trees (T) and derivations (D) and overall semantic expressions (Ψ). PltagStep applies when a new tree is chosen to be integrated with the prefix tree.

$$\frac{N_1 \Downarrow: \{\Sigma_1, Q_1, \Sigma_2\} \qquad N_2 \Uparrow: \{\Sigma_3, ? = Q_2, \Sigma_4\} \qquad D : \{\Psi\}}{D[N_1 \mapsto \text{nodeMerge}(N_1 : \{\Sigma_1, Q_1, \Sigma_2\}, N_2 : \{\Sigma_3, \Sigma_4\})] : \{\Psi \& Q_1 = Q_2\}}\ \textsf{QuantEquate}$$

$$\frac{N_1 \Downarrow: \{\Sigma_1, x_1, \Sigma_2\} \qquad N_2 \Uparrow: \{\Sigma_3, ? = x_2, \Sigma_4\} \qquad D : \{\Psi\}}{D[N_1 \mapsto \text{nodeMerge}(N_1 : \{\Sigma_1, x_1, \Sigma_2\}, N_2 : \{\Sigma_3, \Sigma_4\})] : \{\Psi \& x_1 = x_2\}}\ \textsf{VarEquate}$$

$$\frac{{N_1}_p^p : \{\Sigma_1, \_\_{}_1, \Sigma_2\} \qquad N_2 : \{\Sigma_3\} \qquad \text{anchor}(N_2){:}\{\Sigma_4, Pred(x), \Sigma_5\} \qquad D : \{\Psi\}}{D[N_1 \mapsto \text{nodeMerge}(N_1 : \{\Sigma_1, \_\_{}_1, \Sigma_2\}, N_2 : \{\Sigma_3\})] : \{\Psi \& \_\_{}_1 = \text{Pred}\}}\ \textsf{Verify}$$

Figure 3: Rules for combining nodes. The nodes are attached during the derivation via the nodeMerge operation, with N_1 being the node above ($\Downarrow$), and N_2 being the node below ($\Uparrow$). These hold for substitution and adjunction (for both canonical and prediction trees). The underlying intuition is that the ($\Downarrow$) node will contain the variable equation, and the ($\Uparrow$) node will contain the mention of a variable to be equated. The Verify rule equates the __ variable with the predicate of the verification tree. The equation is appended to the output expression Ψ. Q_2 can also be $\exists$ or another quantifier. VarEquate also applies to event variables. The Σ_n notation represents the prefixes and suffixes of the semantic expressions relative to the mentioned variable or statement. The rules delete the variable assignment statement from the node by concatenating Σ_3 and Σ_4.

from both nodes involved in the integration are included in the semantic expression of the merged node.

4. Optionally, a Resolve step is applied, which eliminates variable assignment statements by replacing variable mentions with their most concrete realization.

Regarding variable assignments at the integration of two trees, the value for quantifier variables can be a constant in the form of a quantifier. Entity variables can be equated with other entity variables, and entity constants (e.g., proper names) are a relatively simple extension to the rules[4]. Verification variables can only be equated with a constant—a predicate name.

We present an example of the processing of a substitution step in figure 4. The S tree for *sleeps* with an open NP substitution node is in the process of having the NP "someone" substituted into it using the substUp operation. So we have already done step 1 of our parsing procedure. Step 2 is visit, such that the semantic expression of the NP is appended to the output expression Ψ. For step 3, the variable assignment statements are then processed by application of QuantEquate and VarEquate. Finally in step 4, the expression is simplified with Resolve.

The Resolve **operation.** From an implementation perspective, resolving variable assignment statements does not really need a separate operation, as references can be maintained such that the assignment is automatically performed without any explicit substitution in the manner of a Prolog inference engine's resolution procedure. The same holds for the variable assignment statements. However, we include explicit mention of this mechanism for ease of expression of the semantic operations as well as to illustrate some degree of convergence with existing formalisms such as (R)MRS, which also has a mechanism to assert relationships between variables *post hoc*.

There is only one condition under which application of Resolve can fail, which is if there is more than one assignment statement connecting the same variable to different constants.

The Resolve rule is defined to be able to apply to the entire output expression. When should it apply? It is defined such that it can be applied at any time; its actual execution will be controlled by the parsing algorithm, e.g., after each parsing operation or at the end of the parse.

There are remaining matters of quantifier scope

[4]A noun phrase like "Peter" will have the associated semantic expression peter&? = peter and will require an additional inference rule to remove the quantifier when it is adjoined or substituted to a node carrying a role. In other words, substituting peter into $Qx\text{ARG1}(e, x)$ should result in ARG1(e, peter). An analogous rule for constant verification that allows $Qx\_\_(x)$ to be verified as peter is also required.

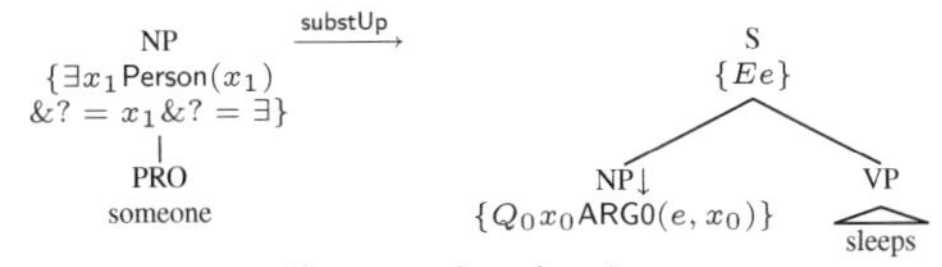

(Syntactic view)

$$\Psi = \exists e Q_0 x_0 \mathsf{ARG0}(e, x_0)$$
(Before substitution starts)

$$\Psi = \exists e Q_0 x_0 \mathsf{ARG0}(e, x_0) \\ \& \exists x_1 \mathsf{Person}(x_1) \&? = x_1 \&? = \exists$$
(Result of visit)

$$\Psi = \exists e Q_0 x_0 \mathsf{ARG0}(e, x_0) \\ \& \exists x_1 \mathsf{Person}(x_1) \&? = x_1 \&? = \exists \\ \& Q_0 = \exists \& x_0 = x_1$$
(Result of QuantEquate and VarEquate)

$$\Psi = \exists e \exists x_0 \mathsf{ARG0}(e, x_0) \& \mathsf{Person}(x_0)$$
(Result of Resolve)

Figure 4: An example incremental step from the semantic perspective.

and semantic well-formedness that must be handled *post hoc* at every step. For example, universal quantifiers require a distinction to be made between the restrictor of the quantified variable and the nuclear scope. It is possible within a neo-Davidsonian representation to perform such representational adjustments easily, as shown by Sayeed and Demberg (2012).

Example Now that we have described the procedure, we provide an example of how this semantic augmentation of PLTAG can represent role labeling and prediction inside the syntactic parsing system. We perform a relevant segment of the parse of example (1-a), "The woman slid the butter to the man." In this sentence, we expect that the parser will already know the expected role of the NP "the man" before it actually receives it. That is, it will know in advance that there is an upcoming NP to be predicted such that it is compatible with a recipient (ARG2) role, and this knowledge will be represented in the incremental output expression.

The minimum lexicon required for our example is contained in figures 5a and 5b. For our illustration, we only include the ditransitive alternation of "slide". Both versions of slide contain all the roles on NP nodes. This parse involves only the prediction of noun phrases, so we only have an NP prediction tree. We presume for the sake of simplicity that the determiner "the" represents the existential quantifier $\exists$.

Our parse begins in figure 5c with "The woman slid", since these are the same in both cases, and it proceeds up to figure 5e with the sentence "The woman slid the butter to the man". We Resolve the assignments at every step for brevity in the examples, and we also apply it to the nodes. By figure 5d, the parser already knows that the ARG2 of "slide" is what is sought. Finally, by figure 5e, the appropriate NP is expected by prediction.

7 Discussion and conclusions

We demonstrated how syntactic prediction and thematic roles can interact in our framework, but we did so with a simple example of prediction: a single noun phrase. Our framework is, however, able to accomodate more complex interactions. In particular, we want to draw attention to an example which can not be modelled by other formalisms which are not fully connected like PLTAG. Consider sentences beginning with "The victim/criminal was violently...". Does the semantic association between "victim" vs. "criminal" and "violently" change the likelihoods of the semantic roles that can be assigned to the subject NP? Does it make an active or a passive voice verb more likely after "violently"? These are the kinds of possible syntactic-semantic interactions for which one will need a flexible but robust formalism such as we have described in this paper: the prediction mechanism allows dependents to jointly affect the expectation of a head even before the head has been encountered. Note that these interactions can also go beyond thematic roles.

In this paper, we have presented a procedure to augment a treebank-extracted PLTAG lexicon with semantic annotations based in a flexible neo-Davidsonian theory of events. Then we have provided the way to combine these representations during incremental parsing in a manner fully synchronized with the existing PLTAG syntactic operations. We demonstrated that we can represent thematic role prediction in a case that is known to be relevant to an on-going stream of psycholinguistic research. Ongoing and future work includes the development of a joint syntactic-semantic statistical model for PLTAG and experimental validation of predictions made by our semantic augmentation. We are also considering higher-order semantic issues such as quantifier scope underspecification in the context of our formalism (Koller et al., 2003).

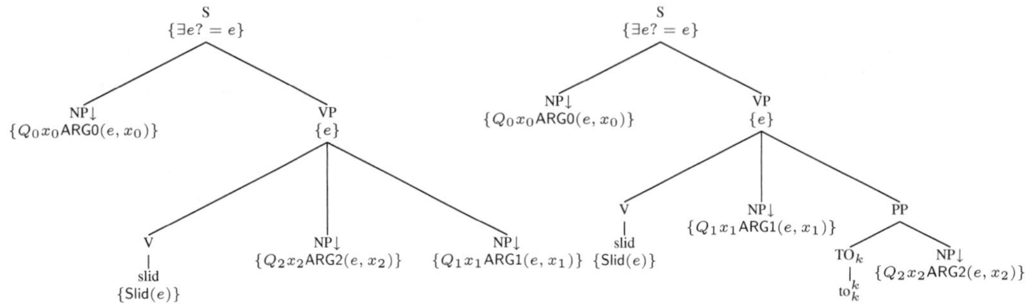

(a) Lexicon: ditransitive alternation of *slid*.

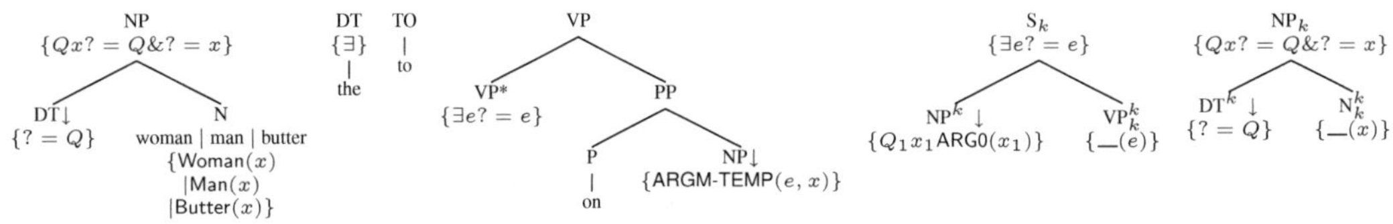

(b) Lexicalized trees and prediction trees.

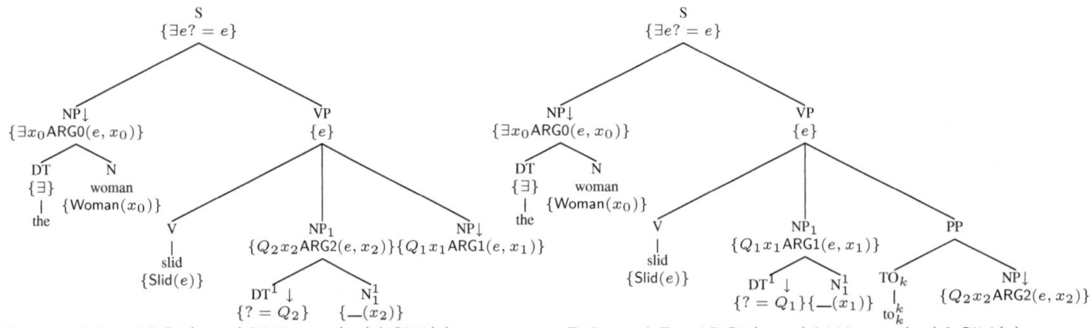

$\exists e? = e \& \exists x_0 \mathsf{ARG0}(e, x_0) \& \mathsf{Woman}(x_0) \& \mathsf{Slid}(e)$
$\& Q_2 x_2 \mathsf{ARG2}(e, x_2) \& ? = Q_2 \& \_\_(x_2) \& Q_1 x_1 \mathsf{ARG1}(e, x_1)$

$\exists e? = e \& \exists x_0 \mathsf{ARG0}(e, x_0) \& \mathsf{Woman}(x_0) \& \mathsf{Slid}(e)$
$\& Q_1 x_1 \mathsf{ARG1}(e, x_1) \& ? = Q_1 \& \_\_(x_1) \& Q_2 x_2 \mathsf{ARG2}(e, x_2)$

(c) Parse of "The woman slid" with respect to the ditransitive alternation, with the syntactic prediction of an NP. Two possibilities still remain. The semantics are identical except for the role of the predicted nominal predicate. The $? = e$ variable assignment statement persists through the derivation, representing the possibility that this sentence is embedded in another.

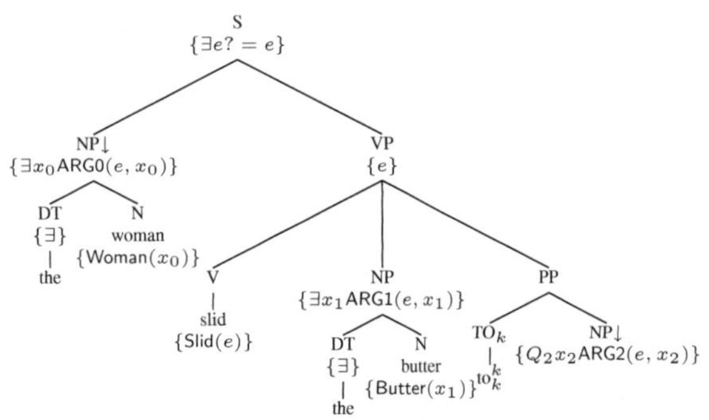

$\exists e? = e \& \exists x_0 \mathsf{ARG0}(e, x_0) \& \mathsf{Woman}(x_0) \& \mathsf{Slid}(e)$
$\& \exists x_1 \mathsf{ARG1}(e, x_1) \& \mathsf{Butter}(x_1) \& Q x_2 \mathsf{ARG2}(e, x_2)$

(d) Parse of "The woman slid the butter…". The arrival of "the butter" greatly reduces the likelihood of the recipient role (ARG2) being the one filled at this point, effectively abolishing the first parse.

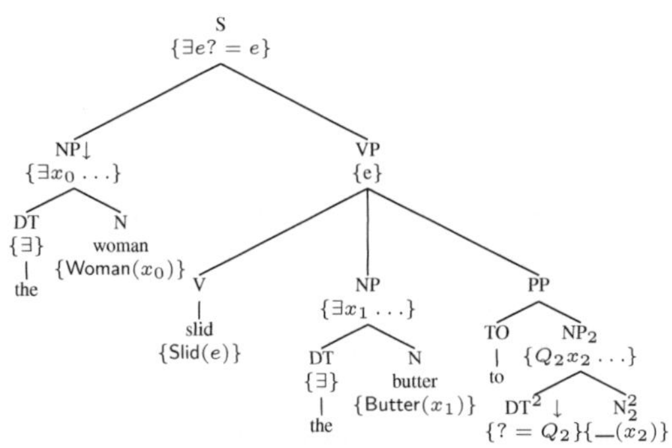

$\exists e? = e \& \exists x_0 \mathsf{ARG0}(e, x_0) \& \mathsf{Woman}(x_0) \& \mathsf{Slid}(e)$
$\& \exists x_1 \mathsf{ARG1}(e, x_1) \& \mathsf{Butter}(x_1) \& Q x_2 \mathsf{ARG2}(e, x_2)$
$\& ? = Q_2 \& \_\_(x_2)$

(e) Parse of "The woman slid the butter to…". *to* is verified and the last NP is expanded via prediction. This gives us the last predicted predicate in the semantic expression. It shares its variable with the ARG2 role, thus thematically restricting its possible verifications.

Figure 5: Excerpt of our example parse.

References

Gerry Altmann and Yuki Kamide. 1999. Incremental interpretation at verbs: Restricting the domain of subsequent reference. *Cognition*, 73(3):247–264.

Ann Copestake. 2007. Semantic composition with (robust) minimal recursion semantics. In *Proc. of the Workshop on Deep Linguistic Processing*.

Vera Demberg and Frank Keller. 2008. A psycholinguistically motivated version of tag. In *Proceedings of the 9th International Workshop on Tree Adjoining Grammars and Related Formalisms. Tübingen*, pages 25–32.

Vera Demberg and Frank Keller. 2009. A computational model of prediction in human parsing: Unifying locality and surprisal effects. In *Proceedings of the 29th meeting of the Cognitive Science Society (CogSci-09)*.

Vera Demberg, Frank Keller, and Alexander Koller. 2014. Parsing with psycholinguistically motivated tree-adjoining grammar. *Computational Linguistics*, 40(1).

Vera Demberg-Winterfors. 2010. *A Broad-Coverage Model of Prediction in Human Sentence Processing*. Ph.D. thesis, University of Edinburgh.

Tim Hunter. 2009. Deriving syntactic properties of arguments and adjuncts from neo-davidsonian semantics. In *Proc. of MOL 2009*, Los Angeles, CA, USA.

Srini Narayanan Daniel Jurafsky. 2002. A bayesian model predicts human parse preference and reading times in sentence processing. In *Advances in Neural Information Processing Systems 14: Proceedings of the 2001 Neural Information Processing Systems (NIPS) Conference*, volume 1, page 59. The MIT Press.

Yuki Kamide, Gerry Altmann, and Sarah L Haywood. 2003a. The time-course of prediction in incremental sentence processing: Evidence from anticipatory eye movements. *Journal of Memory and Language*, 49(1):133–156.

Yuki Kamide, Christoph Scheepers, and Gerry TM Altmann. 2003b. Integration of syntactic and semantic information in predictive processing: Cross-linguistic evidence from german and english. *Journal of Psycholinguistic Research*, 32(1):37–55.

Alexander Koller, Joachim Niehren, and Stefan Thater. 2003. Bridging the gap between underspecification formalisms: Hole semantics as dominance constraints. In *Proc. of EACL 2003*, pages 367–374.

David M Magerman. 1994. *Natural language parsing as statistical pattern recognition*. Ph.D. thesis, Stanford University.

Jeff Mitchell, Mirella Lapata, Vera Demberg, and Frank Keller. 2010. Syntactic and semantic factors in processing difficulty: An integrated measure. In *Proceedings of the 48th Annual Meeting of the Association for Computational Linguistics*, pages 196–206. Association for Computational Linguistics.

Ulrike Padó, Matthew W Crocker, and Frank Keller. 2009. A probabilistic model of semantic plausibility in sentence processing. *Cognitive Science*, 33(5):794–838.

Martha Palmer, Dan Gildea, and Paul Kingsbury. 2003. The proposition bank: An annotated corpus of semantic roles. *Computational Linguistics*, 31(1):71–106.

T. Parsons. 1990. *Events in the semantics of English*. MIT Press, Cambridge, MA, USA.

Philip Resnik. 1992. Left-corner parsing and psychological plausibility. In *In The Proceedings of the fifteenth International Conference on Computational Linguistics, COLING-92*, pages 191–197.

Brian Roark. 2001. Probabilistic top-down parsing and language modeling. *Computational linguistics*, 27(2):249–276.

Asad Sayeed and Vera Demberg. 2012. Incremental neo-davidsonian semantic construction for tag. In *11th Workshop on Tree-Adjoining Grammars and Related Formalisms (TAG+11)*.

Mark Steedman. 2000. *The syntactic process*. MIT Press.

Henry S. Thompson, Mike Dixon, and John Lamping. 1991. Compose-reduce parsing. In *Proceedings of the 29th annual meeting on Association for Computational Linguistics*, pages 87–97, Berkeley, California.

David Vadas and James Curran. 2007. Adding noun phrase structure to the Penn Treebank. In *Proceedings of the 45th Annual Meeting of the Association of Computational Linguistics*, pages 240–247, Prague, Czech Republic, June. Association for Computational Linguistics.

Fei Xia, Martha Palmer, and Aravind Joshi. 2000. A uniform method of grammar extraction and its applications. In *Proceedings of the Joint SIGDAT Conference on Empirical Methods in Natural Language Processing and Very Large Corpora*, pages 53–62.

Evaluating Neighbor Rank and Distance Measures as Predictors of Semantic Priming

Gabriella Lapesa
Universität Osnabrück
Institut für Kognitionswissenschaft
Albrechtstr. 28, 49069 Osnabrück
glapesa@uos.de

Stefan Evert
FAU Erlangen-Nürnberg
Professur für Korpuslinguistik
Bismarckstr. 6, 91054 Erlangen
severt@fau.de

Abstract

This paper summarizes the results of a large-scale evaluation study of bag-of-words distributional models on behavioral data from three semantic priming experiments. The tasks at issue are (i) identification of consistent primes based on their semantic relatedness to the target and (ii) correlation of semantic relatedness with latency times. We also provide an evaluation of the impact of specific model parameters on the prediction of priming. To the best of our knowledge, this is the first systematic evaluation of a wide range of DSM parameters in all possible combinations. An important result of the study is that neighbor rank performs better than distance measures in predicting semantic priming.

1 Introduction

Language production and understanding make extensive and immediate use of world knowledge information that concerns prototypical events. Plenty of experimental evidence has been gathered to support this claim (see McRae and Matzuki, 2009, for an overview). Specifically, a number of priming studies have been conducted to demonstrate that event knowledge is responsible for facilitation of processing of words that denote events and their participants (Ferretti et al., 2001; McRae et al., 2005; Hare et al., 2009). The aim of our research is to investigate to which extent such event knowledge surfaces in linguistic distribution and can thus be captured by Distributional Semantic Models (henceforth, DSMs). In particular, we test the capabilities of bag-of-words DSMs in simulating priming data from the three aforementioned studies.

DSMs have already proven successful in simulating priming effects (Padó and Lapata, 2007; Herdağdelen et al., 2009; McDonald and Brew, 2004). Therefore, in this work, we aim at a more specific contribution to the study of distributional modeling of priming: to identify the *indexes of distributional relatedness* that produce the best performance in simulating priming data and to assess the impact of specific model parameters on such performance. In addition to *distance in the semantic space*, traditionally used as an index of distributional relatedness in DSMs, we also introduce *neighbor rank* as a predictor of priming effects. Distance and a number of rank-based measures are compared with respect to their performance in two tasks: the identification of congruent primes on the basis of distributional relatedness to the targets (we measure accuracy in picking up the congruent prime) and the prediction of latency times (we measure correlation between distributional relatedness and reaction times). The results of our experiments show that neighbor rank is a better predictor than distance for priming data.

Our approach to DSM evaluation constitutes a methodological contribution of this study: we use linear models with performance (accuracy or correlation) as a dependent variable and various model parameters as independent variables, instead of looking for optimal parameter combinations. This approach is robust to overfitting and allows to analyze the influence of individual parameters as well as their interactions.

The paper is structured as follows. Section 2 provides an overview of the modeled datasets. Section 3 introduces model parameters and indexes of distributional relatedness evaluated in this paper, describes the experimental tasks and outlines our statistical approach to DSM evaluation. Section 4 presents results for the accuracy and correlation tasks and evaluates the impact of model parameters on performance. We conclude in section 5 by sketching ongoing work and future developments of our research.

Dataset	Relation	N	$Prime_c$	$Prime_i$	Target	Fac
V-N	AGENT	28	Pay	Govern	Customer	27*
	PATIENT	18	Invite	Arrest	Guest	32*
	PATIENT FEATURE	20	Comfort	Hire	Upset	33*
	INSTRUMENT	26	Cut	Dust	Rag	32*
	LOCATION	24	Confess	Dance	Court	- 5
N-V	AGENT	30	Reporter	Carpenter	Interview	18*
	PATIENT	30	Bottle	Ball	Recycle	22*
	INSTRUMENT	32	Chainsaw	Detergent	Cut	16*
	LOCATION	24	Beach	Pub	Tan	18*
N-N	EVENT-PEOPLE	18	Trial	War	Judge	32*
	EVENT-THING	26	War	Gun	Banquet	33*
	LOCATION-LIVING	24	Church	Gym	Athlete	37*
	LOCATION-THING	30	Pool	Garage	Car	29*
	PEOPLE-INSTRUMENT	24	Hiker	Barber	Compass	45*
	INSTRUMENT-PEOPLE	24	Razor	Compass	Barber	-10
	INSTRUMENT-THING	24	Hair	Scissors	Oven	58*

Table 1: Overview of datasets: thematic relations, number of triples, example stimuli, facilitation effects

2 Data

This section introduces the priming datasets which are the object of the present study. All the experiments we aim to model were conducted to provide evidence for the immediate effect of event knowledge in language processing.

The first dataset comes from Ferretti et al. (2001), who found that verbs facilitate the processing of nouns denoting prototypical participants in the depicted event and of adjectives denoting features of prototypical participants. In what follows, the dataset from this study will be referred to as **V-N dataset**.

The second dataset comes from McRae et al. (2005). In this experiment, nouns were found to facilitate the processing of verbs denoting events in which they are prototypical participants. In this paper, this dataset is referred to as **N-V dataset**.

The third dataset comes from Hare et al. (2009), who found a facilitation effect from nouns to nouns denoting events or their participants. We will refer to this dataset as **N-N dataset**.

Experimental items and behavioral data from these three experiments have been pooled together in a global dataset that contains 404 word **triples** (Target, Congruent Prime, Incongruent Prime). For every triple, the dataset contains mean reaction times for the congruent and incongruent conditions, and a label for the thematic relation involved. Table 1 provides a summary of the experimental data. It specifies the number of triples for every relation in the datasets (*N*) and gives an example triple ($Prime_{congruent}$, $Prime_{incongruent}$, *Target*). Facilitation effects and stars marking significance by participants and items reported in the original studies are also specified for every relation (*Fac*). Relations for which the experiments showed no priming effect are highlighted in bold.

3 Method

3.1 Models

Building on the Distributional Hypothesis (Harris, 1954), DSMs are employed to produce semantic representations of words from patterns of co-occurrence in texts or documents (Sahlgren, 2006; Turney and Pantel, 2010). Semantic representations in the form of distributional vectors are compared to quantify the amount of shared contexts as an empirical correlate of semantic similarity. For the purposes of this study, similarity is understood in terms of topical relatedness (words connected to a particular situation) rather than attributional similarity (synonyms and near-synonyms).

DSMs evaluated in this study belong to the class of bag-of-words models: the distributional vector of a target word consists of co-occurrence counts with other words, resulting in a word-word co-occurrence matrix. The models cover a large vocabulary of target words (27668 words in the untagged version; 31713 words in the part-of-speech tagged version). It contains the stimuli from the datasets described in section 2 and further target words from state-of-the-art evaluation studies (Baroni and Lenci, 2010; Baroni and Lenci, 2011; Mitchell and Lapata, 2008). Contexts are filtered by part-of-speech (nouns, verbs, adjectives, and adverbs) and by frequency thresholds. Neither syntax nor word order were taken into account when gathering co-occurrence information. Distributional models were built using the UCS toolkit[1] and the `wordspace` package for R[2]. The evaluated parameters are:

- **Corpus**: British National Corpus[3]; ukWaC[4]; WaCkypedia_EN[5]; WP500[6]; and a concatenation of BNC, ukWaC, and WaCkypedia_EN (called the *joint corpus*);
- **Window size**: 2, 5, or 15 words to the left and to the right of the target;
- **Part of speech**: no part of speech tags; part of speech tags for targets; part of speech tags for targets and contexts;
- **Scoring measure**: frequency; Dice coefficient; simple log-likelihood; Mutual Information; t-score; z-score;[7]
- **Vector transformation**: no transformation; square root, sigmoid or logarithmic transformation;
- **Dimensionality reduction**: no dimensionality reduction; Singular Value Decomposition to 300 dimensions using randomized SVD (Halko et al., 2009); Random Indexing (Sahlgren, 2005) to 1000 dimensions;
- **Distance measure**: cosine, euclidean or manhattan distance.

3.2 Indexes of Distributional Relatedess

3.2.1 Distance and Rank

The indexes of distributional relatedness described in this section represent alternative perspectives on the semantic representation inferred by DSMs from co-occurrence data.

Given a *target*, a *prime*, and a matrix of distances produced by a distributional model, we test the following indexes of relatedness between *target* and *prime*:

- **Distance**: distance between the vectors of *target* and *prime* in the semantic space;
- **Backward association**: rank of *prime* among the neighbors of *target*, as in Hare et al. (2009);[8]
- **Forward association**: rank of *target* in the neighbors of *prime*;
- **Average rank**: average of backward and forward association.

Indexes of distributional relatedness were considered as an additional parameter in the evaluation, labeled **relatedness index** below. Every combination of the parameters described in section 3.1 with each value of the *relatedness index* parameter defines a DSM. The total number of models evaluated in our study amounts to 38880.

3.2.2 Motivation for Rank

This section provides some motivation for the use of neighbor rank as a predictor of priming effects in DSMs, on the basis of general cognitive principles and of previous modeling experiments.

In distributional semantic modeling, similarity between words is calculated according to Euclidean geometry: the more similar two words are, the closer they are in the semantic space. One of the axioms of spatial models is *symmetry* (Tversky, 1977): the distance between point *a* and point *b* is equal to the distance between point *b* and point *a*. Cognitive processes, however, often violate the symmetry axiom. For example, asymmetric associations are often found in word association norms (Griffiths et al., 2007).

Our study also contains a case of asymmetry. In particular, the results from Hare et al. (2009), which constitute our N-N dataset, show priming from PEOPLE to INSTRUMENTS, but not from INSTRUMENTS to PEOPLE. This asymmetry cannot be captured by distance measures for reasons stated above. However, the use of rank-based indexes allows to overcome the limitation of symmetrical distance measures by introducing directionality (in our case, target $\rightarrow$ prime vs. prime $\rightarrow$ target), and this without discarding the established and proven measures.

Rank has already proven successful in modeling priming effects with DSMs. Hare et al. (2009) conducted a simulation on the N-N dataset using LSA (Landauer and Dumais, 1997) and BEAGLE (Jones and Mewhort, 2007) trained on the TASA corpus. Asymmetric priming was correctly predicted by the context-only version of BEAGLE using rank (namely, rank of prime among neighbors of target, cf. backward rank in section 3.2.1).

Our study extends the approach of Hare et al. (2009) in a number of directions. First, we introduce and evaluate several different rank-based measures (section 3.2.1). Second, we evaluate rank in connection with specific parameters and on

[1]http://www.collocations.de/software.html

[2]http://r-forge.r-project.org/projects/wordspace/

[3]http://www.natcorp.ox.ac.uk/

[4]http://wacky.sslmit.unibo.it/doku.php?id=corpora

[5]http://wacky.sslmit.unibo.it/doku.php?id=corpora

[6]A subset of WaCkypedia_EN containing the initial 500 words of each article, which amounts to 230 million tokens.

[7]See Evert (2004) for a description of these measures and details on the calculation of association scores.

[8]This type of association is labeled as "backward" because it goes from targets to primes, while in the experimental setting targets are shown after primes.

larger corpora. Third, we extend the use of rank-based measures to the distributional simulation of two other experiments on event knowledge (Ferretti et al., 2001; McRae et al., 2005). Note that our simulation differs from the one by Hare et al. (2009) with respect to tasks (they test for a significant difference of mean distances between target and related vs. unrelated prime) and the class of DSMs (we use term-term models, rather than LSA; our models are not sensitive to word order, unlike BEAGLE).

3.3 Tasks and Analysis of Results

The aim of this section is to introduce the experimental tasks whose results will be discussed in section 4 and to describe the main features of the analysis we applied to interpret these results.

Two experiments have been carried out:

- A **classification** experiment: given a target and two primes, distributional information is used to identify the congruent prime. Performance in this task is measured by classification accuracy (section 4.1).
- A **prediction** experiment: the information concerning distributional relatedness between targets and congruent primes is tested as a predictor for latency times. Performance in this task is quantified by Pearson correlation (section 4.2).

Concerning the interpretation of the evaluation results, it would hardly be meaningful to look at the best parameter combination or the average across all models. The best model is likely to be overfitted tremendously (after testing 38880 parameter settings over a dataset of 404 data points). Mean performance is largely determined by the proportions of "good" and "bad" parameter settings among the evaluation runs, which include many non-optimal parameter values that were only included for completeness.

Instead, we analyze the influence of individual DSM parameters and their interactions using linear models with performance (accuracy or correlation) as a dependent variable and the various model parameters as independent variables. This approach allows us to identify parameters that have a significant effect on model performance and to test for interactions between the parameters. Based on the partial effects of each parameter (and significant interactions) we can select a best model in a robust way.

This statistical analysis contains some elements of novelty with respect to the state-of-the-art DSM evaluation. Broadly speaking, approaches to DSM evaluation described in the literature fall into two classes. The first one can be labeled as *best model first*, as it implies the identification of the optimal configuration of parameters on an initial task, considered more basic; the best performing model on the general task is therefore evaluated on other tasks of interest. This is the approach adopted, for example, by Padó and Lapata (2007). In the second approach, described in Bullinaria and Levy (2007; 2012), evaluation is conducted via *incremental tuning of parameters*: parameters are evaluated sequentially to identify the best performing value on a number of tasks. Such approaches to DSM evaluation have specific limitations. The former approach does not assess which parameters are crucial in determining model performance, since its goal is the evaluation of performance of the same model on different tasks. The latter approach does not allow for parameter interactions, considering parameters individually. Both limitations are avoided in the analysis used here.

4 Results

4.1 Identification of Congruent Prime

This section presents the results from the first task evaluated in our study. We used the DSMs to identify which of the two primes is the congruent one based on their distributional relatedness to the target. For every triple in the dataset, the different indexes of distributional relatedness (parameter *relatedness index*) were used to compare the association between the target and the congruent prime with the association between the target and the incongruent prime. Accuracy of DSMs in picking up the congruent prime was calculated on the global dataset and separately for each subset.[9]

Figure 1 displays the distribution of the accuracy scores of all tested models in the task, on the global dataset. All accuracy values are specified as percentages. Minimum, maximum, mean and standard deviation of the accuracy values for the global dataset and for the three subsets are displayed in table 2.

The mean performance on N-N is lower than on

[9]The small number of triples for which no prediction could be made because of missing words in the DSMs were considered mistakes. The coverage of the models ranges from 97.8% to 100% of the triples, with a mean of 99%.

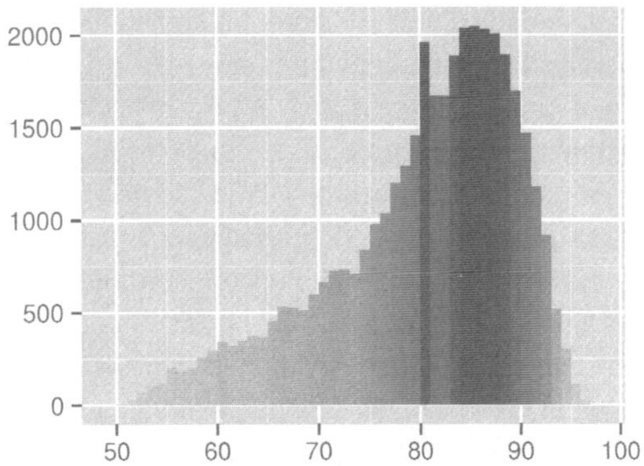

Figure 1: Identification of congruent prime: distribution of accuracy (%) for global dataset

Dataset	Min	Max	Mean	σ
Global	50.2	96.5	80.2	9.2
V-N	45.8	95.8	80.0	8.4
N-V	49.1	99.1	82.7	9.7
N-N	47.6	97.6	78.7	10.0

Table 2: Identification of congruent prime: mean and range for global dataset and subsets

N-V and slightly lower than on V-N. This effect may be interpreted as being due to mediated priming, as no verb is explicitly involved in the N-N relationship. Yet, the relatively high accuracy on N-N and its relatively small difference from N-V and V-N does not speak in favor of a different underlying mechanism responsible for this effect. Indeed, McKoon and Ratcliff (1992) suggested that effects traditionally considered as instances of mediated priming are not due to activation spreading through a mediating node, but result from a direct but weaker relatedness between prime and target words. This hypothesis found computational support in McDonald and Lowe (2000).[10]

4.1.1 Model Parameters and Accuracy

The aim of this section is to assess which parameters have the most significant impact on the performance of DSMs in the task of identification of the congruent prime.

We trained a linear model with the eight DSM parameters as independent variables ($R^2 = 0.70$) and a second model that also includes all two-way interactions ($R^2 = 0.89$). Given the improvement in R^2 as a consequence of the inclusion of two-way interactions in the linear model, we will focus on the results from the model with interactions. Table 3 shows results from the analysis of variance for the model with interactions. For every parameter (and interaction of parameters) we report degrees of freedom (*df*), percentage of explained variance (R^2), and a significance code (*signif*). We only list significant interactions that explain at least 1% of the variance. Even though all parameters and many interactions are highly significant due to the large number of DSMs that were tested, an analysis of their predictive power in terms of explained variance allows us to make distinctions between parameters.

Parameter	df	R^2	signif
corpus	4	7.44	***
window	2	4.39	***
pos	2	0.92	***
score	5	7.39	***
transformation	3	3.79	***
distance	2	22.20	***
dimensionality reduction	2	10.52	***
relatedness index	3	13.67	***
score:transformation	15	4.53	***
distance:relatedness index	12	2.24	***
distance:dim.reduction	4	2.16	***
window:dim.reduction	4	1.73	***

Table 3: Accuracy: Parameters and interactions

Results in table 3 indicate that *distance*, *dimensionality reduction* and *relatedness index* are the parameters with the strongest explanatory power, followed by *corpus* and *score*. *Window* and *transformation* have a weaker explanatory power, while *pos* falls below the 1% threshold. There is a strong interaction between *score* and *transformation*, which has more influence than one of the individual parameters, namely *transformation*.

Figures 2 to 7 display the partial effects of different model parameters (*pos* was excluded because of its low explanatory power). One of the main research questions behind this work was whether neighbor rank performs better than distance in predicting priming data. The partial effect of *relatedness index* in Figure 6 confirms our hypothesis: forward rank achieves the best performance, distance the worst.[11]

Accuracy improves for models trained on bigger corpora (parameter *corpus*, figure 2; corpora are ordered by size) and larger context windows (parameter *window*, figure 3). Cosine is the best performing *distance measure* (figure 4). Interestingly, dimensionality reduction is found to negatively affect model performance: as shown in figure 7, both random indexing (ri) and singular

[10]The interpretation of the N-N results in terms of spreading activation is also rejected by Hare et al. (2009, 163).

[11]Backward rank is equivalent to distance in this task.

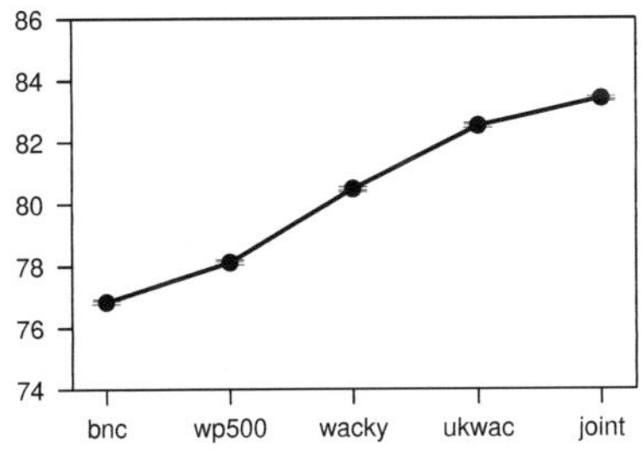

Figure 2: Corpus

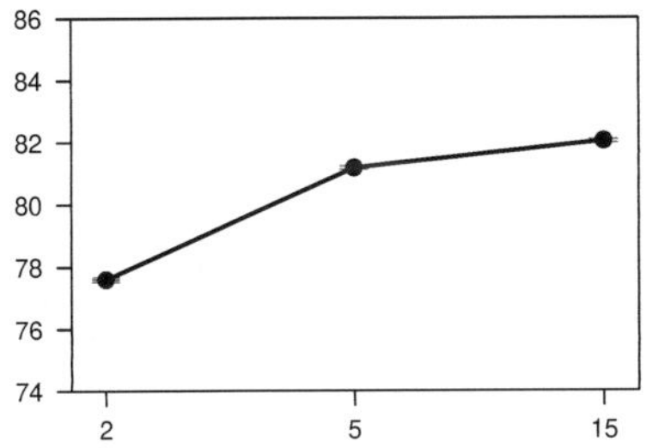

Figure 3: Window

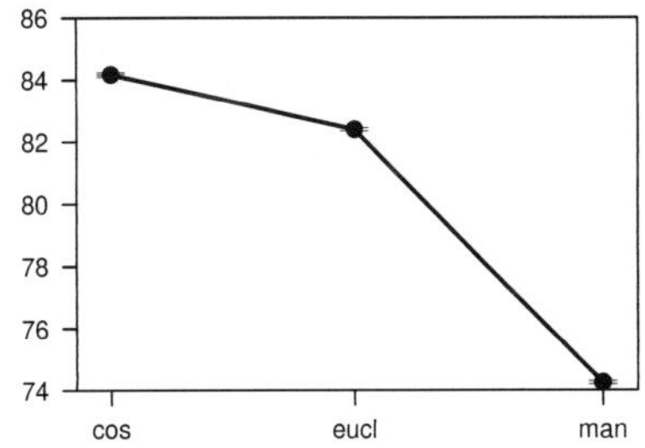

Figure 4: Distance

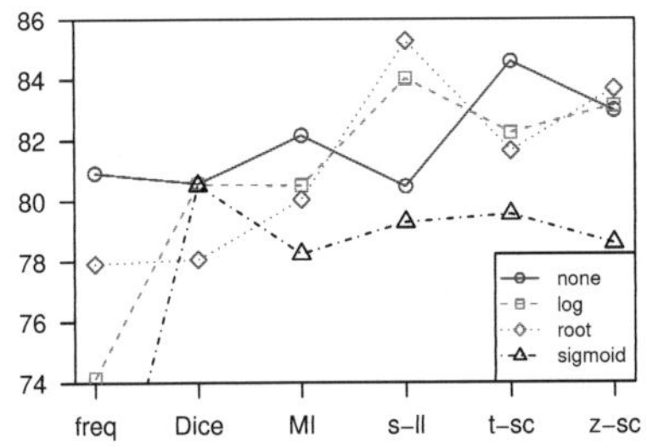

Figure 5: Score + Transformation

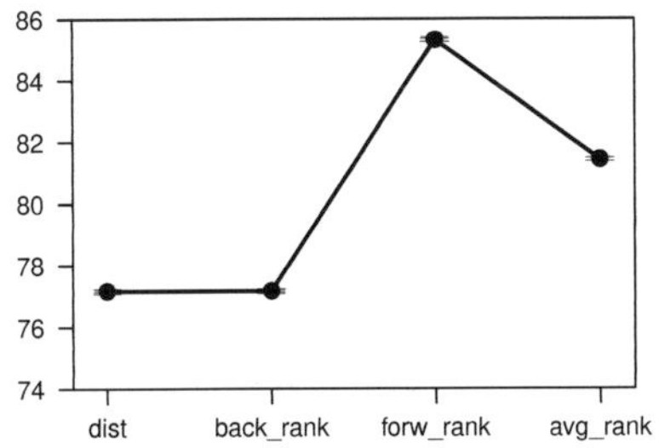

Figure 6: Rel. Index

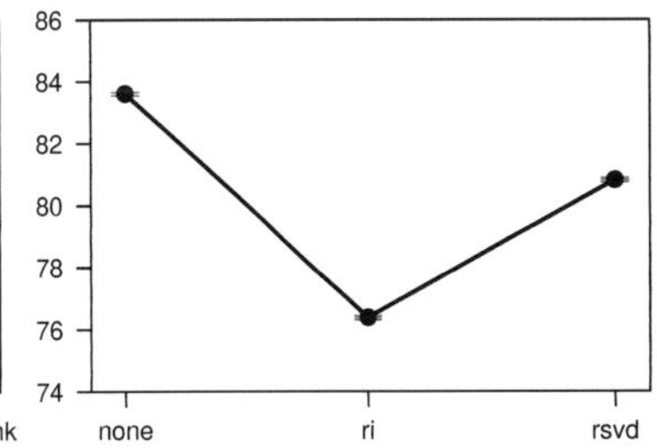

Figure 7: Dim. Reduction

value decomposition (rsvd) cause a decrease in predicted accuracy.

Because of the strong interaction between *score* and *transformation*, only their combined effect is shown (figure 5). Among the scoring measures, stochastic association measures perform better than frequency: in particular log-likelihood (simple-ll), z-score and t-score are the best measures. We can identify a general tendency of *transformation* to lower accuracy. This is true for all scores except log-likelihood: square root and (to a lesser extent) logarithmic transformation result in an improvement for this measure.

Figure 8 displays the interaction between the parameters *distance* and *dimensionality reduction*. Despite a general tendency for *dimensionality reduction* to lower accuracy, we found an interaction between cosine distance and singular value decomposition: in this combination, accuracy remains stable and is even minimally higher compared to no dimensionality reduction.

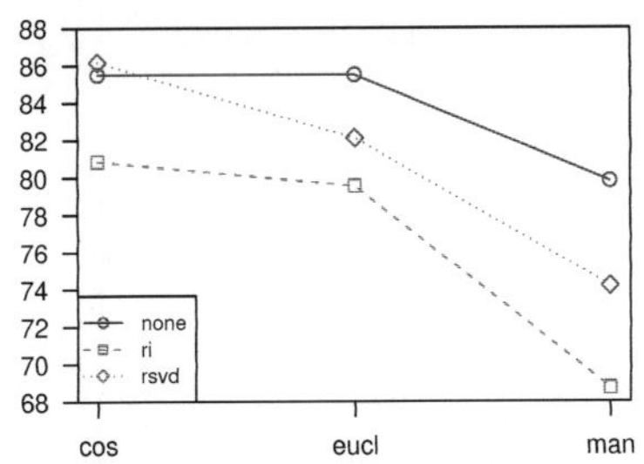

Figure 8: Distance + Dimensionality Reduction

4.2 Correlation to Reaction Times

The results reported in section 4.1 demonstrate that forward rank is the best index for identifying which of the two primes is the congruent one. The aim of this section is to find out whether rank is also a good predictor of latency times. We check correlation between distributional relatedness and reaction times and evaluate the impact of model parameters on this task.

Figure 9 displays the distribution of Pearson correlation coefficient achieved by the different DSMs on the global dataset.

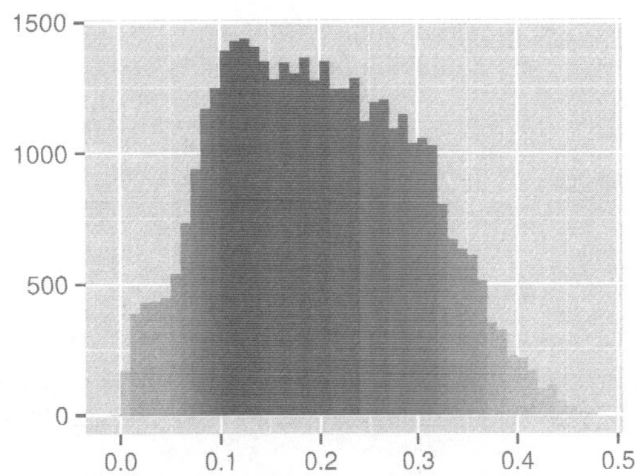

Figure 9: Distribution of Pearson correlation between relatedness and RT in the global dataset

Figure 9 shows that the majority of the models perform rather poorly, and that only few models achieve moderate correlation with RT. DSM performance in the correlation task appears to be less robust to non-optimal parameter settings than in the accuracy task (cf. figure 1).

Minimum, maximum, mean and standard deviation correlation for the global dataset and for the three evaluation subsets are shown in table 4. In all the cases, absolute correlation values are used so as not to distinguish between positive and negative correlation.

Dataset	Min	Max	Mean	σ
Global	-0.26	0.47	0.19	0.10
V-N	-0.34	0.57	0.2	0.12
N-V	-0.35	0.41	0.11	0.06
N-N	-0.29	0.42	0.16	0.09

Table 4: Mean and range of Pearson correlation coefficients on global dataset and subsets

4.2.1 Model Parameters and Correlation

In this section we discuss the impact of different model parameters on correlation with reaction times.

We trained a linear model with absolute Pearson correlation on the global dataset as dependent variable and the eight DSM parameters as independent variables ($R^2 = 0.53$), and a second model that includes two-way interactions ($R^2 = 0.77$). Table 5 is based on the model with interactions; it reports the degrees of freedom (*df*), proportion of explained variance (R^2) and a significance code (*signif*) for every parameter and every interaction of parameters (above 1% of explained variance).

Parameter	df	R^2	signif
corpus	4	7.45	***
window	2	0.47	***
pos	2	0.20	***
score	5	3.03	***
transformation	3	3.52	***
distance	2	4.27	***
dimensionality reduction	2	10.57	***
relatedness index	3	23.40	***
dim.reduction:relatedness index	6	5.21	***
distance:dim.reduction	4	4.11	***
distance:relatedness index	6	3.77	***
score:transformation	15	3.22	***
score:relatedness index	15	1.37	***

Table 5: Correlation: Parameters and interactions

Relatedness index is the most important parameter, followed by *dimensionality reduction* and *corpus*. The explanatory power of the other parameters (*score, transformation, distance*) is lower than for the accuracy task, and two parameters (*window* and *pos*) explain less than 1% of the variance each. By contrast, the explanatory power of interactions is higher in this task. Table 5 shows the five relevant interactions with an overall higher R^2 compared to the accuracy task (cf. table 3).

The partial effect plot for *relatedness index* (figure 14) confirms the findings of the accuracy task: forward rank is the best value for this parameter. The best values for the other parameters, however, show opposite tendencies with respect to the accuracy task. Models trained on smaller corpora (figure 10) perform better than those trained on bigger ones. Cosine is still the best distance measure, but manhattan distance performs equally well in this task (parameter *distance*, figure 12). Singular value decomposition (parameter *dimensionality reduction*, figure 15) weakens the correlation values achieved by the models, but no significant difference is found between random indexing and the unreduced data.

Co-occurrence frequency performs better than statistical association measures and *transformation* improves correlation: figure 13 displays the interaction between these two parameters. *Transformation* has a positive effect for every score, but the optimal transformation differs. Its impact is particularly strong for the Dice coefficient, which reaches the same performance as frequency when combined with a square root transformation.

Let us conclude by discussing the interaction between *distance* and *dimensionality reduction* (figure 16). Based on the partial effects of the individual parameters, any combination of manhattan or cosine distance with random indexing or no dimensionality reduction should be close to optimal. However, the interaction plot reveals that manhattan distance with random indexing is the best combination, outperforming the second best (cosine without dimensionality reduction) by a considerable margin. The positive effect of random indexing is quite surprising and will require further investigation.

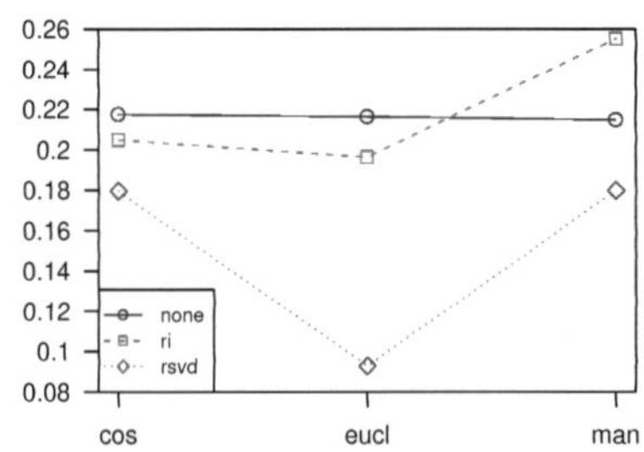

Figure 16: Distance + Dimensionality Reduction

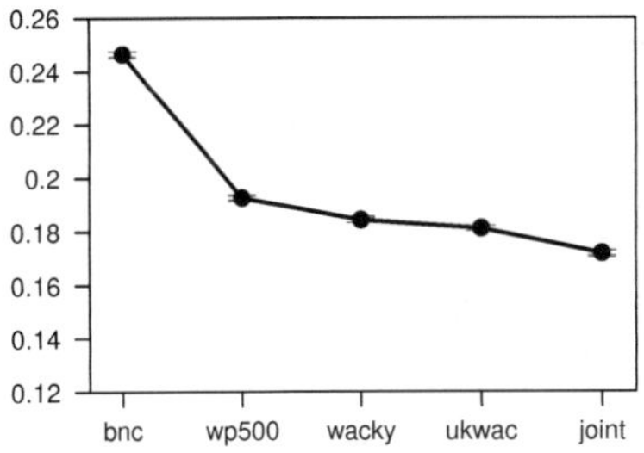

Figure 10: Corpus

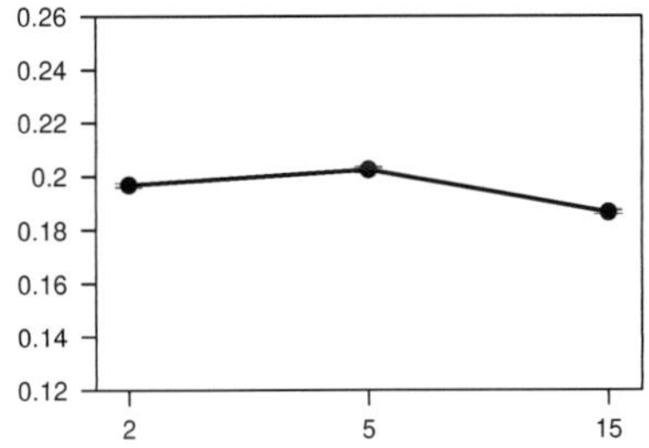

Figure 11: Window

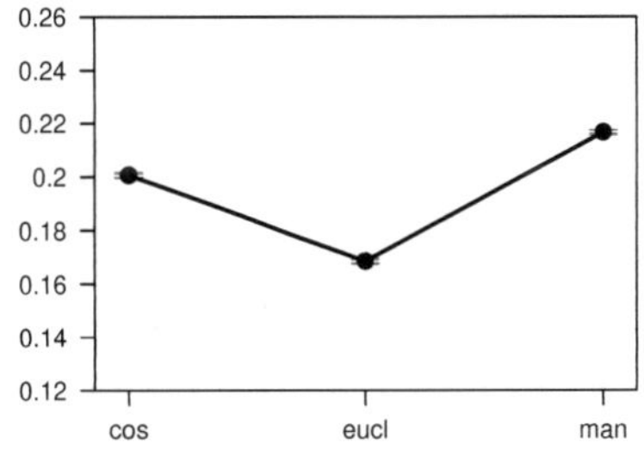

Figure 12: Distance

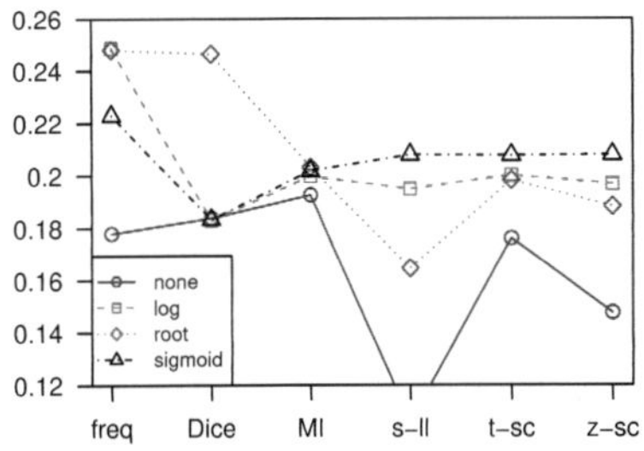

Figure 13: Score + Transformation

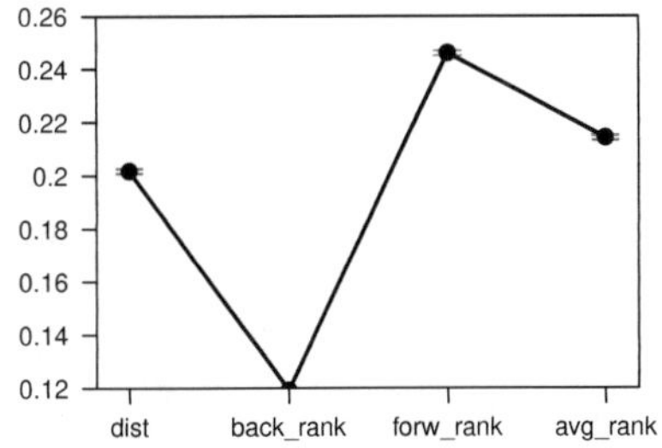

Figure 14: Rel. Index

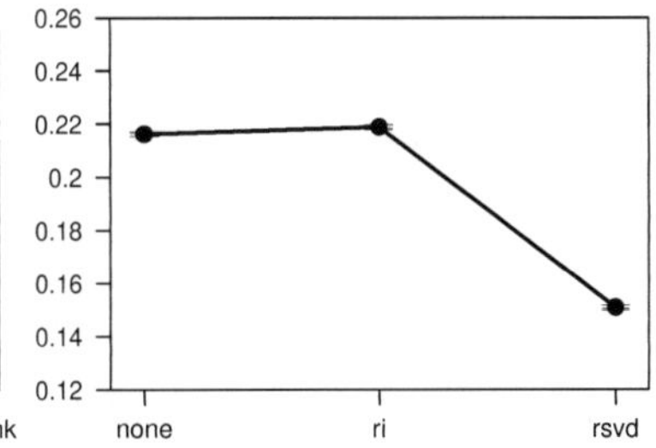

Figure 15: Dim. Reduction

5 Conclusion

In this paper, we presented the results of a large-scale evaluation of distributional models and their parameters on behavioral data from priming experiments. Our study is, to the best of our knowledge, the first systematic evaluation of such a wide range of DSM parameters in all possible combinations. Our study also provides a methodological contribution to the problem of DSM evaluation. We propose to apply linear modeling to determine the impact of different model parameters and their interactions on the performance of the models. We believe that this type of analysis is robust against overfitting. Moreover, effects can be tested for significance and various forms of interactions between model parameters can be captured.

The main findings of our evaluation can be summarized as follows. Forward association (rank of target among the nearest neighbors of the prime) performs better than distance in both tasks at issue: identification of congruent prime and correlation with latency times. This finding confirms and extends the results of previous studies (Hare et al., 2009). The relevance of rank-based measures for cognitive modeling is discussed in section 3.2.2.

Identification of congruent primes on the basis of distributional relatedness between prime and target is improved by employing bigger corpora and by using statistical association measures as scoring functions, while correlation to reaction times is strengthened by smaller corpora and co-occurrence frequency or Dice coefficient. A significant interaction between transformation and scoring function is found in both tasks: considering the interaction between these two parameters turned out to be vital for the identification of optimal parameter values.

Some preliminary analyses of individual thematic relations showed substantial improvements of correlations. Therefore, future work will focus on finer-grained linear models for single relations and on further modeling of reaction times, extending the study by Hutchinson et al. (2008).

Further research steps also include an evaluation of syntax-based models (Baroni and Lenci, 2010; Padó and Lapata, 2007) and term-document models on the tasks tackled in this paper, as well as an evaluation of all models on standard tasks.

Acknowledgments

We are grateful to Ken MacRae for providing us the priming data modeled here and to Alessandro Lenci for his contribution to the development of this study. We would also like to thank the Computational Linguistics group at the University of Osnabrück and the Corpus Linguistics group at the University Erlangen for feedback. Thanks also go to three anonymous reviewers, whose comments helped improve our analysis, and to Sascha Alexeyenko for helpful advice. The first author's PhD project is funded by a Lichtenberg grant from the Ministry of Science and Culture of Lower Saxony.

References

Marco Baroni and Alessandro Lenci. 2010. Distributional memory: A general framework for corpus-based semantics. *Computational Linguistics*, 36(4):1–49.

Marco Baroni and Alessandro Lenci. 2011. How we blessed distributional semantic evaluation. In *Proceedings of the GEMS 2011 Workshop on GEometrical Models of Natural Language Semantics*, GEMS '11, pages 1–10. Association for Computational Linguistics.

John A. Bullinaria and Joseph P. Levy. 2007. Extracting semantic representations from word co-occurrence statistics: A computational study. *Behavior Research Methods*, 39:510–526.

John A. Bullinaria and Joseph P. Levy. 2012. Extracting semantic representations from word co-occurrence statistics: stop-lists, stemming and svd. *Behavior Research Methods*, 44:890–907.

Stefan Evert. 2004. *The Statistics of Word Cooccurrences: Word Pairs and Collocations*. Ph.D. thesis, IMS, University of Stuttgart.

Todd Ferretti, Ken McRae, and Ann Hatherell. 2001. Integrating verbs, situation schemas, and thematic role concepts. *Journal of Memory and Language*, 44(4):516–547.

Thomas L. Griffiths, Mark Steyvers, and Joshua B. Tenenbaum. 2007. Topics in semantic representation. *Psychological Review*, 114:211–244.

Nathan Halko, Per-Gunnar Martinsson, and Joel A. Tropp. 2009. Finding structure with randomness: Stochastic algorithms for constructing approximate matrix decompositions. Technical Report 2009-05, ACM, California Institute of Technology.

Mary Hare, Michael Jones, Caroline Thomson, Sarah Kelly, and Ken McRae. 2009. Activating event knowledge. *Cognition*, 111(2):151–167.

Zelig Harris. 1954. Distributional structure. *Word*, 10(23):146–162.

Amac Herdağdelen, Marco Baroni, and Katrin Erk. 2009. Measuring semantic relatedness with vector space models and random walks. In *Proceedings of the 2009 Workshop on Graph-based Methods for Natural Language Processing*, pages 50–53.

Keith A. Hutchinson, David A. Balota, Michael J. Cortese, and Jason M. Watson. 2008. Predicting semantic priming at the item level. *The Quarterly Journal of Experimental Psychology*, 61(7):1036–1066.

Michael Jones and Douglas Mewhort. 2007. Representing word meaning and order information in a composite holographic lexicon. *Psychological Review*, 114:1–37.

Thomas K. Landauer and Susan T. Dumais. 1997. A solution to Plato's problem: The latent semantic analysis theory of the acquisition, induction, and representation of knowledge. *Psychological Review*, 104:211–240.

Will Lowe and Scott McDonald. 2000. The direct route: mediated priming in semantic space. Technical report, Division of Informatics, University of Edinburgh.

Scott McDonald and Chris Brew. 2004. A distributional model of semantic context effects in lexical processing. In *Proceedings of ACL-04*, pages 17–24.

Gain McKoon and Roger Ratcliff. 1992. Spreading activation versus compound cue accounts of priming: Mediated priming revisited. *Journal of Experimental Psychology: Learning, Memory and Cognition*, 18:1155–1172.

Ken McRae and Kazunaga Matzuki. 2009. People use their knowledge of common events to understand language, and do so as quickly as possible. *Language and Linguistics Compass*, 3(6):1417–1429.

Ken McRae, Mary Hare, Jeffrey L. Elman, and Todd Ferretti. 2005. A basis for generating expectancies for verbs from nouns. *Memory & Cognition*, 33(7):1174–1184.

Jeff Mitchell and Mirella Lapata. 2008. Vector-based models of semantic composition. In *Proceedings of ACL-08: HLT*, pages 236–244, Columbus, Ohio.

Sebastian Padó and Mirella Lapata. 2007. Dependency-based construction of semantic space models. *Computational Linguistics*, 33(2):161–199.

Magnus Sahlgren. 2005. An introduction to random indexing. In *Proceedings of the Methods and Applications of Semantic Indexing Workshop at the 7th International Conference on Terminology and Knowledge Engineering, TKE 2005*.

Magnus Sahlgren. 2006. *The Word-Space Model: Using distributional analysis to represent syntagmatic and paradigmatic relations between words in high-dimensional vector spaces*. Ph.D. thesis, University of Stockolm.

Peter D. Turney and Patrick Pantel. 2010. From frequency to meaning: Vector space models of semantics. *Journal of Artificial Intelligence Research*, 37:141–188.

Amos Tversky. 1977. Features of similarity. *Psychological Review*, 84:327–352.

Concreteness and Corpora: A Theoretical and Practical Analysis

Felix Hill
Computer Laboratory
University of Cambridge
fh295@cam.ac.uk

Douwe Kiela
Computer Laboratory
University of Cambridge
dlk427@cam.ac.uk

Anna Korhonen
Computer Laboratory
University of Cambridge
alk23@cam.ac.uk

Abstract

An increasing body of empirical evidence suggests that *concreteness* is a fundamental dimension of semantic representation. By implementing both a vector space model and a Latent Dirichlet Allocation (LDA) Model, we explore the extent to which concreteness is reflected in the distributional patterns in corpora. In one experiment, we show that that vector space models can be tailored to better model semantic domains of particular degrees of concreteness. In a second experiment, we show that the quality of the representations of abstract words in LDA models can be improved by supplementing the training data with information on the physical properties of concrete concepts. We conclude by discussing the implications for computational systems and also for how concrete and abstract concepts are represented in the mind

1 Introduction

A growing body of theoretical evidence emphasizes the importance of concreteness to semantic representations. This fact has not been widely exploited in NLP systems, despite its clear theoretical relevance to tasks such as word-sense induction and compositionality modeling. In this paper, we take a first step towards integrating concreteness into NLP by testing the extent to which it is reflected by the superficial (distributional) patterns in corpora. The motivation is both theoretical and practical: We consider the implications for the development of computational systems and also for how concrete and abstract concepts are represented in the human mind. Experimenting with two popular methods of extracting lexical representations from text, we show both that these approaches are sensitive to concreteness and that their performance can be improved by adapting their implementation to the concreteness of the domain of application. In addition, our findings offer varying degrees of support to several recent proposals about conceptual representation.

In the following section we review recent theoretical and practical work. In Section 3 we explore the extent to which concreteness is reflected by Vector-Space Models of meaning (VSMs), and in Section 4 we conduct a similar analysis for (Bayesian) Latent Dirichlet Allocation (LDA) models. We conclude, in Section 5, by discussing practical and theoretical implications.

2 Related work

2.1 Concreteness

Empirical evidence indicates important cognitive differences between abstract concepts, such as *guilt* or *obesity,* and concrete concepts, such as *chocolate* or *cheeseburger.* It has been shown that concrete concepts are more easily learned and remembered than abstract concepts, and that language referring to concrete concepts is more easily processed (Schwanenflugel, 1991). There are cases of brain damage in which either abstract or concrete concepts appear to be specifically impaired (Warrington, 1975), and functional magnetic resonance imaging (fMRI) studies implicate overlapping but partly distinct neural systems in the processing of the two concept types (Binder et al., 2005). Further, there is increasing evidence that concrete concepts are represented via intrinsic properties whereas abstract representations encode extrinsic relations to other concepts (Hill et al., in press). However, while these studies together suggest that concreteness is fundamental to human conceptual representation, much remains to be understood about the precise cognitive basis of the abstract/concrete distinction. Indeed, the majority of theoretically motivated studies of conceptual representation focus on concrete domains, and comparatively little has been established empirically about abstract concepts.

Despite this support for the cognitive importance of concreteness, its application to computational semantics has been limited to date. One possible reason for this is the difficulty in measuring lexical concreteness using corpora alone (Kwong, 2008). Turney et al. (2011) overcome this hurdle by applying a semi-supervised method to quantify noun concreteness. Using this data, they show that a disparity in the concreteness between elements of a construction can facilitate metaphor identification. For instance, in the expressions *kill the process* or *black comedy*, a verb or adjective that generally occurs with a concrete argument takes an abstract argument. Turney et al. show that a supervised classifier can exploit this effect to correctly identify 79% of adjective-noun and verb-object constructions as literal or metaphorical. Although these results are clearly promising, to our knowledge Turney et al.'s paper is unique in integrating corpus-based methods and concreteness in NLP systems.

1.2 Association / similarity

A proposed distinction between abstract and concrete concepts that is particularly important for the present work relates to the semantic relations *association* and (*semantic*) *similarity* (see e.g. Crutch et al. 2009; Resnik, 1995). The difference between these relations is exemplified by the concept pairs {*car, petrol*} and {*car, van*}. *Car* is said to be (semantically) similar to *van*, and associated with (but not similar to) *petrol*. Intuitively, the basis for the similarity of *car* and *bike* may be their common physical features (wheels) or the fact that they fall within a clearly definable category (modes of transport). In contrast, the basis for the association between *car* and *petrol* may be that they are often found together or the clear functional relationship between them. The two relations are neither mutually exclusive nor independent; *bike* and *car* are related to some degree by both association and similarity.

Based on fresults of behavioral experiments, Crutch et al. (2009) make the following proposal concerning how association and similarity interact with concreteness:

(C) *The conceptual organization of abstract concepts is governed by association, whereas the organization of concrete concepts is governed by similarity.*

Crutch et al.'s hypothesis derives from experiments in which participants selected the odd-one-out from lists of five words appearing on a screen. The lists comprised either concrete or abstract words (based on ratings of six informants) connected either by similarity (e.g. dog, wolf, fox etc.; theft, robbery, stealing etc.) or association (dog, bone, collar etc.; theft, law, victim etc.), with an unrelated odd-one-out item in each list. Controlling for frequency and position, subjects were both significantly faster and more accurate if the related words were either abstract and associated or concrete and similar. These results support (C) on the basis that decision times are faster when the related items form a more coherent group, rendering the odd-one out more salient. Hill et al. (in press) tested the same hypothesis on a larger scale, analyzing over 18,000 concept pairs scored by human annotators for concreteness as well as the strength of association between them. They found a moderate interaction between concreteness and the correlation between association strength and similarity (as measured using WordNet), but concluded that the strength of the effect was not sufficiently strong to either confirm or refute (C).

Against this backdrop, the present work examines how association, similarity and concreteness are reflected in LDA models and, first, VSMs. In both cases we test Hypothesis (C) and related theoretical proposals, and discuss whether these findings can lead to better performing semantic models.

3 Vector Space Models

Vector space models (VSMs) are perhaps the most common general method of extracting semantic representations from corpora (Sahlgren, 2006; Turney & Pantel, 2010). Words are represented in VSMs as points in a (geometric) vector space. The dimensions of the space correspond to the model features, which in the simplest case are high frequency words from the corpus. In such models, the position of a word representation along a given feature dimension depends on how often that word occurs within a specified proximity to tokens of the feature word in the corpus. The exact proximity required is an important parameter for model implementation, and is referred to as the *context window*. Finally, the degree to which two word representations are related can be calculated as some function of the distance between the corresponding points in the semantic space.

3.1 Motivation

VSMs are well established as a method of quantifying relations between word concepts and have achieved impressive performance in related NLP tasks (Sahlgren, 2006; Turney & Pantel, 2010). In these studies, however, it is not always clear exactly which semantic relation is best reflected by the implemented models. Indeed, research has shown that by changing certain parameter settings in the standard VSM architecture, models can be adapted to better reflect one relation type or another. Specifically, models with smaller context windows are reportedly better at reflecting similarity, whereas models with larger windows better reflect association. (Agirre et al., 2009; Peirsman et al., 2008)

Our experiments in this section aim first to corroborate these findings by testing how models of varying context window sizes perform on empirical data of both association and similarity. We then test if this effect differentially affects performance on concrete and abstract words.

3.2 Method

We employ a conventional VSM design, extracting representations from the (unlemmatised) British National Corpus (Leech et al., 1994) with stopwords removed. In the vector representation of each noun, our dimension features are the 50,000 most frequently occurring (non-stopword) words in the corpus. We experiment with window sizes of three, five and nine (one, two and four words either side of the noun, counting stopwords). Finally, we apply pointwise mutual information (PMI) weighting of our co-occurrence frequencies, and measure similarity between weighted noun vectors by the cosine of the angle between them in the vector space.

To evaluate modeling of association, we use the University of South Florida (USF) Free-association Norms (Nelson & McEvoy, 2012). The USF data consist of over 5,000 words paired with their *free associates*. To elicit free associates, more than 6,000 participants were presented with cue words and asked to "*write the first word that comes to mind that is meaningfully related or strongly associated to the presented word*". For a cue word *c* and an associate *a*, the *forward association strength* (*association*) from *c* to *a* is the proportion of participants who produced *a* when presented with *c*. *association* is thus a measure of the strength of an associate relative to other associates of that cue. The USF data is well suited to our purpose because many cues and associates in the data have a concreteness score, taken from either the norms of Paivio, Yuille and Madigan (1968) or Toglia and Battig (1978). In both cases contributors were asked to rate words based on a scale of 1 (very abstract) to 7 (very concrete).[1] We extracted the all 2,230 nouns from the USF data for which concreteness scores were known, yielding a total of 15,195 noun-noun pairs together with concreteness and *association* values.

Although some empirical word-similarity datasets are publically available, they contain few if any abstract words (Finkelstein et al., 2002; Rubenstein & Goodenough, 1965). Therefore to evaluate similarity modeling, we use Wu-Palmer Similarity (*similarity*) (Wu & Palmer, 1994), a word similarity metric based on the position of the senses of two words in the WordNet taxonomy (Felbaum, 1998). *similarity* can be applied to both abstract and concrete nouns and achieves a high correlation, with human similarity judgments (Wu & Palmer, 1994).[2]

3.3 Results

In line with previous studies, we observed that VSMs with smaller window sizes were better able to predict *similarity*. The model with window size 3 achieves a higher correlation with similarity (Spearman rank r_s = -0.29) than the model with window size 9 (r_s = -0.25). However, the converse effect for association was not observed: Model correlation with *association* was approximately constant over all window sizes. These effects are illustrated in Fig. 1.

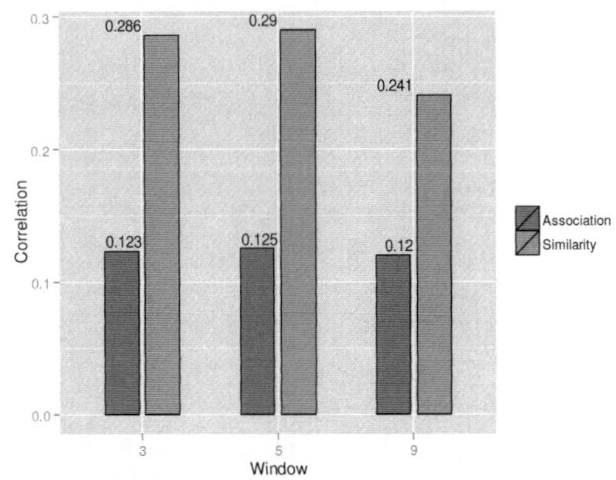

[1]Although concreteness is well understood intuitively, it lacks a universally accepted definition. It is often described in terms of reference to sensory experience (Paivio et al., 1968), but also connected to specificity; *rose* is often considered more concrete than *flora*. The present work does not address this ambiguity.

[2] similarity achieves a Pearson correlation of r = .80 on the 30 concrete word pairs in the Miller & Charles (1991) data.

Figure 1: Spearman correlations between VSM output and *association* and *similarity* for different window sizes.

In addressing the theoretical Hypothesis (C) we focused on the output of our VSM of window size five, although the same trends were observed over all three models. Over all 18,195 noun-noun pairs the correlation between the model output and *association* was significant (r_s = 0.13, $p < 0.001$) but notably lower than the correlation with *similarity* (r_s = -0.29, $p < 0.001$). To investigate the effect of concreteness, we ranked each pair in our sample by the total concreteness of both nouns, and restricted our analysis to the 1000 most concrete and 1000 most abstract pairs. The models captured *association* better over the abstract pairs than concrete concepts, but reflected *similarity* better over the concrete concepts. The strength of this effect is illustrated in Fig. 2.

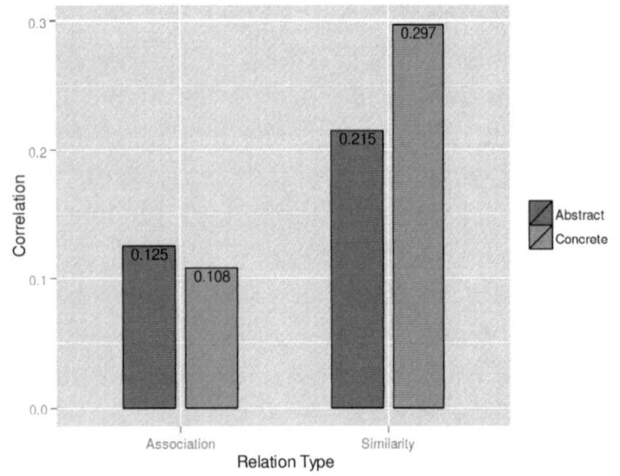

Figure 2: Spearman correlation values between VSM output and *similarity* and *association* over subsets of concrete and abstract pairs.

Given that small window sizes are optimal for modeling similarity, and that WSMs appear to model similarity better over concrete concepts than over abstract concepts, we explored whether different window sizes were optimal for either abstract or concrete word pairs. When comparing the model output to *association*, no interaction between window size and concreteness was observed. However, there was a notable interaction when considering performance in modeling *similarity*. As illustrated in Fig. 3, performance on concrete word pairs is better for smaller window sizes, whereas with abstract word pairs a larger window size is preferable.

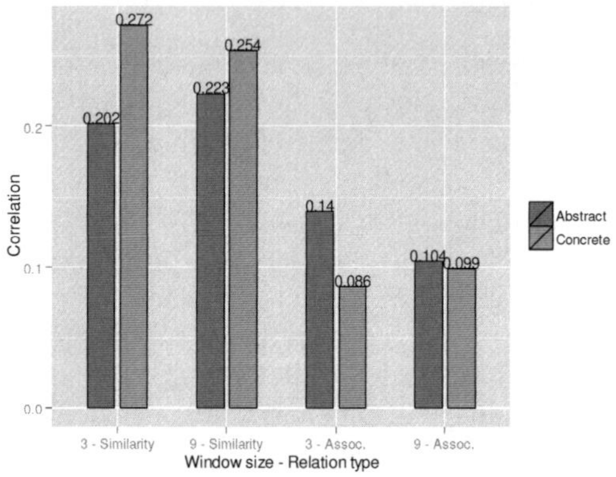

Figure 3: Spearman correlation values between VSM output and similarity and association for different window sizes over abstract and concrete word pair subsets

3.4 Conclusion

Our results corroborate the body of VSM research that reports better performance from small window sizes in modeling similarity. A likely explanation for this finding is that similarity is a paradigmatic relation: Two similar entities can be plausibly exchanged in most linguistic contexts. Small context windows emphasize proximity, which loosely reflects structural relationships such as verb-object, ensuring that paradigmatically related entities score highly. Models with larger context windows cannot discern paradigmatically and syntagmatically related entities in this way. The performance of our models on the association dataset did not support the converse conclusion that larger window sizes perform better. Overall, each of the three models was notably better at capturing similarity than association. This suggests that the core architecture of WSMs is not well suited to modeling association. Indeed, 'first order' models that directly measure word co-occurrences, rather than connecting them via features, seem to perform better at this task (Chaudhari et al., 2011). This fact is consistent with the view that association is a more basic or fundamental semantic relation from which other more structured relations are derived.

The fact that the USF association data reflects the instinctive first response of participants when presented with a cue word is important for interpreting the results with respect to Hypothesis (C). Our findings suggest that VSMs are better able to model this data for abstract word pairs than for concrete word pairs. This is consistent with the idea that language fundamentally determines which abstract concepts come to be associated or connected in the mind. Conversely, the fact that the model reflects associations between concrete words less well suggests that the importance of extra-linguistic information is lower for connecting concrete concepts in this instinctive way. Indeed, it seems plausible that the process by which concrete concepts become associated involves visualization or some other form of perceptual reconstruction. Consistent with Hypothesis (C), this reconstruction, which is not possible for abstract concepts, would naturally reflect *similarity* to a greater extent than linguistic context alone.

Finally, when modeling similarity, the advantage of a small window increases as the words become more concrete. Similarity between concrete concepts is fundamental to cognitive theories involving the well studied notions of prototype and categorization (Rosch, 1975; Rogers & McClelland, 2003). In contrast, the computation of abstract similarity is intuitively a more complex cognitive operation. Although the accurate quantification of abstract similarity may be beyond existing corpus-based methods, our results suggest that a larger context window could in fact be marginally preferable should VSMs be applied to this task.

Overall, our findings show that the design of VSMs can be tailored to reflect particular semantic relations and that this in turn can affect their performance on different semantic domains, particularly with respect to concreteness. In the next section, we investigate whether the same conclusions should apply to a different class of distributional model.

4 Latent Dirichlet Allocation Models

LDA models are trained on corpora that are divided into sections (typically documents), exploiting the principle that words appearing in the same document are likely to have similar meanings. In an LDA model, the sections are viewed as having been generated by random sampling from unknown latent dimensions, which are represented as probability distributions (*Dirichlet* distributions) over words. Each document can then be represented by a probability distribution over these dimensions, and by considering the meaning of the dimensions, the meaning of the document can be effectively characterized. More importantly, because each latent dimension clusters words of a similar meaning, the output of such models can be exploited to provide high quality lexical representations (Griffiths et al., 2007). Such a word representation encodes the extent to which each of the latent dimensions influences the meaning of that word, and takes the form of a probability distribution over these dimensions. The degree to which two words are related can then be approximated by any function that measures the similarity or difference between distributions.

4.1 Motivation

In recent work, Andrews et al. (2009) explore ways in which LSA models can be modified to improve the quality of their lexical representations. They propose that concepts are acquired via two distinct information sources: *experiential data* – the perceptible properties of objects, and *distributional data* – the superficial patterns of language. To test this hypothesis, Andrews et al. construct three different LDA models, one trained on experiential data, one trained in the conventional manner on running text, and one trained on the same text but with the experiential data appended. They evaluate the quality of the lexical representations in the three models by calculating the Kulback-Leibler divergence between the representation distributions to measure how closely related two words are (Kullback & Leibler, 1951). When this data was compared with the USF association data, the combined model performed better than the corpus-based model, which in turn performed better than the features-only model. Andrews et al. concluded that both experiential and distributional data are necessary for the acquisition of good quality lexical representations.

As well as suggesting a way to improve the performance of LDA models on NLP tasks by supplementing the training data, the approach taken by Andrews et al. may be useful for better understanding the nature of the abstract/concrete distinction. In recent work, Hill et al. (in press) present empirical evidence that concrete concepts are represented in terms of intrinsic features or properties whereas abstract concepts are represented in terms of connections to other (concrete and abstract) concepts. For example, the features [legs], [tail], [fur], [barks] are all central aspects of the concrete representation of *dog*, whereas the representation of the abstract concept *love* encodes connections to other concepts such as *heart*, *rose*, *commitment* and *happiness* etc. If a *feature-based* representation is understood to be constructed from physical or perceptible properties (which themselves may be basic or fundamental concrete representations), Hill et al.'s characterization of concreteness can be summarized as follows:

(H) *Concreteness correlates with the degree to which conceptual representations are feature-based*

Because such differences in representation structure would in turn entail differences in the computation of similarity, (H) is closely related to a proposal of Markman and Stilwell (2001; see also Gentner & Markman, 2007):

(M) *Computing similarity among concrete concepts involves a feature-comparison operation, whereas similarity between abstract concepts is a structural, analogy-like, comparison.*

The findings of Andrews et al. do not address (H) or (M) directly, for two reasons. Firstly, they evaluate their model on a set that includes no abstract concepts. Secondly, they compare their model output to association data without testing how well it reflects similarity. In this section we therefore reconstruct the Andrews models and evaluate how well they reflect both association and similarity across a larger set of abstract and concrete concepts.

4.2 Method/materials

We reconstruct two of the three models developed by Andrews et al. (2009), excluding the features-only model because of the present focus on corpus-based approaches. However, while the experiential data applied in the Andrews et al. combined model was that collected by Vigliocco et al. (2004), we use the publicly available McRae feature production norms (McRae et al., 2005). The McRae data consist of 541 concrete noun concepts together with features for each elicited from 725 participants. In the data collection, *feature* was understood in a very loose sense, so that participants were asked to list both physical and functional properties of the nouns in addition to encyclopedic facts. However, for the present work, we filter out those features that were not perceptual properties using McRae et al.'s feature classes, leaving a total of 1,285 feature types, such as [has_claws] and [made_of_brass]. The importance of each feature to the representation of a given concept is reflected by the proportion of participants who named that feature in the elicitation experiment. For each noun concept we therefore extract a corresponding probability distribution over features.

The model design and inference are identical to those applied by Andrews et al. Our distributional model contains 250 latent dimensions and was trained using a Gibbs Sampling algorithm on approximately 7,500 sections of the BNC with stopwords removed.[3] The combined model contains 350 latent dimensions, and was trained on the same BNC data. However, for each instance of one of the 541 McRae concept words, a feature is drawn at random from the probability distribution corresponding to that word and appended to the training data. The latent dimensions in the combined model therefore correspond to probability distributions both over words and over features. This leads to an important difference between how words come to be related in the distributional model and in the combined model. Both models infer connections between words by virtue of their occurrence either in the same document or in pairs of documents for which the same latent dimensions are prominent. In the distributional model, it is the words in a document that determines which latent dimensions are ultimately prominent, whereas the in combined model it is both the words and the features in that document. Therefore, in the combined model, two words can come to be related because they occur not only in documents whose words are related, but also in documents whose features are related. For words in the McRae data, this has the effect of strengthening the relationship between words with common features. More interestingly, because it alters which latent dimensions are most prominent for each document, it should also influence the relationship between words not in the McRae data.

We evaluate the performance of our models in reflecting free association (*association*) and similarity (*similarity*). To obtain test items we rank the 18,195 noun-noun pairs from the USF data by the product of the two (BNC) word frequencies and select the 5,000 highest frequency pairs.

4.3 Results

As expected, the correlation of the combined model output with *association* was greater than the correlation of the distributional model output. Notably, however, as illustrated in Fig. 4, we observed far greater differences between the combined and the distributional models when comparing to *similarity*. Over all noun pairs, the addition of features in the combined model im-

[3] Code for model implementation was taken from Mark Andrews : http://www.mjandrews.net/code/index.html

proved the correlation with *similarity* from Spearman $r_s = 0.09$ to $r_s = 0.15$.

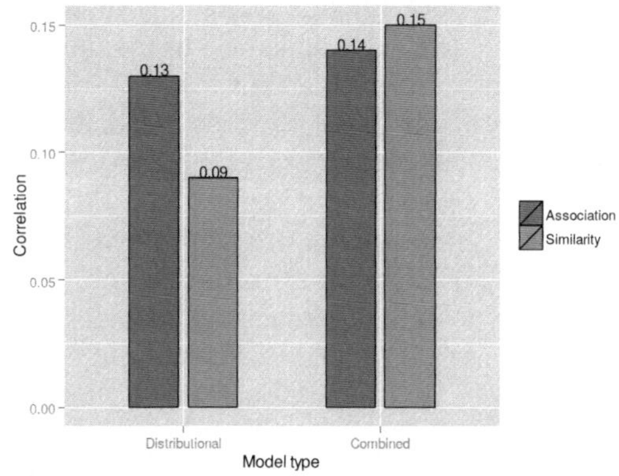

Figure 4: Spearman correlations between distributional and combined model outputs, *similarity* and *association*

In order to address Hypothesis (C) (Section 2.2), we analyzed the output of the combined model on subsets of the 1000 most abstract and concrete word pairs in our data as before. Perhaps surprisingly, as shown in Fig. 5, when comparing with *similarity*, the model performed better over abstract pairs, whereas when comparing with *association* the model performed better over concrete pairs. However, when these concrete pairs were restricted to those for which at least one of the two words was in the McRae data, and hence to which features had been appended in the corpus, the ability of the model to reflect *similarity* increased significantly.

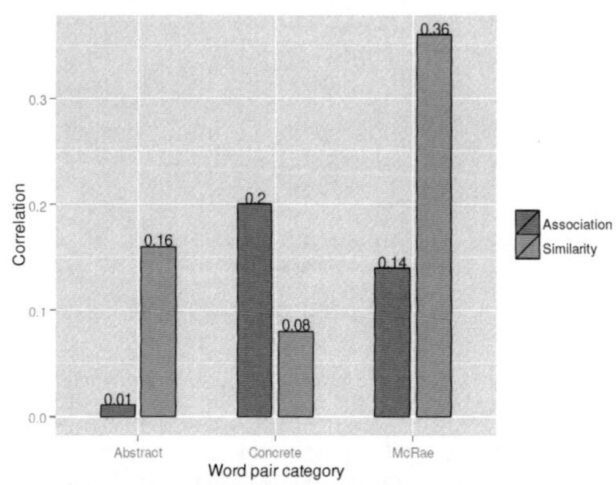

Figure 5: Spearman correlations between combined model output and *similarity* and *association* on different word pair subsets

Finally, to address hypotheses (H) and (M) we compared the previous analysis of the combined model output to the equivalent output from the distributional model. Surprisingly, as shown in Fig. 6, the ability of the model to reflect *association* over abstract pairs seemed to reduce with the addition of features to the training data. Nevertheless, in all other cases the combined model outperformed the distributional model. Interestingly, the combined model advantage when comparing with *similarity* was roughly the same over both abstract and concrete pairs. However, when these pairs contained at least one word from the McRae data, the combined model was indeed significantly better at modeling *similarity*, consistent with Hypotheses (M) and (H).

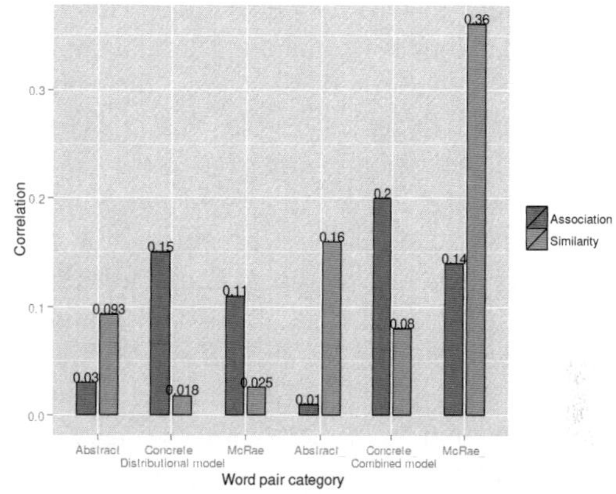

Figure 6: Comparison between distributional model and combined model output correlations with *similarity* and *association* over different word pair subsets

4.4 Conclusion

Our findings corroborate the main conclusion of Andrews et al., that the addition of experiential data improves the performance of the LDA model in reflecting association. However, they also indicate that the advantage of feature-based LDA models is far more significant when the objective is to model similarity.

The findings are also consistent with, if not suggestive of, the theoretical hypotheses (H) and (M). Clearly, the property features in the combined model training data enable it to better model both similarity and association between those concepts to which the features correspond. However, this benefit is greater when modeling similarity than when modeling association. This suggests that the similarity operation is indeed based on features to a greater extent than association. Moreover, this effect is far greater for the concrete words for which the features were added than over the other words pairs we tested. Whilst this is not a sound test of hypothesis (H) (no attempt was made to add 'features' of abstract concepts to the model), it is certainly consistent with the idea that features or properties are a more important aspect of concrete representations than of abstract representations.

Perhaps the most interesting aspect of the combined model is how the addition of feature information in the training data for certain words influences performance on words for which features were not added. In this case, our findings suggest that the benefit when modeling similarity is marginally greater than when modeling association, an observation consistent with Hypothesis (M). A less expected observation is that, between words for which features were not added, the advantage of the combined model over the distributional model in modeling similarity was equal if not greater for abstract than for concrete concepts. We hypothesize that this is because abstract representations naturally inherit any reliance on feature information from the concrete concepts with which they participate. In contrast, highly concrete representations do not encode relations to other concepts and therefore cannot inherit relevant feature information in the same way. Under this interpretation, the concrete information from the McRae words would propagate more naturally to abstract concepts than to other concrete concepts. As a result, the highest quality representations in the combined model would be those of the McRae words, followed by those of the abstract concepts to which they closely relate.

5 Discussion

This study has investigated how concreteness is reflected in the distributional patterns found in running text corpora. Our results add to the body of evidence that abstract and concrete concepts are represented differently in the mind. The fact that VSMs with small windows are particularly adept at modeling relations between concrete concepts supports the view that similarity governs the conceptual organization of concrete concepts to a greater extent than for abstract concepts. Further, the performance of our LSA models on different tasks and across different word pairs is consistent with the idea that concrete representations are built around features, whereas abstract concepts are not.

More practically, we have demonstrated that vector space models can be tailored to reflect either similarity or association by adjusting the size of the context window. This in turn indicates a way in which VSMs might be optimized to either abstract or concrete domains. Our experiments with Latent Dirichlet Allocation corroborate a recent proposal that appending training data with perceptible feature or property information for a subset of concrete nouns can significantly improve the quality of the model's lexical representations. As expected, this effect was particularly salient for representations of words for which features were appended to the training data. However, the results show that this information can propagate to words for which features were not appended, in particular to abstract words.

The fact that certain perceptible aspects of meaning are not exhaustively reflected in linguistic data is a potentially critical obstacle for corpus-based semantic models. Our findings suggest that existing machine learning techniques may be able to overcome this by adding the required information for words that refer to concrete entities and allowing this information to propagate to other elements of language. In future work we aim to investigate specifically whether this hypothesis holds for particular parts of speech. For example, we would hypothesize that verbs inherit a good degree of their meaning from their prototypical nominal arguments.

References

Agirre, E., Alfonseca, E., Hall, K., Kravalova, J. Pasca, K,. & Soroa,A. 2009. A Study on Similarity and Relatedness Using Distributional and WordNet-based Approaches. *In Proceedings of NAACL-HLT 2009.*

Andrews, M., Vigliocco, G. & Vinson, D. 2009. Integrating experiential and distributional data to learn semantic represenations. *Psychological Review,* 116(3), 463-498.

Barsalou, L. 1999. Perceptual symbol systems. *Behavioral and Brain Sciences*, 22, 577-609.

Binder, J., Westbury, C., McKiernan, K., Possing, E., & Medler, D. 2005. Distinct brain systems for processing concrete and abstract concepts. *Journal of Cognitive Neuroscience* 17(6), 905-917.

Chaudhari, D., Damani, O., & Laxman, S. 2011. Lexical Co-occurrence, Statistical Significance, and Word Association. *EMNLP 2011,* 1058-1068.

Crutch, S., Connell, S., & Warrington, E. 2009. The different representational frameworks underpinning abstract and concrete knowledge: evidence from odd-one-out judgments. *Quarterly Journal of Experimental Psychology*, 62(7), 1377-1388.

Felbaum, C. 1998. *WordNet: An Electronic Lexical Database.* Cambridge, MA: MIT Press.

Finkelstein, L., Gabrilovich, Matias, Rivlin, Solan, Wolfman & Ruppin. 2002. Placing Search in Context: The Concept Revisited. *ACM Transactions on Information Systems, 20*(1):116-131.

Gentner, D., & Markman, A. 1997. Structure mapping in analogy and similarity. *American Psychologist*, 52. 45-56.

Griffiths, T., Steyvers, M., & Tenembaum, J. 2007. Topics in semantic representation. *Psychological Review*, 114 (2), 211-244.

Hill, F., Korhonen, A., & Bentz, C. A quantitative empricial analysis of the abstract/concrete distinction. *Cognitive Science*. In press.

Kullback, S., & Leibler, R.A. 1951. On Information and Sufficiency. *Annals of Mathematical Statistics* 22 (1): 79–86.

Kwong, O, Y. 2008. A Preliminary study on inducing lexical concreteness from dictionary definitions. *22nd Pacific Asia Conference on Language, Information and Computation*, 235–244.

Leech, G., Garside, R. & Bryant, R. 1994. Claws4: The tagging of the British National Corpus. *COL-ING 94*, Lancaster: UK.

Markman, A, & Stilwell, C. 2001. Role-governed categories. *Journal of Theoretical and Experimental Artificial Intelligence,* 13, 329-358.

McRae, K., Cree, G. S., Seidenberg, M. S., & McNorgan, C. 2005. Semantic feature production norms for a large set of living and nonliving things. *Behavior Research Methods*, 37, 547-559

Miller, G., & Charles, W. 1991. Contextual correlates of semantic similarity. *Language and Cognitive Processes*, *6*(1).

Nelson, D., & McEvoy, C. 2012. The University of South Florida Word Association, Rhyme and Word Fragment Norms. *Retrieved online from: http://web.usf.edu/FreeAssociation/Intro.html*.

Paivio, A., Yuille, J., & Madigan, S. 1968. Concreteness, imagery, and meaningfulness values for 925 nouns. *Journal of Experimental Psychology Monograph Supplement,* 76(1, Pt. 2).

Peirsman, y., Heylen, K. & Geeraerts, D. 2008. Size Matters. Tight and Loose Context Definitions in English Word Space Models. *In Proceedings of the ESSLLI Workshop on Distributional Lexical Semantics, Hamburg, Germany*

Resnik, P. 1995. Using Information Content to Evaluate Semantic Similarity in a Taxonomy. *Proceedings of IJCAI-95*.

Rogers, T., & McLelland, J. 2003. *Semantic Cognition*. Cambridge, Mass: MIT Press.

Rosch, E. 1975. Cognitive representations of semantic categories. *Journal of Experimental Psychology: General,* 104(3), (September 1975), pp. 192–233.

Rubenstein, H., & Goodenough, J. 1965. Contextual correlates of synonymy. *Communications of the ACM* 8(10), 627-633.

Sahlgren, M. 2006. *The Word-Space Model: Using distributional analysis to represent syntagmatic and paradigmatic relations between words in high-dimensional vector spaces*. Ph.D. dissertation, Department of Linguistics, Stockholm University.

Schwanenflugel, P. 1991. *Why are abstract concepts hard to understand?* In P. Schwanenflugel. The psychology of word meanings (pp. 223-250). Hillsdale, NJ: Erlbaum.

Toglia, M., & Battig, W. 1978. *Handbook of semantic word norms*. Hillsdale, N.J: Erlbaum.

Turney, P, & Pantel, P. 2010. From frequency to meaning: Vector space models of semantics. *Journal of Artificial Intelligence Research (JAIR)*, 37, 141-188.

Turney,P., Neuman, Y., Assaf,.D, Cohen, Y. 2011. Literal and Metaphorical Sense Identification through Concrete and Abstract Context. *EMNLP 2011*: 680-690

Vigliocco, G., Vinson, D. P., Lewis, W., & Garrett, M. F. 2004. Reprssenting the meanings of object and action words: The featural and unitary semantic space hypothesis. *Cognitive Psychology*, 48, 422–488.

Warrington, E. (1975). The selective impairment of semantic memory. *Quarterly Journal of Experimental Psychology* 27(4), 635-657.

Wu, Z., Palmer, M. 1994. Verb semantics and lexical selection. *In: Proceedings of the 32nd Annual Meeting of the Associations for Computational Linguistics. 133–138.*

On the Information Conveyed by Discourse Markers

Fatemeh Torabi Asr
MMCI Cluster of Excellence
Saarland University
Germany
fatemeh@coli.uni-saarland.de

Vera Demberg
MMCI Cluster of Excellence
Saarland University
Germany
vera@coli.uni-saarland.de

Abstract

Discourse connectives play an important role in making a text coherent and helping humans to infer relations between spans of text. Using the Penn Discourse Treebank, we investigate what information relevant to inferring discourse relations is conveyed by discourse connectives, and whether the specificity of discourse relations reflects general cognitive biases for establishing coherence. We also propose an approach to measure the effect of a discourse marker on sense identification according to the different levels of a relation sense hierarchy. This will open a way to the computational modeling of discourse processing.

1 Introduction

A central question in psycholinguistic modeling is the development of models for human sentence processing difficulty. An approach that has received a lot of interest in recent years is the information-theoretic measure of *surprisal* (Hale, 2001). Recent studies have shown that surprisal can successfully account for a range of psycholinguistic effects (Levy, 2008), as well as account for effects in naturalistic broad-coverage texts (Demberg and Keller, 2008; Roark et al., 2009; Frank, 2009; Mitchell et al., 2010). : what work of Roark and Frank you mean here? Under the notion of the Uniform Information Density hypothesis (UID, Levy and Jaeger, 2007; Frank and Jaeger, 2008), surprisal has also been used to explain choices in language production: When their language gives people the option to choose between different linguistic encodings, people tend to choose the encoding that distributes the information more uniformly across the sentence (where the information conveyed by a word is its surprisal).

When using surprisal as a cognitive model of processing difficulty, we hypothesize that the processing difficulty incurred by the human when processing the word is proportional to the update of the interpretation, i.e. the information conveyed by the word (Hale, 2001; Levy, 2008). We can try to estimate particular aspects of the information conveyed by a word, e.g., the information conveyed about the syntactic structure of the sentence, the semantic interpretation, or about discourse relations within the text.

This paper does not go all the way to proposing a model of discourse relation surprisal, but discusses first steps towards a model for the information conveyed by discourse connectors about discourse relations, based on available resources like the Penn Discourse Treebank (Prasad et al., 2008). First, we quantify how unambiguously specific discourse relations are marked by their typical connectors (Section 4.1) and test whether easily inferable relations are on average marked more ambiguously than relations which are less expected according to the default assumption of a reader. This idea is shaped with respect to the UID hypothesis: expected relations can afford to be signaled by weaker markers and less expected ones should be marked by strong connectors in order to keep the discourse-level information density smooth throughout the text (Section 4.2). We then investigate in more detail the types of ambiguity that a reader might face when processing discourse relations. While some ambiguities lie in discourse connectors, it also happens that more than one relation exist at the same time between two text spans. We show that some discourse markers also signal the presence of several relations (Section 5). In computational modeling as well as laboratory setups, one should therefore have a strategy to deal with the different types of ambiguities. Finally, we ask what granularity of distinction from other discourse relations (with respect to the PDTB relation sense hierarchy) each English discourse connective conveys (Section 6).

2 Discourse Relations and their Markers

A cognitive approach to discourse processing emphasizes on the procedural role of the connectives to constrain the way readers relate the propositions in a text (Blakemore, 1992; Blass, 1993). Experimental findings suggest that these markers can facilitate the inference of specific discourse relations (Degand and Sanders, 2002), and that discourse connectors are processed incrementally Köhne and Demberg (2013). People can however infer discourse relations also in the absence of discourse connecotrs, relying on the propositional content of the sentences and their world-knowledge (Hobbs, 1979; Asher and Lascarides, 1998). Asr and Demberg (2012b) point out that similar inferences are also necessary for discourse relations which are only marked with a weak connector which can be used for many relations, such as *and*. Furthermore, we know that the inference of discourse relations is affected by a set of general cognitive biases. To illuminate the role of these factors let's have a look at (1). While the type of relation between the two events is clearly inferable in (1-a) and (1-b) due to the discourse connectives, in (1-c), the reader would have to access their knowledge, e.g., about Harry (from larger context) or the usual affairs between bosses and employees, in order to construct a discourse relation.

(1) a. The boss was angry because Harry skipped the meeting (`reason`).
b. The boss was angry, so Harry skipped the meeting (`result`).
c. The boss was angry and Harry skipped the meeting.

Here, not only both `reason` and `result` interpretations but even an independent parallel relation (simple `Conjunction`) between the two events are possible to be inferred as a relatively neutral connective, i.e., *and* is used. Levinson (2000) notes in his discussion on presumptive meanings that *"when events are conjoined they tend to be read as temporally successive and if at all plausible, as causally linked"*. If this is true then the `result` reading is most probable for (1-c). General preferences of this kind have been investigated via experimental approaches (Segal et al., 1991; Murray, 1997; Sanders, 2005; Kuperberg et al., 2011). Segal et al. (1991) and Murray (1997) argue that readers expect a sentence to be continuous with respect to its preceding context (the continuity hypothesis). Continuous discourse relations in terms of congruency and/or temporality are consequently easier to process than the discontinuous ones. Sanders (2005) proposes that causal relatedness entails the maximum degree of coherence in a text, therefore readers always start by attempting to find cause-consequence relations between neighboring sentences (the causality-by-default hypothesis). In a similar vein, Kuperberg et al. (2011) shows that readers face comprehension difficulty when sentences in short text spans cannot be put into causal relation and no marker of other relations (e.g., `Concession`) is available.

Taken together, these findings suggest that world knowledge, general cognitive biases, and linguistic features of the sentences such as the presence of a weak or strong marker contribute to the relational inference. With a look back to the information theoretic approach to the linguistic patterns, one could hypothesize that when one factor is strongly triggering expectation for a specific type of relation the other factors could remain silent in order to keep the information distribution uniform. With this perspective, Asr and Demberg (2012a) tested whether the predictability of discourse relations due to general cognitive biases (towards causality and continuity) can explain the presence vs. absence of the discourse connectors. They found that connectors were more likely to be dropped in the more predictable (causal or continuous) relations than in others. Our investigation of the explicit relations in this paper (the first experiment) looks into this question in a stricter manner considering **how much** information a connective delivers about discourse relations. Since this information is

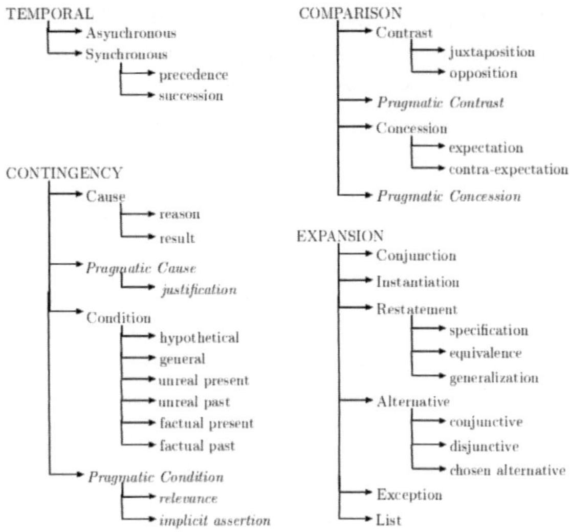

Figure 1: Hierarchy of senses in PDTB (Prasad et al., 2008)

closely related to the ambiguities a connective removes (or maybe adds to the context) in the course of reading, we dedicate a separate section in this paper to illuminate different types of ambiguities. Also, a more detail question would be **what types** of information a connective can convey about one or several discourse relations. To our best of knowledge there has been no corpus-based study so far about this last point which we will try to model in our third experiment.

3 Penn Discourse Treebank

The Penn Discourse Treebank (PDTB, Prasad et al., 2008) is a large corpus annotated with discourse relations, (covering the Wall Street Journal part of the Penn Treebank). The annotation includes sentence connectives, spans of their arguments and the sense of discourse relations implied by the connectives. The relation labels are chosen according to a hierarchy of senses (Figure 1). Annotators were asked to find the *Explicit* discourse connectives and respectively select a sense (as much specific as possible) from the hierarchy. For neighboring sentences where no explicit marker existed in the original text they were asked to first insert a suitable connective between the two arguments and then annotate a relation sense, in this case categorized as *Implicit*. If an expression — not belonging to the list of constituted connectives — in one of the involved sentences is already indicative of a specific relation, then instead they marked that expression and put the relation into the *AltLex* category. In all of our experiments only the explicit relation are considered. Some connectives were annotated with two sense labels in the PDTB. In our analyses below, we count these text spans twice (i.e., once for each sense), resulting in a total of 19,458 relation instances.

4 Are Unexpected Relations Strongly Marked?

4.1 Markedness Measure

Point-wise mutual information (pmi) is an information-theoretic measure of association between two factors. For our purpose of measuring the markedness degree of a relation r in the corpus, we calculate the normalized *pmi* of it with any of the connectives, written as c that it co-occurs with:

$$npmi(r;c) = \frac{pmi(r;c)}{-\log p(r,c)} = \frac{\log \frac{p(r,c)}{p(r)p(c)}}{-\log p(r,c)} = \frac{\log p(r)p(c)}{\log p(r,c)} - 1$$

npmi is calculated in base 2 and ranges between -1 and 1. For our markedness measure, we scale it to the interval of $[0,1]$ and weigh it by the probability of the connector given the relation.

$$0 < \frac{npmi(r;c)+1}{2} < 1$$

$$markedness(r) = \sum_c p(c|r)\frac{npmi(r;c)+1}{2}$$

Intuitively, the markedness measure tells us whether a relation has very specific markers (high markedness) or whether it is usually marked by connectors that also mark many other relations (low markedness).

4.2 Discourse Expectations and Marker Strength

Given the markedness measure, we are now able to test whether those relations which are more expected given general cognitive biases

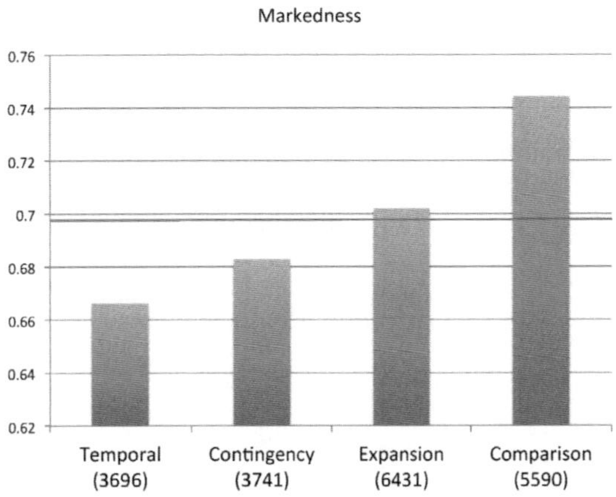

Figure 2: Markedness of level-1 explicit relations in the PDTB (frequencies of the relations given in brackets).

(expecting continuous and causal relations) are marked less strongly than e.g. discontinuous relations. Figure 2 compares the markedness associated to the explicit relations of the PDTB when the first level relation sense distinction is considered.

Figure 2 shows that COMPARISON relations exhibit higher markedness than other relations, meaning that discontinuity is marked with little ambiguity, i.e. markers of COMPARISON relations are only very rarely used in other types of discourse relations. COMPARISON relations are exactly those relations which were classified in Asr and Demberg (2012a) as a class of discontinuous relations. Further experimental evidence also shows that these relations are more likely to cause processing difficulty than others when no connector is present (Murray, 1997), and that their markers have a more strongly disruptive effect than other markers when used incorrectly. Under the information density view, these observations can be interpreted as markers for comparison relations causing a larger context update. The high markedness of COMPARISON relations is thus in line with the hypothesis that unpredictable relations are marked strongly.

CONTINGENCY relations, on the other hand, exhibit a lower score of markedness. This indeed complies with the prediction of the causality-by-default hypothesis (Sanders, 2005) in conjunction with the UID hypothesis: causal relations can still be easily inferred even in the presence of ambiguous connectives because they are preferred by default.

As also discussed in Asr and Demberg (2012a), some types of EXPANSION relations are continuous while others are discontinuous; finding that the level of markedness is near the average of all relations therefore comes as no surprise.

More interesting is the case of TEMPORAL relations: these relations have low markedness, even though this class includes continuous (temporal succession) relations as well as discontinuous (temporal precedence) relations, and we would thus have expected a higher level of markedness than we actually find. Even when calculating markedness at the more fine-grained relation distinction level, did not find a significant difference between the markedness of the temporally forward vs. backward relations. A low level of markedness means that the connectors used to mark temporal relations are also used to mark other relations, in particular, temporal connectives are often used to mark CONTINGENCY relations. This observation brings us to the question of general patterns of ambiguity in discourse markers and the ambiguity of discourse relations themselves, see Section 5.

5 Ambiguous Connective vs. Ambiguous Relation

Some discourse connectives (e.g., *since*, which can be temporal or causal, or *while*, which can be temporal or contrastive) are ambiguous. In this section, we would like to distinguish between three different types of ambiguity (all with respect to the PDTB relation hierarchy):

1. A connector expressing different relations, where it is possible to say that one but not the other relation holds between the text spans, for example *since*.

2. A connector expressing a class of relations but being ambiguous with respect to the subclasses of that relation, for example *but*, which always expresses a COMPARISON relationship but may express any subtype of the comparison relation.

3. the ambiguity inherent in the relation between two text spans, where several rela-

Relation pair	#R1 (total)	#R2 (total)	#Pair	χ^2
T.Synchrony–CON.Cause.reason	507 (1594)	353 (1488)	187	1.08E+00
T.Asynchronous.succession–CON.Cause.reason	189 (1101)	353 (1488)	159	2.43E+02 ***
E.Conjunction–CON.Cause.result	352 (5320)	162 (752)	140	2.22E+02 ***
T.Synchrony–EXP.Conjunction	507 (1594)	352 (5320)	123	5.43E+01 ***'
T.Synchrony–CON.Condition.reneral	507 (1594)	70 (362)	52	1.67E+01 ***
T.Synchrony–COM.Contrast.juxtaposition	507 (1594)	77 (1186)	45	1.97E+00
T.Asynchronous.precedence–E.Conjunction	66 (986)	352 (5320)	36	1.15E+01 ***
T.Synchrony–COM.Contrast	507 (1594)	37 (2380)	28	9.55E+00 ***
T.Synchrony–COM.Contrast.opposition	507 (1594)	28 (362)	21	6.78E+00 **

Table 1: Most frequent co-occurring relations in the PDTB, their frequency among multi-labels (and in the entire corpus)

tions can be identified to hold at the same time.

The first and second notion of ambiguity refer to what we so far have been talking about: we showed that some connectors mark can mark differnt types of relations, and that some connectives marking a general relation type but not marking specific subrelations.

The third type of ambiguity is also annotated in the PDTB. Relations which are ambiguous by nature are either labeled with a coarse-grained sense in the hierarchy (e.g., `COMPARISON.Contrast` the second most frequent label in the corpus chosen by the annotators when they could not agree on a more specific relation sense), or are labelled with two senses. Table 1 lists which two relation senses were most often annotated to hold at the same time in the PDTB, along with the individual frequency (also frequency in the entire corpus inside brackets). Sub-types of `Cause` and `TEMPORAL` relations appear most often together, while `TEMPORAL.Synchrony` is a label that appears significantly more than expected among the multi-label instances, even with a higher frequency than that of `EXPANSION.Conjunction`, the most frequent label in the corpus. Such observations confirm the existence of the third type of ambiguity in discourse relations.

Interestingly, these inherently ambiguous relations also have their own specific markers, such as *meanwhile* which occurs in about 70% of its instances with two relation senses[1].

[1]This connective is mostly labeled with `TEMPORAL.Synchrony` and `EXPANSION.Conjunction`. Interestingly these two labels appear together significanly less frequently than expected (as marked in the table with ***') but when such a cooccurrance happened in the corpus it has been for the connective *meanwhile*.

On the other hand, other well-known ambiguous connectors like *since* rarely mark inherently ambiguous relations, and most often can be identified as one specific relation sense by looking at the content of the arguments. The importance of the possibility to annotate a second sense and hence explicitly mark the inherently ambiguous relations has also been pointed out by Versley (2011). In fact, a connective like *meanwhile* can be thought of as delivering information not only about the possible relation senses it can express, but also about the fact that two discourse relations hold simultaneously.

In conclusion, it is possible that more than one discourse relation hold between two text spans. We believe that taking into account the different types of ambiguity in discourse relations can also benefit automatic discourse relation classification methods, that so far ignore multiple relation senses. Relations with two senses mostly include one temporal sense. This also (at least partially) explains the low level of markedness of temporal relations in Figure 2. Of particular interest is also the finding that there seem to be specific connectors such as *meanwhile* which are used to mark inherently ambiguous relations.

6 Type of Information Conveyed by a Discourse Connector

In this experiment, we focus on the differences among individual connectives in reflecting information about discourse relations from coarse to fine grained granularity.

6.1 Measure of Information Gain

The mutual information between two discrete variables which is indicative of the amount of uncertainty that one removes for inference of the other, can be decomposed in the following manner:

$$I(X;Y) = \sum_c p(c) \sum_r p(r|c) \log \frac{p(r|c)}{p(r)}$$

The inner sum is known as *Kullback-Leibler divergence* or relative entropy of the distribution of relations p(r) independent of the connector c and the distribution of relations $p(r|c)$ after observing c[2]. The relative entropy thus quantifies in how far knowing the connector c changes the distribution of relations.

$$gain(c) = D_{KL}(p(r|c)||p(r))$$

This formulation also allows us to calculate the change in distribution for different levels of the PDTB relation sense hierarchy and thus to analyse which connectors convey information about which level of the hierarchy. We define the measure of *enhancement* to formalize this notion:

$$enhancement_{xy}(c) = gain_y(c) - gain_x(c)$$

The enhancement$_{xy}(c)$ indicates the amount of information delivered by cue c for the classification of the instances into finer-grained relation subtypes. For example, enhancement$_{01}$(*because*) describes how much information gain *because* provides for distinguishing the level-1 relations it marks from other relations. Similarly, high enhancement$_{23}$(*because*) indicates that this connective is important for distinguishing among level 3 relations (here, distinguishing `CONTINGENCY.Cause.reason` from `CONTINGENCY.Cause.result` relations), while low enhancement$_{23}$(*if*) indicates that *if* does not contribute almost any information for distinguishing among the subtypes of the `CONTINGENCY.Condition` relation.

[2]Note that this formulation is closely related to surprisal: Levy (2008) shows that $surprisal(w_{k+1}) = -\log P(w_{k+1}|w_1..w_k)$ is equivalent to the KL divergence $D(P(T|w_{1..j+1})||P(T|w_{1..j}))$ for "any stochastic generative process P, conditioned on some (possibly null) external context, that generates complete structures T, each consisting at least partly of surface strings to be identified with serial linguistic input". Note however that in our current formulation of a discourse relation, the simplification to general structure-independent surprisal does not hold ($D_{KL}(p(r|c)||p(r)) \neq -\log p(c)$) because our relations (as they are defined here) do not satisfy the above condition for T, in particular, $P(r,c) \neq P(r)$.

6.2 Connective Help in Hierarchical Classification

Figure 3 shows the amount of enhancement for 27 frequent (> 100 occurrences) connectives in the corpus in three transitions, namely from no information to the first level classification, from first to the second level and from second to the third. Most of the connectives contribute most strongly at the coarsest level of classification, i.e., their L1-Root enhancement is the highest. In particular, we find that some of the most frequent connectives such as *but*, *and*, and *also* only help distinguishing discourse relation meaning at the coarsest level of the PDTB relation hierarchy, but contribute little to distinguish among e.g. different subtypes of `COMPARISON` or `EXPANSION`. An interesting observation is also that frequent markers of comparison relations *but*, *though*, *still* and *however* provide almost no information about the second or third level of the hierarchy.

Another group of connectors, *for example*, *instead*, *indeed* and *or* contribute significantly more information in transition from the first to the second level. These are specific markers of some level-2 relation senses. Among these, *instead* and *or* even help more for the deepest classification[3].

Temporal and causal connectives such as *before*, *after*, *so*, *then* ,*when* and *thus* have more contribution to the deepest classification level. This reflects the distinctions employed in the definition of the third level senses which has a direct correlation with the temporal ordering, i.e., forward vs. backward transition between the involved sentences. In other words, regardless of whatever high-level class of relation such markers fit in, the temporal information they hold make them beneficial for the 3rd level classification.

There are also a few connectives (*if*, *indeed*, *for example*) that convey a lot of information about the distinctions made at the first and second level of the hierarchy, but not about the third level. The reason for this is either that the third level distinction can only be made based on the propositional information in the

[3]Markers of `EXPANSION.Alternative.conjunction` and `EXPANSION.Alternative.chosen alternative` respectively.

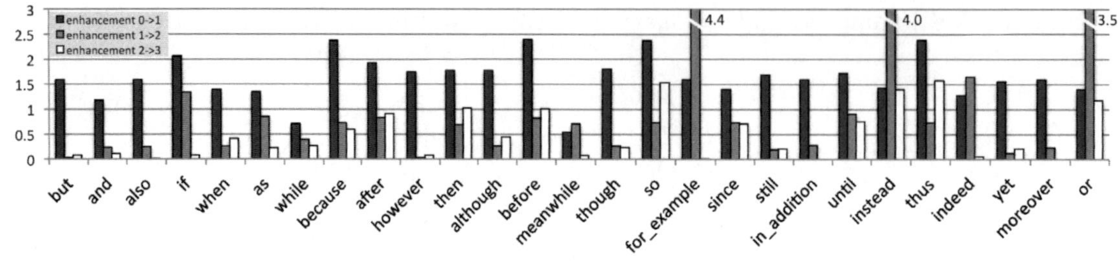

Figure 3: Enhancement through three levels of relation sense classification obtained by 27 most frequent connectives in the PDTB — ordered left to right by frequency.

arguments (this is the case for the sub-types of conditionals), or that the connector usually marks a relation which does not have a third level (e.g., *for example* is a good marker of the `EXPANSION.Instantiation` relation which does not have any subtypes).

It is worth noting that a sum over enhancements obtained in the three levels results in the total relative entropy the distribution of discourse relations before vs. after encountering the connective. As expected, ambiguous connectors of the first type of ambiguity (*while*, *since*, *when*) convey a little bit of information at each level of distinction, while overall information gain is relatively small. Ambiguous connectors of the second type of ambiguity (e.g., *but*, *and*, *if*) convey almost no information about specific sub-types of relations. Finally, markers of inherently ambiguous relations (*meanwhile*) stand out for very low information gain at all levels.

6.3 Discussion

The notion of the information conveyed by a discourse connector about a discourse relation can also help to explain two previous findings on the relative facilitative effect of causal and adversative connectors, that at first glance seem contradictory.

While Murray (1997) showed a generally more salient effect for a group of adversative cues such as *however*, *yet*, *nevertheless* and *but* compared with causal connectives *therefore*, *so*, *thus* and *consequently*, others reported different patterns when particular pairs of connectives were compared: Caron et al. (1988) found greater inference activity and recall accuracy for *because* sentences than sentences connected with *but*. Also, Millis and Just (1994) found a faster reading time and better response to the comprehension questions in the case of *because* than that of *although* sentences. Interestingly, by looking at Figure 3, we find that *because* is a more constraining connective than *but* and even *although*, given that the information gain obtain by this connective in all levels of relation classification is greater than that of *but* and *although*. While adversative connectives are reliable signals to distinguish comparison relations in a high-level from the other three major types of relations, most causal connectives deliver specific information down to the finer grains. In particular, *because* is a distinguished marker of the `reason` relation; hence, it should be associated with a more constraining discourse effect, while a generally used connective such as *but* can serve as the marker of a variety of adversative relations, e.g., a simple `Contrast` vs. a `Concession` relation.

The information-theoretic view can also account for the larger facilitating effect of highly constraining causal and adversative connectives on discourse comprehension compared to additive connectives such as *and*, *also* and *moreover* (Murray, 1995, 1997; Ben-Anath, 2006). We also can see from the Figure 3 that the mentioned additive connectives show a relatively lower sum of enhancement.

In summary, the broad classification of a discourse connector (Murray, 1997; Halliday and Hasan, 1976) is not the only factor that determines how constraining it is, or how difficult it will be to process. Instead, one should look at its usage in different context (i.e., specificity of the connective usage in the natural text). For example, based on the measurements presented in the Figure 3 we would expect a relatively high constraining effect of the connectives such as *for example* and *instead*. Note however that these predictions strongly depend on the discourse relation sense inventory and the discourse relation hierarchy. In particular, it is important to ask in how far computational linguistics resources, like the PDTB, reflect the inference processes in humans – in how far are the sense distinction and hierarchical classification cognitively adequate?

7 Discussion and Conclusion

Discourse Relation Hierarchy and Feature Space Dimensions Psycholingusitic models that need to be trained on annotated data from computational linguistics resources also have to be concerned about the psycholinguistic adequacy of the annotation. In particular, for a model of discourse relation surprisal, we need to ask which discourse relations are relevant to humans, and which distinctions between relations are relevant to them? For example, it may be possible that the distinction between cause and consequence (3rd level PDTB hierarchy) is more important in the inference process than the distinction between conjunction and list (2nd level PDTB hierarchy). Given the fact that more than one discourse relation (or none) can hold between two text segments, one should also ask whether a hierarchy is the right way to think about the discourse relation senses at all – it might be more adequate to think about discourse connectives conveying information about temporality, causality, contrast etc, with each connector possibly conveying information about more than one of these aspects at the same time.

These questions are also relevant for automatic discourse relation identification: many approaches to discourse relation identification have simplified the task to only distinguish between e.g. the level-1 sense distinctions, or level-2 distinctions (Versley, 2011; Lin et al., 2011; Hernault et al., 2011; Park and Cardie, 2012), but may be missing to differentiate aspects that are important also for many text interpretation tasks, such as distinguishing between causes and consequences.

Towards discourse relation surprisal A computational model of discourse relation surprisal would have to take the actual local context into account, i.e. factors other than just the connective, and model the interplay of different factors in the arguments of the discourse relation. We would then be in a position to argue about the predictability of a specific instance of a discourse relation, as opposed to arguing based on general cognitive biases such as the causality-by-default or continuity hypotheses.

From the three studies in this paper, we note that our findings so far are compatible with a surprisal account at the discourse relation level: The first study showed that discourse relations that seem to cause a larger context update are marked by less ambiguous connectives than relations for which less information needs to be conveyed in order to be inferred. This is in line with the UID and the *continuity* and *causality-by-default* hypotheses put forth by Murray (1997) and Sanders (2005). The second study then went on to show that one can distinguish several types of ambiguity among discourse relations, in particular, more than one relation can hold between two propositions, and there are some connectives which express this inherent ambiguity. In the third study, we also showed that the effect of particular discourse markers varies with respect to their contribution in different levels of relation classification. Some connectives such as the majority of the adversative ones, simply help to distinguish contrastive relations from other classes, while those with a temporal directionality contribute most in the deeper level of the PDTB hierarchical classification. The enhancement measure introduced in this paper can be employed for measuring the effect of any discriminative feature through the hierarchical classification of the relations. This work is a first step towards the computational modeling of the discourse processing with respect to the linguistic markers of the abstract discourse relations. In future work, we would like to look at the contribution of different types of relational markers including sentence connectives, sentiment words, implicit causality verbs, negation markers, event modals etc., which in the laboratory setup have proven to affect the expectation of the readers about an upcoming discourse relation (Kehler et al., 2008; Webber, 2013).

References

Asher, N. and Lascarides, A. (1998). Bridging. *Journal of Semantics*, 15(1):83–113.

Asr, F. T. and Demberg, V. (2012a). Implicitness of discourse relations. In *Proceedings of COLING*, Mumbai, India.

Asr, F. T. and Demberg, V. (2012b). Measuring the strength of the discourse cues. In *workshop on the Advances in Discourse Analysis and its Computational Aspects*, Mumbai, India.

Ben-Anath, D. (2006). The role of connectives in text comprehension. *Teachers College, Columbia University Working Papers in TESOL & Applied Linguistics*, 5(2).

Blakemore, D. (1992). *Understanding utterances: An introduction to pragmatics.* Blackwell Oxford.

Blass, R. (1993). Are there logical relations in a text? *Lingua*, 90(1-2):91–110.

Caron, J., Micko, H. C., and Thuring, M. (1988). Conjunctions and the recall of composite sentences. *Journal of Memory and Language*, 27(3):309–323.

Degand, L. and Sanders, T. (2002). The impact of relational markers on expository text comprehension in l1 and l2. *Reading and Writing*, 15(7):739–757.

Demberg, V. and Keller, F. (2008). Data from eye-tracking corpora as evidence for theories of syntactic processing complexity. *Cognition*, 109(2):193–210.

Frank, A. and Jaeger, T. (2008). Speaking rationally: Uniform information density as an optimal strategy for language production. *Proceedings of the 28th meeting of the Cognitive Science Society.*

Frank, S. (2009). Surprisal-based comparison between a symbolic and a connectionist model of sentence processing. In *Proceedings of the 31st annual conference of the cognitive science society*, pages 1139–1144.

Hale, J. (2001). A probabilistic earley parser as a psycholinguistic model. In *Second meeting of the North American Chapter of the Association for Computational Linguistics on Language technologies 2001*, pages 1–8.

Halliday, M. and Hasan, R. (1976). *Cohesion in English.* Longman (London).

Hernault, H., Bollegala, D., and Ishizuka, M. (2011). Semi-supervised discourse relation classification with structural learning. *Computational Linguistics and Intelligent Text Processing*, pages 340–352.

Hobbs, J. R. (1979). Coherence and coreference. *Cognitive science*, 3(1):67–90.

Kehler, A., Kertz, L., Rohde, H., and Elman, J. L. (2008). Coherence and coreference revisited. *Journal of Semantics*, 25(1):1–44.

Köhne, J. and Demberg, V. (2013). The timecourse of processing discourse connectives. In *Proceedings of the 35th Annual Meeting of the Cognitive Science Society.*

Kuperberg, G., Paczynski, M., and Ditman, T. (2011). Establishing causal coherence across sentences: An ERP study. *Journal of Cognitive Neuroscience*, 23(5):1230–1246.

Levinson, S. (2000). *Presumptive Meanings: The Theory of Generalized Conversational Implicature.* The MIT Press.

Levy, R. (2008). Expectation-based syntactic comprehension. *Cognition*, 106(3):1126–1177.

Levy, R. and Jaeger, T. F. (2007). Speakers optimize information density through syntactic reduction. In *Advances in Neural Information Processing Systems.*

Lin, Z., Ng, H., and Kan, M. (2011). Automatically evaluating text coherence using discourse relations. In *Proceedings of the 49th Annual Meeting of the Association for Computational Linguistics: Human Language Technologies-Volume 1*, pages 997–1006.

Millis, K. and Just, M. (1994). The influence of connectives on sentence comprehension. *Journal of Memory and Language.*

Mitchell, J., Lapata, M., Demberg, V., and Keller, F. (2010). Syntactic and semantic factors in processing difficulty: An integrated measure. In *Proceedings of the 48th Annual Meeting of the Association for Computational Linguistics*, pages 196–206.

Murray, J. (1995). Logical connectives and local coherence. *Sources of Coherence in Reading*, pages 107–125.

Murray, J. (1997). Connectives and narrative text: The role of continuity. *Memory and Cognition*, 25(2):227–236.

Park, J. and Cardie, C. (2012). Improving implicit discourse relation recognition through feature set optimization. In *Proceedings of the 13th Annual Meeting of the Special Interest Group on Discourse and Dialogue*, pages 108–112. Association for Computational Linguistics.

Prasad, R., Dinesh, N., Lee, A., Miltsakaki, E., Robaldo, L., Joshi, A., and Webber, B. (2008). The Penn Discourse Treebank 2.0. In *Proceedings of the 6th International Conference on Language Resources and Evaluation*, pages 2961–2968.

Roark, B., Bachrach, A., Cardenas, C., and Pallier, C. (2009). Deriving lexical and syntactic expectation-based measures for psycholinguistic modeling via incremental top-down parsing. In *Proceedings of the 2009 Conference on Empirical Methods in Natural Language Processing*, pages 324–333, Singapore. Association for Computational Linguistics.

Sanders, T. (2005). Coherence, causality and cognitive complexity in discourse. In *Proceedings/Actes SEM-05, First International Symposium on the Exploration and Modelling of Meaning*, pages 105–114.

Segal, E., Duchan, J., and Scott, P. (1991). The role of interclausal connectives in narrative structuring: Evidence from adults' interpretations of simple stories. *Discourse Processes*, 14(1):27–54.

Versley, Y. (2011). Towards finer-grained tagging of discourse connectives. In *Proceedings of the Workshop Beyound Semantics: Corpus-based Investigations of Pragmatic and Discourse Phenomena.*

Webber, B. (2013). What excludes an alternative in coherence relations? In *Proceedings of the IWCS.*

Incremental Grammar Induction from Child-Directed Dialogue Utterances*

Arash Eshghi
Interaction Lab
Heriot-Watt University
Edinburgh, United Kingdom
eshghi.a@gmail.com

Julian Hough and Matthew Purver
Cognitive Science Research Group
Queen Mary University of London
London, United Kingdom
{julian.hough, mpurver}@eecs.qmul.ac.uk

Abstract

We describe a method for learning an incremental semantic grammar from data in which utterances are paired with logical forms representing their meaning. Working in an inherently incremental framework, Dynamic Syntax, we show how words can be associated with probabilistic procedures for the incremental projection of meaning, providing a grammar which can be used directly in incremental probabilistic parsing and generation. We test this on child-directed utterances from the CHILDES corpus, and show that it results in good coverage and semantic accuracy, without requiring annotation at the word level or any independent notion of syntax.

1 Introduction

Human language processing has long been thought to function incrementally, both in parsing and production (Crocker et al., 2000; Ferreira, 1996). This incrementality gives rise to many characteristic phenomena in conversational dialogue, including unfinished utterances, interruptions and compound contributions constructed by more than one participant, which pose problems for standard grammar formalisms (Howes et al., 2012). In particular, examples such as (1) suggest that a suitable formalism would be one which defines grammaticality not in terms of licensing strings, but in terms of constraints on the *semantic* construction process, and which ensures this process is common between parsing and generation.

(1) A: I burnt the toast.
B: But did you burn ...
A: Myself? Fortunately not.
[where "did you burn myself?" if uttered by the same speaker is ungrammatical]

One such formalism is Dynamic Syntax (DS) (Kempson et al., 2001; Cann et al., 2005); it recognises no intermediate layer of syntax, but instead reflects grammatical constraints via constraints on the word-by-word incremental construction of meaning, underpinned by attendant concepts of underspecification and update.

Eshghi et al. (2013) describe a method for inducing a probabilistic DS lexicon from sentences paired with DS semantic trees (see below) representing not only their meaning, but their function-argument structure with fine-grained typing information. They apply their method only to an artificial corpus generated using a known lexicon. Here, we build on that work to induce a lexicon from real child-directed utterances paired with less structured Logical Forms in the form of TTR Record Types (Cooper, 2005), thus providing less supervision. By assuming only the availability of a small set of general compositional semantic operations, reflecting the properties of the lambda calculus and the logic of finite trees, we ensure that the lexical entries learnt include the grammatical constraints and corresponding compositional semantic structure of the language. Our method exhibits incrementality in two senses: incremental learning, with the grammar being extended and refined as each new sentence becomes available; resulting in an inherently incremental, probabilistic grammar for parsing and production, suitable for use in state-of-the-art incremental dialogue systems (Purver et al., 2011) and for modelling human-human dialogue.

* We are grateful to Ruth Kempson for her support and helpful discussions throughout this work. We also thank the CMCL'2013 anonymous reviewers for their constructive criticism. This work was supported by the EPSRC, RISER project (Ref: EP/J010383/1), and in part by the EU, FP7 project, SpaceBook (Grant agreement no: 270019).

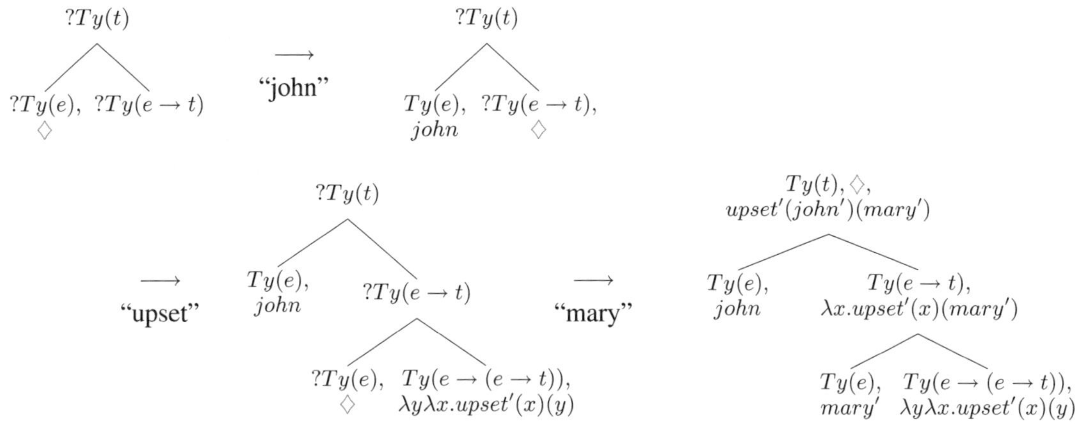

Figure 1: Incremental parsing in DS producing semantic trees: *"John upset Mary"*

2 Background

2.1 Grammar Induction and Semantics

We can view existing grammar induction methods along a spectrum from supervised to unsupervised. Fully supervised methods take a parsed corpus as input, pairing sentences with syntactic trees and words with their syntactic categories, and generalise over the phrase structure rules to learn a grammar which can be applied to a new set of data. Probabilities for production rules sharing a LHS category can be estimated, producing a grammar suitable for probabilistic parsing and disambiguation e.g. a PCFG (Charniak, 1996). While such methods have shown great success, they presuppose detailed prior linguistic information and are thus inadequate as human grammar learning models. Fully unsupervised methods, on the other hand, proceed from unannotated raw data; they are thus closer to the human language acquisition setting, but have seen less success. In its pure form —positive data only, without bias— unsupervised learning is computationally too complex ('unlearnable') in the worst case (Gold, 1967). Successful approaches involve some prior learning or bias (see (Clark and Lappin, 2011)) e.g. a set of known lexical categories, a probability distribution bias (Klein and Manning, 2005) or a semi-supervised method with shallower (e.g. POS-tag) annotation (Pereira and Schabes, 1992).

Another point on the spectrum is *lightly* supervised learning: providing information which constrains learning but with little or no lexico-syntactic detail. One possibility is the use of *semantic* annotation, using sentence-level propositional Logical Forms (LF). It seems more cognitively plausible, as the learner can be said to be able to understand, at least in part, the meaning of what she hears from evidence gathered from (1) her perception of her local, immediate environment given appropriate biases on different patterns of individuation of entities and relationships between them, and (2) helpful interaction, and joint focus of attention with an adult (see e.g. (Saxton, 1997)). Given this, the problem she is faced with is one of separating out the contribution of each individual linguistic token to the overall meaning of an uttered linguistic expression (i.e. decomposition), while maintaining and generalising over several such hypotheses acquired through time as she is exposed to more utterances involving each token.

This has been successfully applied in Combinatorial Categorial Grammar (CCG) (Steedman, 2000), as it tightly couples compositional semantics with syntax (Zettlemoyer and Collins, 2007; Kwiatkowski et al., 2010; Kwiatkowski et al., 2012); as CCG is a lexicalist framework, grammar learning involves inducing a lexicon assigning to each word its syntactic and semantic contribution. Moreover, the grammar is learnt incrementally, in the sense that the learner collects data over time and does the learning sentence by sentence.

Following this approach, Eshghi et al. (2013) outline a method for inducing a DS grammar from semantic LFs. This brings an added dimension of incrementality: not only is learning sentence-by-sentence incremental, but the grammar learned is inherently word-by-word incremental (see section 2.2 below). However, their method requires a higher degree of supervision than (Kwiatkowski et al., 2012): the LFs assumed are not simply flat semantic formulae, but full DS semantic trees (see e.g. Fig. 1) containing information about the function-argument structure required for their composition, in addition to fine grained type and formula annotations. Further, they test their method only on artificial data created using a known, manually-specified DS grammar. In contrast, in this paper we provide an approach which can learn from LFs without any compositional structure information, and test it on real language data; thus providing the first practical learning system for an explicitly incremental grammar that we are aware of.

2.2 Dynamic Syntax (DS)

Dynamic Syntax (Kempson et al., 2001; Cann et al., 2005) is a parsing-directed grammar formalism, which models the word-by-word incremental processing of linguistic input. Unlike many other formalisms, DS models the incremental building up of *interpretations* without presupposing or indeed recognising an independent level of syntactic processing. Thus, the output for any given string of words is a purely *semantic* tree representing its predicate-argument structure; tree nodes correspond to terms in the lambda calculus, decorated with labels expressing their semantic type (e.g. $Ty(e)$) and formula, with beta-reduction determining the type and formula at a mother node from those at its daughters (Figure 1).

These trees can be *partial*, containing unsatisfied requirements for node labels (e.g. $?Ty(e)$ is a requirement for future development to $Ty(e)$), and contain a *pointer* $\diamondsuit$ labelling the node currently under development. Grammaticality is defined as parsability: the successful incremental construction of a tree with no outstanding requirements (a *complete* tree) using all information given by the words in a sentence. The complete sentential LF is then the formula decorating the root node – see Figure 1. Note that in these trees, leaf nodes do not necessarily correspond to words, and may not be in linear sentence order; syntactic structure is not explicitly represented, only the structure of semantic predicate-argument combination.

2.2.1 Actions in DS

The parsing process is defined in terms of conditional *actions*: procedural specifications for monotonic tree growth. These include general structure-building principles (*computational actions*), putatively independent of any particular natural language, and language-specific actions associated with particular lexical items (*lexical actions*). The latter are what we learn from data here.

Computational actions These form a small, fixed set, which we assume as given here. Some merely encode the properties of the lambda calculus and the logical tree formalism itself, LoFT (Blackburn and Meyer-Viol, 1994) – these we term *inferential* actions. Examples include THINNING (removal of satisfied requirements) and ELIMINATION (beta-reduction of daughter nodes at the mother). These actions are language-independent, cause no ambiguity, and add no new information to the tree; as such, they apply non-optionally whenever their preconditions are met.

Other computational actions reflect the fundamental predictivity and dynamics of the DS framework. For example, *-ADJUNCTION introduces a single *unfixed* node with underspecified tree position (replacing feature-passing or type-raising concepts for e.g. long-distance dependency); and LINK-ADJUNCTION builds a paired ("linked") tree corresponding to semantic conjunction (licensing relative clauses, apposition and more). These actions represent possible parsing strategies and can apply optionally whenever their preconditions are met. While largely language-independent, some are specific to language type (e.g. INTRODUCTION-PREDICTION in the form used here applies only to SVO languages).

Lexical actions The lexicon associates words with lexical actions; like computational actions, these are sequences of tree-update actions in an IF..THEN..ELSE format, and composed of explicitly procedural *atomic* tree-building actions such as `make` (creates a new daughter node), `go` (moves the pointer), and `put` (decorates the pointed node with a label). Figure 2 shows an example for a proper noun, *John*. The action checks whether the pointed node (marked as $\diamondsuit$) has a requirement for type e; if so, it decorates it with type e (thus satisfying the requirement), formula $John'$ and the bottom restriction $\langle\downarrow\rangle\bot$ (meaning that the node cannot have any daughters). Otherwise the action aborts, i.e. the word *'John'* cannot be parsed in the context of the current tree.

Graph-based Parsing & Generation These actions define the parsing process. Given a sequence of words $(w_1, w_2, ..., w_n)$, the parser starts from the *axiom* tree T_0 (a requirement to construct a complete propositional tree, $?Ty(t)$), and applies the corresponding lexical actions $(a_1, a_2, \ldots, a_n)$, optionally interspersing computational actions.

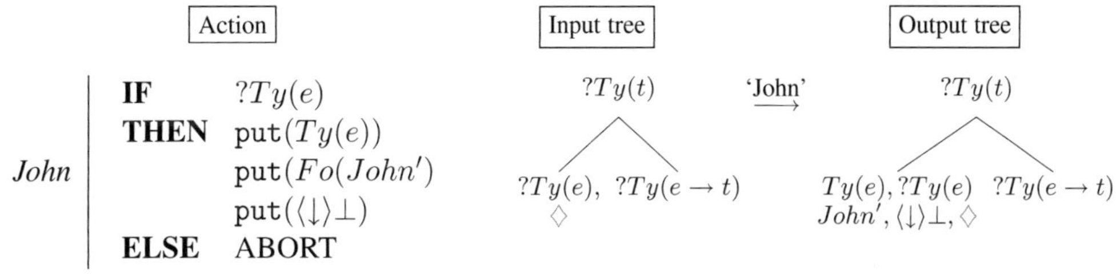

Figure 2: Lexical action for the word 'John'

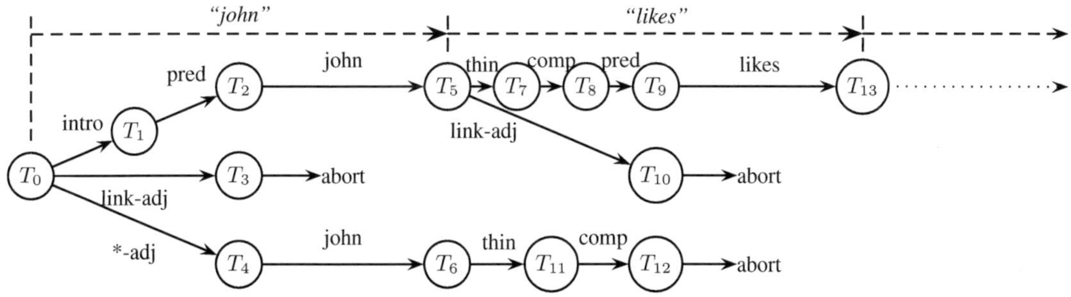

Figure 3: DS parsing as a graph: actions (edges) are transitions between partial trees (nodes).

This parsing process can be modelled as a directed acyclic graph (DAG) rooted at T_0, with partial trees as nodes, and computational and lexical actions as edges (i.e. transitions between trees) (Sato, 2011). Figure 3 shows an example: here, *intro*, *pred* and **adj* correspond to the computational actions INTRODUCTION, PREDICTION and *-ADJUNCTION respectively; and 'john' is a lexical action. Different DAG paths represent different parsing strategies, which may succeed or fail depending on how the utterance is continued. Here, the path $T_0 - T_3$ will succeed if *'John'* is the subject of an upcoming verb ("John upset Mary"); $T_0 - T_4$ will succeed if *'John'* turns out to be a left-dislocated object ("John, Mary upset").

This incrementally constructed DAG makes up the entire *parse state* at any point. The rightmost nodes (i.e. partial trees) make up the current maximal semantic information; these nodes with their paths back to the root (tree-transition actions) make up the *linguistic context* for ellipsis and pronominal construal (Purver et al., 2011). Given a conditional probability distribution $P(a|w,T)$ over possible actions a given a word w and (some set of features of) the current partial tree T, we can parse probabilistically, constructing the DAG in a best-first, breadth-first or beam parsing manner.

Generation uses exactly the same actions and structures, and can be modelled on the same DAG with the addition only of a *goal* tree; partial trees are checked for subsumption of the goal at each stage. The framework therefore inherently provides both parsing and generation that are word-by-word incremental and interchangeable, commensurate with psycholinguistic results (Lombardo and Sturt, 1997; Ferreira and Swets, 2002) and suitable for modelling dialogue (Howes et al., 2012). While standard grammar formalisms can of course also be used with incremental parsing or generation algorithms (Hale, 2001; Collins and Roark, 2004; Clark and Curran, 2007), their string-based grammaticality and lack of inherent parsing-generation interoperability means examples such as (1) remain problematic.

3 Method

Our task here is to learn an incremental DS grammar; following Kwiatkowski et al. (2012), we assume as input a set of sentences paired with their semantic LFs. Eshghi et al. (2013) outline a method for inducing DS grammars from semantic *DS trees* (e.g. Fig. 1), in which possible lexical entries are incrementally hypothesized, constrained by subsumption of the target tree for the sentence. Here, however, this structured tree information is not available to us; our method must therefore constrain hypotheses via compatibility with the sentential LF, represented as Record Types of Type Theory with Records (TTR).

3.1 Type Theory with Records (TTR)

Type Theory with Records (TTR) is an extension of standard type theory shown useful in semantics and dialogue modelling (Cooper, 2005; Ginzburg, 2012). It is also used for representing non-linguistic context such as the visual perception of objects (Dobnik et al., 2012), suggesting potential for embodied learning in future work.

Some DS variants have incorporated TTR as the semantic LF representation (Purver et al., 2011; Hough and Purver, 2012; Eshghi et al., 2012). Here, it can provide us with the mechanism we need to constrain hypotheses in induction by restricting them to those which lead to *subtypes* of the known sentential LF.

In TTR, logical forms are specified as *record types* (RTs), sequences of *fields* of the form $[\, l : T \,]$ containing a label l and a type T. RTs can be witnessed (i.e. judged true) by *records* of that type, where a record is a sequence of label-value pairs $[\, l = v \,]$, and $[\, l = v \,]$ is of type $[\, l : T \,]$ just in case v is of type T.

$$R_1 : \begin{bmatrix} l_1 & : T_1 \\ l_{2=a} & : T_2 \\ l_{3=p(l_2)} & : T_3 \end{bmatrix} \quad R_2 : \begin{bmatrix} l_1 & : T_1 \\ l_2 & : T_{2'} \end{bmatrix} \quad R_3 : []$$

Figure 4: Example TTR record types

Fields can be *manifest*, i.e. given a singleton type e.g. $[\, l : T_a \,]$ where T_a is the type of which only a is a member; here, we write this using the syntactic sugar $[\, l_{=a} : T \,]$. Fields can also be *dependent* on fields preceding them (i.e. higher) in the record type – see R_1 in Figure 4. Importantly for us here, the standard subtyping relation $\sqsubseteq$ can be defined for record types: $R_1 \sqsubseteq R_2$ if for all fields $[\, l : T_2 \,]$ in R_2, R_1 contains $[\, l : T_1 \,]$ where $T_1 \sqsubseteq T_2$. In Figure 4, $R_1 \sqsubseteq R_2$ if $T_2 \sqsubseteq T_{2'}$, and both R_1 and R_2 are subtypes of R_3.

Following Purver et al. (2011), we assume that DS tree nodes are decorated not with simple atomic formulae but with RTs, and corresponding lambda abstracts representing functions from RT to RT (e.g. $\lambda r : [\, l_1 : T_1 \,].[\, l_{2=r.l_1} : T_1 \,]$ where $r.l_1$ is a *path* expression referring to the label l_1 in r) – see Figure 5. The equivalent of conjunction for linked trees is now RT *extension* (concatenation modulo relabelling – see (Cooper, 2005; Fernández, 2006)). TTR's subtyping relation now allows a record type at the root node to be inferred for any partial tree, and incrementally further specified via subtyping as parsing proceeds (Hough and Purver, 2012).

We assume a field $head$ in all record types, with this corresponding to the DS tree node type. We also assume a neo-Davidsonian representation of

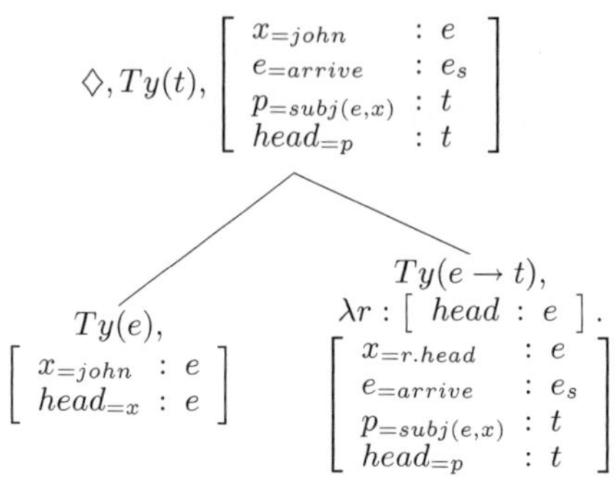

Figure 5: DS-TTR tree

predicates, with fields corresponding to the event and to each semantic role; this allows all available semantic information to be specified incrementally via strict subtyping (e.g. providing the $subj()$ field when subject but not object has been parsed) – see Figure 5 for an example.

3.2 Problem Statement

Our induction procedure now assumes as input:

- a known set of DS computational actions.
- a set of training examples of the form $\langle S_i, R_{T_i} \rangle$, where $S_i = \langle w_1 \ldots w_n \rangle$ is a sentence of the language and R_{T_i} – henceforth referred to as the *target RT* – is the record type representing the meaning of S_i.

The output is a grammar specifying the possible lexical actions for each word in the corpus. Given our data-driven approach, we take a probabilistic view: we take this grammar as associating each word w with a probability distribution θ_w over lexical actions. In principle, for use in parsing, this distribution should specify the posterior probability $p(a|w, T)$ of using a particular action a to parse a word w in the context of a particular partial tree T. However, here we make the simplifying assumption that actions are conditioned solely on one feature of a tree, the semantic type Ty of the currently pointed node; and that actions apply exclusively to one such type (i.e. ambiguity of type implies multiple actions). This simplifies our problem to specifying the probability $p(a|w)$.

In traditional DS terms, this is equivalent to assuming that all lexical actions have a simple IF clause of the form IF $?Ty(X)$; this is true of most lexical actions in existing DS grammars (see Fig. 2), but not all. Our assumption may therefore lead to over-generation – inducing actions which can parse some ungrammatical strings – we must rely on the probabilities learned to make such parses unlikely, and evaluate this in Section 4. Given this, our focus here is on learning the THEN clauses of lexical actions: sequences of DS atomic actions such as *go*, *make*, and *put* (Fig. 2), but now with attendant posterior probabilities. We will henceforth refer to these sequences as *lexical hypotheses*. We first describe how we construct lexical hypotheses from individual training examples; we then show how to generalise over these, while incrementally estimating corresponding probability distributions.

3.3 Hypothesis construction

DS is *strictly monotonic*: actions can only *extend* the current (partial) tree T_{cur}, deleting nothing except satisfied requirements. Thus, we can hypothesise lexical actions by incrementally exploring the space of all monotonic, well-formed extensions T of T_{cur}, whose maximal semantics R is a supertype of (extendible to) the target R_T (i.e. $R \sqsubseteq R_T$). This gives a bounded space described by a DAG equivalent to that of section 2.2.1: nodes are trees; edges are possible extensions; paths start from T_{cur} and end at any tree with LF R_T . Edges may be either known computational actions or new *lexical hypotheses*. The space is further constrained by the properties of the lambda-calculus and the modal tree logic LoFT (not all possible trees and extensions are well-formed).[1]

Hypothesising increments In purely semantic terms, the hypothesis space at any point is the possible set of TTR increments from the current LF R to the target R_T. We can efficiently compute and represent these possible increments using a *type lattice* (see Figure 6),[2] which can be constructed for the whole sentence before processing each training example. Each edge is a RT R representing an *increment* from one RT, R_j, to another, R_{j+1}, such that $R_j \wedge R_I = R_{j+1}$ (where $\wedge$ represents record type intersection (Cooper, 2005)); possible parse DAG paths must correspond to some path through this lattice.

Hypothesising tree structure These DAG paths can now be hypothesised with the lattice as a constraint: hypothesising possible sequences of actions which extend the tree to produce the required semantic increment, while the increments themselves constitute a search space of their own which we explore by traversing the lattice.

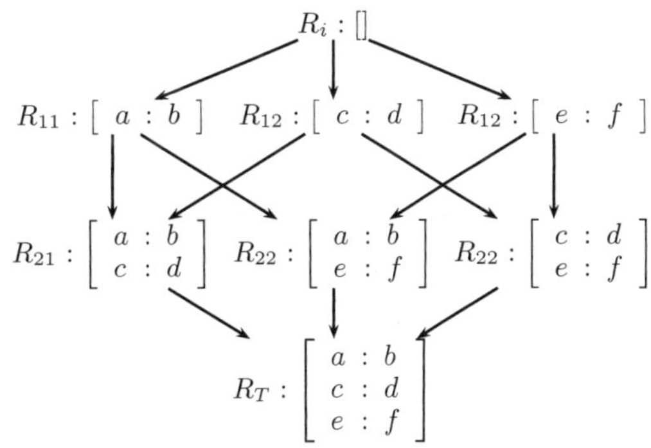

Figure 6: RT extension hypothesis lattice

The lexical hypotheses comprising these DAG paths are divide into two general classes: (1) *tree-building* hypotheses, which hypothesise appropriately typed daughters to compose a given node; and (2) *content* hypotheses, which decorate leaf nodes with appropriate formulae from R_i (non-leaf nodes then receive their content via beta-reduction/extension of daughters).

Tree-building can be divided into two general options: functional decomposition (corresponding to the addition of daughter nodes with appropriate types and formulae which will form a suitable mother node by beta-reduction); and type extension (corresponding to the adjunction of a linked tree whose LF will extend that of the current tree, see Sec. 3.1 above). The availability of the former is constrained by the presence of suitable *dependent* types in the LF (e.g. in Fig. 5, $p = subj(e, x)$ depends on the fields with labels x and e, and could therefore be hypothesised as the body of a function with x and/or e as argument). The latter is more generally available, but constrained by sharing of a label between the resulting linked trees.

Figure 7 shows an example: a template for functional decomposition hypotheses, extending a node with some type requirement $?Ty(X)$ with daughter nodes which can combine to satisfy that requirement – here, of types Y and $Y \rightarrow X$. Specific instantiations are limited to a finite set of types: e.g. $X = e \rightarrow t$ and $Y = e$ is allowed, but higher types for Y are not. We implement these constraints by packaging together permitted sequences of tree updates as macros, and using these macros to hypothesise DAG paths commensurate with the lattice.

Finally, semantic content decorations (as se-

[1] We also prevent arbitrary type-raising by restricting the types allowed, taking the standard DS assumption that noun phrases have semantic type e (rather than a higher type as in Generalized Quantifier theory) and common nouns their own type cn, see Cann et al. (2005), chapter 3 for details.

[2] Clark (2011) similarly use a *concept* lattice relating strings to their contexts in syntactic grammar induction.

IF	$?Ty(X)$
THEN	$make(\langle\downarrow_0\rangle); go(\langle\downarrow_0\rangle)$
	$put(?Ty(Y)); go(\langle\uparrow\rangle)$
	$make(\langle\downarrow_1\rangle); go(\langle\downarrow_1\rangle)$
	$put(?Ty(Y \rightarrow X)); go(\uparrow)$
ELSE	ABORT

Figure 7: Tree-building hypothesis

quences of `put` operations) are hypothesised for the leaf nodes of the tree thus constructed; these are now determined entirely by the tree structure so far hypothesised and the target LF R_T.

3.4 Probabilistic Grammar Estimation

This procedure produces, for each training sentence $\langle w_1 \ldots w_n \rangle$, all possible sequences of actions that lead from the axiom tree T_0 to a tree with the target RT as its semantics. These must now be split into n sub-sequences, hypothesising a set of word boundaries to form discrete word hypotheses; and a probability distribution estimated over this (large) word hypothesis space to provide a grammar that can be useful in parsing. For this, we apply the procedure of Eshghi et al. (2013).

For each training sentence $S = \langle w_1 \ldots w_n \rangle$, we have a set HT of possible *Hypothesis Tuples* (sequences of word hypotheses), each of the form $HT_j = \langle h_1^j \ldots h_n^j \rangle$, where h_i^j is the word hypothesis for w_i in HT_j. We must estimate a probability distribution θ_w over hypotheses for each word w, where $\theta_w(h)$ is the posterior probability $p(h|w)$ of a given word hypothesis h being used to parse w. Eshghi et al. (2013) define an incremental version of Expectation-Maximisation (Dempster et al., 1977) for use in this setting.

Re-estimation At any point, the Expectation step assigns each hypothesis tuple HT_j a probability based on the current estimate θ'_w:

$$p(HT_j|S) = \prod_{i=1}^{n} p(h_i^j|w_i) = \prod_{i=1}^{n} \theta'_{w_i}(h_i^j) \quad (2)$$

The Maximisation step then re-estimates $p(h|w)$ as the normalised sum of the probabilities of all observed tuples HT_j which contain h, w:

$$\theta''_w(h) = \frac{1}{Z} \sum_{\{j|h,w \in HT_j\}} \prod_{i=1}^{n} \theta'_{w_i}(h_i^j) \quad (3)$$

where Z is the appropriate normalising constant summed over all the HT_j's.

Incremental update The estimate of θ_w is now updated incrementally at each training example: the new estimate θ_w^N is a weighted average of the previous estimate θ_w^{N-1} and the new value from the current example θ''_w from equation (3):

$$\theta_w^N(h) = \frac{N-1}{N}\theta_w^{N-1}(h) + \frac{1}{N}\theta''_w(h) \quad (4)$$

$$\lambda e.not(aux|do(v|have(pro|he, det|a(x, n|hat(x)), e), e), e)$$
$$\downarrow$$
$$\left[\begin{array}{lll} e_{=have} & : & es \\ p3_{=not(e)} & : & t \\ p2_{=do\text{-}aux(e)} & : & t \\ r & : & \left[\begin{array}{lll} x & : & e \\ p_{=hat(x)} & : & t \\ head_{=x} & : & e \end{array}\right] \\ x2_{=\epsilon(r.head,r)} & : & e \\ x1_{=he} & : & e \\ p1_{=object(e,x2)} & : & t \\ p_{=subject(e,x1)} & : & t \\ head_{=e} & : & es \end{array}\right]$$

Figure 8: Conversion of LFs from FOL to TTR.

For the first training example, a uniform distribution is assumed; when subsequent examples produce new previously unseen hypotheses these are assigned probabilities uniformly distributed over a held-out probability mass.

4 Experimental Setup

Corpus We tested our approach on a section of the Eve corpus within CHILDES (MacWhinney, 2000), a series of English child-directed utterances, annotated with LFs by Kwiatkowski et al. (2012) following Sagae et al. (2004)'s syntactic annotation. We convert these LFs into semantically equivalent RTs; e.g. Fig 8 shows the conversion to a record type for "He doesn't have a hat".

Importantly, our representations remove all part-of-speech or syntactic information; e.g. the *subject*, *object* and *indirect object* predicates function as purely semantic role information expressing an event's participants. This includes e.g. $do\text{-}aux(e)$ in (8), which is taken merely to represent temporal/aspectual information about the event, and could be part of any word hypothesis.

From this corpus we selected 500 short utterance-record type pairs. The minimum utterance length in this set is 1 word, maximum 7, mean 3.7; it contains 1481 word tokens of 246 types, giving a type:token ratio of 6.0). We use the first 400 for training and 100 for testing; the test set also has a mean utterance length of 3.7 words, and contains only words seen in training.

Evaluation We evaluate our learner by comparing the record type semantic LFs produced using the induced lexicon against the gold standard LFs, calculating precision, recall and f-score using a method similar to Allen et al. (2008).

	Coverage %	Precision	Recall	F-Score
Top-1	59	0.548	0.549	0.548
Top-2	85	0.786	0.782	0.782
Top-3	92	0.854	0.851	0.851

Table 1: Results: parse coverage & accuracy using the top N hypotheses induced in training.

Each field has a potential score in the range [0,1]. A method $maxMapping(R_1, R_2)$ constructs a mapping from fields in R_1 to those in R_2 to maximise alignment, with fields that map completely scoring a full 1, and partially mapped fields receiving less, depending on the proportion of the R_1 field's representation that subsumes its mapped R_2 field;e.g. a unary predicate field in $RT2$ such as $\left[\ p_{=there(e)}\ :\ t\ \right]$ could score a maximum of 3 - 1 for correct type t, 1 for correct predicate $there$ and 1 for the subsumption of its argument e; we use the total to normalise the final score. The potential maximum for any pair is therefore the number of fields in R_1 (including those in embedded record types). So, for hypothesis H and goal record type G, with N_H and N_G fields respectively:

(5) $precision = maxMapping(H, G)/N_H$
$recall = maxMapping(H, G)/N_G$

5 Results

Table 1 shows that the grammar learned achieves both good parsing coverage and semantic accuracy. Using the top 3 lexical hypotheses induced from training, 92% of test set utterances receive a parse, and average LF f-score reaches 0.851.

We manually inspected the learned lexicon for instances of ambiguous words to assess the system's ability to disambiguate (e.g. the word *''s'* (is) has three different senses in our corpus: (1) auxiliary, e.g. *"the coffee's coming"*; (2) verb predicating NP identity, e.g. *"that's a girl"*; and (3) verb predicating location, e.g. *"where's the pencil"*). From these the first two were in the top 3 hypotheses (probabilities p=0.227 and p=0.068). For example, the lexical entry learned for (2) is shown in Fig. 9.

However, less common words fared worse: e.g. the double object verb *'put'*, with only 3 tokens, had no correct hypothesis in the top 5. Given sufficient frequency and variation in the token distributions, our method appears successful in inducing the correct incremental grammar. However, the complexity of the search space also limits the possibility of learning from larger record types, as the space of possible subtypes used for hypothesising

$$
\begin{array}{ll}
\textbf{IF} & ?Ty(e \rightarrow t) \\
\textbf{THEN} & \mathtt{make}(\langle\downarrow_0\rangle); \mathtt{go}(\langle\downarrow_0\rangle) \\
& \mathtt{put}(?Ty(e)) \\
& \mathtt{go}(\langle\uparrow_0\rangle) \\
& \mathtt{make}(\langle\downarrow_1\rangle); \mathtt{go}(\langle\downarrow_1\rangle) \\
& \mathtt{put}(Ty(e \rightarrow (e \rightarrow t))) \\
& \mathtt{put}(Fo(\\
& \lambda r1 : \left[\ head\ :\ e\ \right] \\
& \lambda r2 : \left[\ head\ :\ e\ \right] . \\
& \left[\begin{array}{ll} x1_{=r1.head} & : e \\ x2_{=r2.head} & : e \\ e_{=eq} & : e_s \\ p1_{=subj(e,x2)} & : t \\ p2_{=obj(e,x1)} & : t \\ head_{=e} & : t \end{array}\right])) \\
& \mathtt{put}(\langle\downarrow\rangle\bot) \\
\textbf{ELSE} & \text{ABORT}
\end{array}
$$

Figure 9: Action learned for second sense of 'is'

tree structure grows exponentially with the number of fields in the type. Therefore, when learning from longer, more complicated sentences, we may need to bring in further sources of bias to constrain our hypothesis process further (e.g. learning from shorter sentences first).

6 Conclusions

We have outlined a novel method for the induction of a probabilistic grammar in an inherently incremental and semantic formalism, Dynamic Syntax, compatible with dialogue phenomena such as compound contributions and with no independent level of syntactic phrase structure. Assuming only general compositional mechanisms, our method learns from utterances paired with their logical forms represented as TTR record types. Evaluation on a portion of the CHILDES corpus of child-directed dialogue utterances shows good coverage and semantic accuracy, which lends support to viewing it as a plausible, yet idealised, language acquisition model.

Future work planned includes refining the method outlined above for learning from longer utterances, and then from larger corpora e.g. the Groningen Meaning Bank (Basile et al., 2012), which includes more complex structures. This will in turn enable progress towards large-scale incremental semantic parsers and allow further investigation into semantically driven language learning.

References

James F. Allen, Mary Swift, and Will de Beaumont. 2008. Deep Semantic Analysis of Text. In Johan Bos and Rodolfo Delmonte, editors, *Semantics in Text Processing. STEP 2008 Conference Proceedings*, volume 1 of *Research in Computational Semantics*, pages 343–354. College Publications.

Valerio Basile, Johan Bos, Kilian Evang, and Noortje Venhuizen. 2012. Developing a large semantically annotated corpus. In *Proceedings of the Eight International Conference on Language Resources and Evaluation (LREC 2012)*, pages 3196–3200, Istanbul, Turkey.

Patrick Blackburn and Wilfried Meyer-Viol. 1994. Linguistics, logic and finite trees. *Logic Journal of the Interest Group of Pure and Applied Logics*, 2(1):3–29.

Ronnie Cann, Ruth Kempson, and Lutz Marten. 2005. *The Dynamics of Language*. Elsevier, Oxford.

Eugene Charniak. 1996. *Statistical Language Learning*. MIT Press.

Stephen Clark and James Curran. 2007. Wide-coverage efficient statistical parsing with CCG and log-linear models. *Computational Linguistics*, 33(4):493–552.

Alexander Clark and Shalom Lappin. 2011. *Linguistic Nativism and the Poverty of the Stimulus*. Wiley-Blackwell.

Alexander Clark. 2011. A learnable representation for syntax using residuated lattices. In Philippe Groote, Markus Egg, and Laura Kallmeyer, editors, *Formal Grammar*, volume 5591 of *Lecture Notes in Computer Science*, pages 183–198. Springer Berlin Heidelberg.

Michael Collins and Brian Roark. 2004. Incremental parsing with the perceptron algorithm. In *Proceedings of the 42nd Meeting of the ACL*, pages 111–118, Barcelona.

Robin Cooper. 2005. Records and record types in semantic theory. *Journal of Logic and Computation*, 15(2):99–112.

Matthew Crocker, Martin Pickering, and Charles Clifton, editors. 2000. *Architectures and Mechanisms in Sentence Comprehension*. Cambridge University Press.

A.P. Dempster, N.M. Laird, and D. B. Rubin. 1977. Maximum likelihood from incomplete data via the EM algorithm. *Journal of the Royal Statistical Society. Series B (Methodological)*, 39(1):1–38.

Simon Dobnik, Robin Cooper, and Staffan Larsson. 2012. Modelling language, action, and perception in type theory with records. In *Proceedings of the 7th International Workshop on Constraint Solving and Language Processing (CSLP12)*, pages 51–63.

Arash Eshghi, Julian Hough, Matthew Purver, Ruth Kempson, and Eleni Gregoromichelaki. 2012. Conversational interactions: Capturing dialogue dynamics. In S. Larsson and L. Borin, editors, *From Quantification to Conversation: Festschrift for Robin Cooper on the occasion of his 65th birthday*, volume 19 of *Tributes*, pages 325–349. College Publications, London.

Arash Eshghi, Matthew Purver, and Julian Hough. 2013. Probabilistic induction for an incremental semantic grammar. In *Proceedings of the 10th International Conference on Computational Semantics (IWCS 2013) – Long Papers*, pages 107–118, Potsdam, Germany, March. Association for Computational Linguistics.

Raquel Fernández. 2006. *Non-Sentential Utterances in Dialogue: Classification, Resolution and Use*. Ph.D. thesis, King's College London, University of London.

Fernanda Ferreira and Benjamin Swets. 2002. How incremental is language production? evidence from the production of utterances requiring the computation of arithmetic sums. *Journal of Memory and Language*, 46:57–84.

Victor Ferreira. 1996. Is it better to give than to donate? Syntactic flexibility in language production. *Journal of Memory and Language*, 35:724–755.

Jonathan Ginzburg. 2012. *The Interactive Stance: Meaning for Conversation*. Oxford University Press.

E. Mark Gold. 1967. Language identification in the limit. *Information and Control*, 10(5):447–474.

John Hale. 2001. A probabilistic Earley parser as a psycholinguistic model. In *Proceedings of the 2nd Conference of the North American Chapter of the Association for Computational Linguistics*, Pittsburgh, PA.

Julian Hough and Matthew Purver. 2012. Processing self-repairs in an incremental type-theoretic dialogue system. In *Proceedings of the 16th SemDial Workshop on the Semantics and Pragmatics of Dialogue (SeineDial)*, pages 136–144, Paris, France, September.

Christine Howes, Matthew Purver, Rose McCabe, Patrick G. T. Healey, and Mary Lavelle. 2012. Predicting adherence to treatment for schizophrenia from dialogue transcripts. In *Proceedings of the 13th Annual Meeting of the Special Interest Group on Discourse and Dialogue (SIGDIAL 2012 Conference)*, pages 79–83, Seoul, South Korea, July. Association for Computational Linguistics.

Ruth Kempson, Wilfried Meyer-Viol, and Dov Gabbay. 2001. *Dynamic Syntax: The Flow of Language Understanding*. Blackwell.

Dan Klein and Christopher D. Manning. 2005. Natural language grammar induction with a generative constituent-context mode. *Pattern Recognition*, 38(9):1407–1419.

Tom Kwiatkowski, Luke Zettlemoyer, Sharon Goldwater, and Mark Steedman. 2010. Inducing probabilistic CCG grammars from logical form with higher-order unification. In *Proceedings of the 2010 Conference on Empirical Methods in Natural Language Processing*, pages 1223–1233, Cambridge, MA, October. Association for Computational Linguistics.

Tom Kwiatkowski, Sharon Goldwater, Luke Zettlemoyer, and Mark Steedman. 2012. A probabilistic model of syntactic and semantic acquisition from child-directed utterances and their meanings. In *Proceedings of the Conference of the European Chapter of the Association for Computational Linguistics (EACL)*.

Vincenzo Lombardo and Patrick Sturt. 1997. Incremental processing and infinite local ambiguity. In *Proceedings of the 1997 Cognitive Science Conference*.

Brian MacWhinney. 2000. *The CHILDES Project: Tools for Analyzing Talk*. Lawrence Erlbaum Associates, Mahwah, New Jersey, third edition.

Fernando Pereira and Yves Schabes. 1992. Inside-outside reestimation from partially bracketed corpora. In *Proceedings of the 30th Annual Meeting of the Association for Computational Linguistics*, pages 128–135, Newark, Delaware, USA, June. Association for Computational Linguistics.

Matthew Purver, Arash Eshghi, and Julian Hough. 2011. Incremental semantic construction in a dialogue system. In J. Bos and S. Pulman, editors, *Proceedings of the 9th International Conference on Computational Semantics*, pages 365–369, Oxford, UK, January.

Kenji Sagae, Brian MacWhinney, and Alon Lavie. 2004. Adding syntactic annotations to transcripts of parent-child dialogs. In *Proceedings of the 4th International Conference on Language Resources and Evaluation (LREC)*, pages 1815–1818, Lisbon.

Yo Sato. 2011. Local ambiguity, search strategies and parsing in Dynamic Syntax. In E. Gregoromichelaki, R. Kempson, and C. Howes, editors, *The Dynamics of Lexical Interfaces*. CSLI Publications.

Matthew Saxton. 1997. The contrast theory of negative input. *Journal of Child Language*, 24(1):139–161.

Mark Steedman. 2000. *The Syntactic Process*. MIT Press, Cambridge, MA.

Luke Zettlemoyer and Michael Collins. 2007. Online learning of relaxed CCG grammars for parsing to logical form. In *Proceedings of the Joint Conference on Empirical Methods in Natural Language Processing and Computational Natural Language Learning (EMNLP-CoNLL)*.

Author Index